The

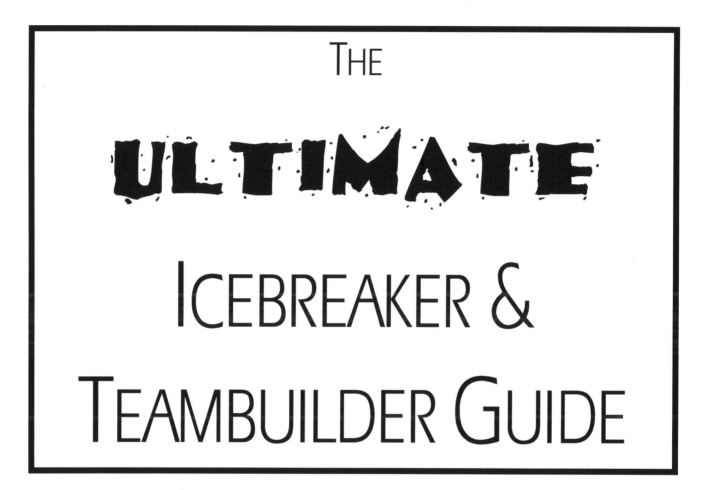

ULTIMATE
Icebreaker &
Teambuilder Guide

Jon Tucker

Thanks to my higher education
colleagues and friends over the years –
Richard McKinnon, Craig Thompson,
Rebecca Hancock, Renae Beal,
Greg Mead, Kim Williamson,
Dana Kelly, D Tobiassen-Baitinger,
Christa Sandelier, Wendy Wallace,
Guy Arnesen, Dave McKelfresh,
Jody Donovan, Denise Galey,
Shondra Russell, Aaron Worley,
Don Boderman, Craig Wimmer,
Mark Keller and Patrick Moser...
to name just a few!

Thanks to my family and my parents
for helping me grow and develop into
a professional, yet playful educator!

© 2007 by Western Oregon University for Jon Tucker. All rights reserved.
Lulu.com Publishing

ultimateicebreaker@yahoo.com

ISBN 978-1-4303-0693-1

TABLE OF CONTENTS

WELCOME TO THE ULTIMATE

ICEBREAKER AND TEAMBUILDER GUIDE!

This guide was designed so that you (as a facilitator) would have access to a large number of activities that are appropriate for a wide variety of audiences. The author works in the higher education area, but almost all of these activities will fit in high school or professional environments. For those of us that work in higher education (and specifically in student affairs), we often understand that the need for icebreakers and teambuilders is great, especially when working with college students. It is imperative for effective trainers to be able to "set the tone" and spark interest in participants, regardless of age or environment. From the office to the classroom…

> **How many times have you been in a gathering of people and started the activity with some sort of icebreaker?**

> **How many times have you worked with a group and found you were looking for an activity to help build group cohesiveness?**

This guide will provide you with over 200 different icebreakers and teambuilders with a specific emphasis on group dynamics, building energy and "breaking the ice."

These activities are divided into categories and sections to help you pinpoint a collection to meet your needs.

> **Need something for the spur-of-the-moment and have no materials?**

No problem, inside are a variety of activities for you!

> **Do you want to do something meaningful with an established group? Or maybe want something that will push the group further?**

It's covered in this guide!

These activities are tried and true. They have been practiced and done in actual environments. Some of them you may recognize from practice. Some may have different names. Some of these activities may make you sit back and say, "Yeah, I remember that!" Some of these activities have changed over the years, but are still valuable for groups who may never have seen them before!

In addition, there are a few facilitation questions for each activity to help you "debrief" the exercise with your participants. This facilitation is often where the bulk of the learning takes place and I can't emphasize enough how important that component is! Look at the exercise, determine what facilitation questions work for your group, and add additional questions to suit your needs.

Some Ropes Course and other activities in this guide could pose some risk for participants and it is imperative that a facilitator have a discussion about the importance of safety prior to starting any activity that has a risk of injury.

Enjoy the resources provided here in this guide and I hope that it provides you with hours of effective activities to meet a variety of needs!

USING THIS GUIDE

This guide uses some terminology and descriptions for specific activities. These definitions are used to provide similar language throughout. Some activities fall under a specific category, but could very well fit into multiple categories. Many of these activities can be adapted in other ways. Feel free to adapt exercises to best fit the needs within your own group!

<u>Definitions of Terms</u>

- **Icebreakers** – activities meant to energize a group, make them familiar with each other or otherwise break down barriers that exist to facilitate greater learning or interaction in the future. These are often meant for fun and typically do not have a topical "message" or "learning opportunity" for facilitation. This guide lists a couple of questions to ask for a quick follow-up to these activities if you would like to process them.

- **Name Games** – activities that are meant for participants to learn the names of others in the group in a fun and interactive way. Often used with new groups when learning names is important. These activities are more like icebreakers in feel, style and content.

- **Ropes Course Activities** – these are high energy and higher risk activities meant to challenge a group mentally and often physically as well. It is best done with groups that do, or will, interact on an on-going basis. Safety is a <u>huge</u> part of these activities and it is imperative that the facilitator be well-prepared for the exercise as well as the more in-depth facilitation questions that will follow.

- **Teambuilders** – These interactive exercises promote group problem-solving, relationship-building or group dynamics. They may focus on an <u>issue</u> that the group may be facing or is likely to face. These activities are best for groups that have some project, work, or initiatives that they will be doing as a group. Communication and group dynamics are often areas of focus for these activities.

- **Risk Level** – this refers to the degree of self-disclosure or personal risk that an activity can provoke, or how deeply the activity may expose personal aspects of a person's life. It can also refer to the risk level for potential injury or the potential to get very wet! You will often know which based upon the description of the activity. Be prepared in advance and anticipate questions from your participants. Do not force people to say or do anything that they are not ready for!
  Risk of injury could be anything from a sprained ankle to a broken bone or something more serious for some very high-energy activities. Although this risk is minimal with proper precautions, as a facilitator you should do everything you can to reduce the potential for risk. Eliminate trip hazards and facilitate a question/answer session about safety prior to any active exercise.

Here are some general definitions for risk level in this book:

- **Low** – Little self-disclosure or exposure to injury intended in activity.
- **Medium** – Some self-disclosure expected although level is determined by participants. Stronger possibility of activity involving some risk for injury. Discuss safety with the group prior to beginning activity.
- **High** – Activity involves potential for significant self-disclosure or involves running or effort that can impose a chance for physical injury. Facilitator must make efforts for participants to be aware of these risks.

- **Activity Level** – refers to how much physical activity, movement or sweat may be involved with the activity! Here are some general definitions used in this book:
  - **Low** – Sedentary activity or walking possible during the exercise.
  - **Medium** – Movement likely, some movement or quickness possible.
  - **High** – Definite movement involved with extended action and high energy.
- **Time Required** – <u>estimates</u> on the amount of time you would use to facilitate the activity. As a facilitator, you may have to anticipate more time for larger groups or for more extensive processing of questions.

<u>NOTE:</u>   Some of the risk and activity level designations, as well as the recommended numbers of participants are based upon the author's experience. You may need to adjust these numbers based upon your experience and the nature of the group. In some cases, activities can be broken down into subgroups to allow a larger number of people to participate.

<u>How to Use the Indices</u>

Use the indices provided at the back of the guide to look at what kind of activities you wish to do with the group. There are separate sections that sort the activities into the following categories:

- Category (Icebreaker, Teambuilder, etc.)
- Alphabetical
- Number of Participants
- Materials
- Risk Level
- Activity Level

There are <u>over 200</u> different activities in this guide, but the list is NOT complete. If you would like to include other unique activities for future editions, please e-mail those to me at <u>ultimateicebreaker@yahoo.com</u> and I'll include them in future editions, giving you credit as the source! In addition, efforts have been made to cite original sources of some of the activities in this guide in the reference page. Original sources of some activities may not be known. If you have documentation showing the original source of an activity, please contact the author so that corrections to this guide can be made for future editions and updates.

<u>ENJOY THE GUIDE!</u>

SUCCESSFUL FACILITATION

When conducting any sort of icebreaker or teambuilder training, it is imperative that the facilitator be prepared for the activity and have a fair idea of what will happen with his or her group. Some considerations may be: age/maturity of the group, size of the group, familiarity, how "touchy-feely" is the group, etc. This next section will talk about tools and methods for successful facilitators.

Facilitation Philosophy

Successful facilitators will walk into each activity and see it as an opportunity to achieve an objective or two with group learning and development. One of the primary purposes of doing an activity is to encourage groups to either develop and grow, or reach some understanding about a specific topic area. As long as the facilitator goes into the exercise with the mindset that "our group is going to accomplish something," the participants themselves will be more invested in what is going on. An activity without a purpose may be viewed as a waste of time (theirs and yours!)

Prior to any activity presented in this or other guides, the facilitator should be able to answer the following questions:

- What is the purpose of this activity? What will this activity provide for the group?
- Does this group of participants need or want the objectives to be provided?
- Do I have the materials necessary? Is the group at the appropriate place for the level of risk for the activity? Is there an adequate space or facility for this activity?
- Do I have enough time for the activity and the important facilitation that will follow?

Only when a facilitator can comfortably answer these questions is s/he ready to present the activity for the group. You must know the group well enough to be able to set up an activity. There have been too many times when an activity was planned that the group wasn't prepared for!

Facilitation Questions

This guide provides facilitators with a few questions following each activity. These questions are designed to provide for engagement and participant learning. When developing your own questions, ask yourself:

- What kind of answer do I expect from this question? Will I get honest answers? How will I respond to answers that I don't expect?
- Will this question address an area of learning that the activity focuses on? For example, if the activity addresses communication issues, will the question hit on this area?

- Is the question at a depth that is appropriate for how well the group knows each other? For example, you wouldn't ask people to share some secret if they have just met ten minutes ago.

Some of the best facilitation questions may ask participants to determine what they <u>saw</u>, what they <u>thought</u> and what they <u>felt</u>. (Seeing, Thinking and Feeling) These three areas are similar, but get at different learning styles. What a participant saw may or may not be congruent with feelings and thoughts.

I would encourage facilitators to follow up and keep the lessons of these activities in mind for future learning. It is always effective later on in training or in a group to say, "Remember when we did the _____ activity? How does this relate to…?" Many participants will expect something tangible to come out of an activity. Some will want to know how it relates to "real life" situations. As a facilitator, think about this issue and discuss it with group organizers or participants themselves. Tailor your facilitation questions to specific topics within a group. If a group has been dealing with issues of conflict lately, then address facilitation questions to this area. A teambuilding activity can only build a team successfully if it addresses issues found within the team!

As a facilitator, you will find that some of these activities fit well with your style and others will not. I recommend that you match those you like best with those that you feel are most effective! Feel free to adapt or change activities around to better suit your needs!

Facilitation Challenges

Leading an activity can be difficult if you are faced with people that are uninterested in the activity or being involved with the group. When you are faced with resistance or hesitancy, there are a few ways you can approach the issue:

- Address the concerns directly. Ask the group why they are hesitant to participate in the activity. As a facilitator, encourage a realistic dialogue about the issues and concerns. It is often through that conversation you can engage the group into participating.

- Discuss varied learning styles. Every person learns differently so you must engage people in visual, auditory and kinesthetic learning opportunities. Ask that everyone participate so that learning and the experience can be equal to everyone in the group.

- Ask that people participate and tell them that you'll provide an opportunity to address concerns during the facilitation that follows the activity.

- Leave the decision of whether to do the activity up to the group. You might wish to postpone the activity until the energy level or group is ready for the exercise. As a facilitator, have a back-up plan in case problems arise with any activity.

Adapting Exercises – Ability and Diversity

These activities are written as if every person participating did not have an ability impairment. Most of these activities could be adapted to meet the needs of a diverse group with some pre-planning on the part of the facilitator. Inclusivity is VITAL to any organization or group and that includes which activities or exercises you plan for a group or organization.

- Do not assume that everyone in a brand new group will be homogenous in nature. Anticipate different levels of physical ability or activity levels.

- Allow people to "opt out" if something makes someone feel uncomfortable, particularly with the active icebreakers. Ask these people to assume alternative roles such as cheerleader, heckler, motivator, team captain, strategist, etc.

- Do not assume by looking at someone that s/he can or cannot do an activity. The best thing to do is ask prior to the exercise.

- Plan ahead. Ask yourself what you would do if someone in your group was in a wheelchair or blind. How might you adapt the activity? Would you do better with an alternative exercise?

If you have questions or need further suggestions, you can also e-mail the author at ultimateicebreaker@yahoo.com. Good luck!

NAME GAMES

Name games are the perfect activity at an initial gathering of people who may not know each other, but should! The following are some activities that will encourage people to get to know the names of other participants and have some fun in the process!

ADJECTIVE NAME GAME

Number of People:	Between 8-30
Materials:	None
Activity Level:	Low
Risk Level:	Low
Time Required:	8-20 minutes

The participants should form a circle and then each person is required to think of an adjective that describes him/her AND starts with the same letter as his/her first name. An example might be: "Silly Sally" or "Rockin' Roberto". Each participant will yell out that new name and from there, the activity will proceed around the circle. The second person would then repeat the first person's name and then state his/her own adjective and name. The third would then say the first, the second, and so on. The game continues until everyone in the circle has gone. It is also a good idea for the facilitator or whoever needs to remember the names the most to go LAST!

Facilitation Questions:

- Why do we do this activity?
- Why did you choose your specific adjective?
- Were there adjectives used that surprised you? Why?
- What were other options for adjectives you considered?
- How did it feel trying to remember names? Will you be more or less likely to remember people now?
- What was challenging about this activity?
- What names are most memorable? Why?

Ultimate Icebreaker & Teambuilder Guide © 2007

BLANKET NAME GAME

Number of People:	Between 10-30
Materials:	One large blanket (one you can't see through)
Activity Level:	Low
Risk Level:	Low
Time Required:	6-15 minutes

Participants should divide themselves into two equal groups. Each group should sit together on their own side of the room facing other members of the group. Have two neutral volunteers (or facilitators) hold up a blanket between the two groups so they cannot see each other. Once ready, a member of each group should move quietly up to his/her side of the blanket and face the blanket without touching it. When ready, the facilitators should drop the blanket and each person at the blanket should try to say the name of the person on the other side. Whoever says the other person's name first, wins. Whoever loses joins the winning team. The game continues until everyone has had a chance to play at least two times or so.

Facilitation Questions:

- What is the purpose of this activity?
- How did it feel to be "on the spot?"
- What names are most memorable? Why?
- What were some memorable moments with this activity?
- What was the competitive nature of this activity like for you?

BUTT SPELLING

Number of People:	Between 10-50
Materials:	None
Activity Level:	Low
Risk Level:	Medium
Time Required:	8-15 minutes

This is a physical activity that will break down barriers of embarrassment and reticence in a group. Participants should stand in a circle facing the middle. One at a time, each person should attempt to spell out their first names (or other words created by the facilitators) by moving their behinds in the shape of the letters of their name. Everyone on the outside circle should wait for a cue and then say the name (or word) out loud all at once. Continue around the circle until everyone has gone. Note that there could be body issue/harassment concerns with this activity, so know your group prior to deciding whether to do this exercise.

Facilitation Questions:

- Why do we do this activity?
- What letters were most difficult?
- What was challenging about this activity? What did you enjoy most?
- How did it feel for some of you to get outside of your comfort zone?

CONCENTRATION

Number of People:	Between 10-30
Materials:	None
Activity Level:	Low
Risk Level:	Low
Time Required:	6-20 minutes

Participants should sit in a circle, facing inwards. One person is designated as the leader and will set the pace for the game. Everyone will repeat the pattern: *slap*, *slap* (hands should pat one thigh and then the other), *snap*, *snap* (snap fingers of one hand then the other). The leader sets the rhythm for the activity. S/he will first say his/her name during the slaps and then someone else's name in the group during the snaps. The person whose name is said must respond on the next set of slaps with his/her own name and then also choose someone else during the snaps. If the player does this correctly, the game continues. If it isn't done quickly enough or is off the beat, that player must get up and sit to the right of the leader and everyone else shifts down to fill in the seats. The game continues until the group has learned names well. The pace of the slaps and snaps can be as slow or as fast as desired!

An example by Jon could look like this:	*Slap*	*Slap*	"Jon"
	Snap	*Snap*	"Janice"
Then Janice would go next:	*Slap*	*Slap*	"Janice"
	Snap	*Snap*	"Monica"

Facilitation Questions:

- What was challenging about this activity?
- How did the tempo affect your performance and remembering names?
- What did you find about people speeding up?
- How did you try to maintain your concentration? What distracted you?
- Were you competitive with this activity? Was there a fear of failure?
- What might you do differently next time?

FUNNY FACE

Number of People: Between 6-40

Materials: None

Activity Level: Low

Risk Level: Low

Time Required: 4-8 minutes

Participants should arrange themselves in a circle and the facilitator will explain that everyone is to introduce themselves to the rest of the people and make the funniest-looking face that they can. Crinkling eyebrows, contorting cheeks or odd movements with eyes are all acceptable. Introductions should be in the form of, "My name is Billy and this is my funny face…" Everyone can also be asked to try to duplicate the funny face given by the person introducing him/herself. Participants should all play and go around the circle until everyone has gone.

Facilitation Questions:

- Why do we do this activity?
- What was memorable about this activity?
- What images are burned in your brain?

GROUP JUGGLE

Number of People:	Between 10-35
Materials:	Balls or other soft objects (Beanbags, etc.)
Activity Level:	Low
Risk Level:	Low
Time Required:	10-25 minutes

The group should start by standing in a circle a little more than shoulder-width apart, facing the middle. The leader should start with an object in their hand (something soft - a tennis ball, beanbag or even roll of toilet paper!) The leader will state his/her name, say another person's name from the group, and then gently toss the object to that group member. That group member will reply, "Thank you <leader's name>". That person will then say another name and then toss the item to that person, and so on, continuing the cycle. Once everyone has been picked, the item should end with the original leader. It helps during the first round to have everyone that has already tossed the object to cross his or her arms to prevent repetition. After the first time through, explain that you'll now continue that same pattern, but add more and more objects so that there may be several objects being tossed simultaneously, all keeping that same pattern. Remember to keep the names and introductions going! If an object is dropped, you may elect to have it start all over again with the initial leader to make the activity more challenging. It also works well to mix up the sizes and types of objects with various other safe items! The facilitator could also quiz people of names at the end of the program to make sure there is a focus on names as well as the tossing activity.

Facilitation Questions:
- Why do we do this activity?
- What was challenging about this activity?
- How did you feel about the tossing and catching during this exercise?
- Where did you find your concentration going? On the names or on the juggling? Why was that?

HERE I AM

Number of People:	Between 10-25
Materials:	Paper, tape and markers
Activity Level:	Low
Risk Level:	Low
Time Required:	5-10 minutes

Participants should stand in a circular arrangement. Explain that this name game will give people an opportunity to identify themselves to the group in a rhythmic pattern. Ask everyone to write their names on the piece of paper and tape it on the floor near them or to their chairs. Give everyone a few minutes to look at the names and faces of the others in the room. After that time the facilitator should ask everyone to then stand up and find a different seat in the room, next to someone else's nametag. The facilitator will randomly designate someone to start the activity. The rhythm should be three claps and then one snap. The beat should be slow to start out and then potentially faster as the game goes on. The person starting will establish the beat and will say someone's name. That person called will then say, "Here I am" prior to the third clap and on the snap, call out someone else's name. This pattern repeats until someone makes a mistake. Someone that makes a mistake can leave the circle or it can force everyone to get up and switch chairs. As another alternative, the group can do a "point and name" activity where one person then points at a nametag and challenges another person to correctly say who is the person in the circle that has that name.

Facilitation Questions:

- Why do we do this activity?
- What was challenging about this activity?
- How did you feel during this activity?
- What kind of pressure did you feel?
- How did you keep track of the rhythm and names at the same time?

HUMAN BINGO

Number of People:	Between 10-150
Materials:	Writing instruments and bingo cards
Activity Level:	Low
Risk Level:	Low
Time Required:	6-15 minutes

Everyone should be given a bingo card and have something to write with. You may create your own bingo card or use the example on the next page. The idea behind the game is to have everyone interact and mingle with each other while finding something out about the people in the room. The object of the bingo activity is to try and get every square on the bingo card with the name or initials of people in the group.

Explain that participants should go up to someone and introduce themselves. S/he should then talk with and ask if that person has taken part or fits a square on the bingo card. If the answer is "yes", then that person should initial the card. If that person hasn't done anything left on the card, then the participant would have to move on to someone else. Depending upon the number of people participating, you can require that they can only have (at most) one or two items on the card initialed by the same person. That way each person is asked to meet more people in the group. You can alternatively have a prize, candy or other goodies available for people that finish their cards. The cards can be in any size you wish, from a 9-square card on up to a 36-square card or even larger. The larger the card, the longer the activity takes.

Facilitation Questions:

- What did you learn about others during this activity?
- Let's go around and see who initialed which boxes. Who initialed for...?
- Were there surprises? What were they?
- What questions do you have for anyone else about their names in a specific box?

BINGO

Ever fallen out of a tree.	Been in a band.	Can speak at least 3 languages.	Has at least 3 other siblings.	Has an odd hobby or interest.
Can do a cartwheel right now.	Can make an odd noise.	Has ever driven 30 MPH over the speed limit.	Can tell a joke on command.	Has never been out of the country.
Still watches cartoons.	Identifies with the Cookie Monster.	Has ever bungee jumped or skydived.	Has won an award that they are proud of.	Can say the alphabet backwards.
Once thought they were a superhero.	Can cook really well.	Played a varsity sport in high school.	Seen any movie more than five times.	Knows any popular song on the radio by heart.
Had a <u>really</u> embarrassing moment	Has dated more than one person at the same time.	Had a GPA of higher than 3.5 in high school.	Thinks cows are cute.	Is excited and motivated for the group/team.

I'M A GIGOLO

Number of People:	Between 10-35
Materials:	None
Activity Level:	Low
Risk Level:	Low
Time Required:	5-12 minutes

Ask participants to form a circle stand up about an arms-length apart. The leader of the activity will explain the rules of this exercise, saying that she will start off by saying his or her name and then say, "My hands are high" while raising his/her hands above his/her head. S/he will then say, "My feet are low" and lower the hands to touch knees (or close to them). Lastly, s/he will say, "This is how I gigolo." The leader will then do a unique little dance for the group. Following this, everyone else in the circle will repeat the motions and sayings that the leader did until the final one when they say, "This is how <leader's name> gigolos" and everyone copies the leader's dance move or jig. Repeat this around the circle until everyone has had a chance to show his or her dance move and name.

Facilitation Questions:
- Why do we do this activity?
- What was challenging about this activity?
- What names are most memorable? Why?
- What barriers were broken down by doing this activity?

INTRODUCTION INTERVIEW

Number of People:	Between 8-30 in pairs
Materials:	None
Activity Level:	Low
Risk Level:	Low
Time Required:	8-25 minutes

Ask participants to pair up with someone that they do not know. Explain that for two minutes, each person will need to talk to her/his partner (without stopping and for the entire two minutes) about her/himself. Topics could include high school, family, hobbies, academic areas, memorably moments, etc. This may be difficult for some people and easier for others. When done, the roles should then switch for another two minutes. When completed, each person in the pair (if time and group size allow) should introduce and provide a brief summary about their partner to the rest of the group using the information gathered in the interview. If the group size prohibits everyone from sharing, put the pairs into groups of 6 or 8 or so and then conduct the interviews in those larger groups. As an alternative, the exercise can be done so that the listener is told to provide no body language or non-verbal feedback. This can be done in conjunction with a discussion about the importance of feedback and two-way communication.

Facilitation Questions:

- Why do we do this activity?
- What was challenging about this activity?
- What was memorable about this exercise?
- How much do you feel you know about the people around you compared to when you began?

MOTION NAME GAME

Number of People:	Between 8-30
Materials:	None
Activity Level:	Medium
Risk Level:	Low
Time Required:	6-30 minutes

The group should start of in a circle, facing inwards about arm's length apart. This exercise is similar to the Adjective Name Game except that instead of inventing an adjective with a name, each person will repeat their name and create some motion or quick action that represents them in some way. Someone can do a somersault, wave to the group or make some other silly motion. The next person in the group must then repeat that person's name and activity and then do her/his own. This repeats until the entire circle has gone. The last person will then have done everyone's name and motion before doing his/her own!

Facilitation Questions:

- How are you feeling?
- What was challenging about this activity?
- What motions did you NOT want to do and why?

MY THREE OBJECTS

Number of People:	Between 4-40
Materials:	Assorted markers and nametags
Activity Level:	Low
Risk Level:	Low
Time Required:	8-30 minutes

This activity is good to start a group off at the very beginning of a training or orientation. Distribute markers to participants and give each person a blank nametag. Everyone should then be asked to print their name in big letters on the top part of their nametag and then asked to draw three things on their nametag that represents who they are on the bottom portion of the tag. After everyone has completed drawing, participants should be asked to go around the group and share their names, what they drew on the tag, and why it is important to them.

Facilitation Questions:

- How did you choose your objects?
- What was challenging about this activity?
- What did you want to know more about?

SHABUYA (sha-BOO-ya) ROLL CALL

Number of People:	Between 8-24
Materials:	None
Activity Level:	Low
Risk Level:	Low
Time Required:	8-20 minutes

This is an individual introduction activity. Tell each participant that s/he will be coming up with a short rhyme to introduce him/herself to the rest of the group while the rest of the participants follow up with "background vocals". The pattern for the roll call goes as follows: "My name is _____." Everyone else says, "Yeah!" in between each line of the song. The singer will then say the next three lines of the rhyme, saying something about him/herself with the lyrics. After the fourth and final line the audience members will yell, "Roll Call! Shabuya, shabuya, shabuya roll call, shabuya, shabuya, shabuya roll call." This pattern will be repeated for every individual. The next person in line should be prepared to go at this point and introduce him/herself.

The pattern for the person to introduce him/herself is to prepare four short lines, the first of which gives his/her name. The second and fourth verses should rhyme and the participant has the option to rhyme the first and third, or all four if s/he desires. This activity should be accompanied by clapping and stomping. Encourage people to be funny and characteristic of him/herself during introductions! An example could be:

Participant		Audience
"My name is Ronnie"	→	<Yeah!>
"And I love hockey"	→	<Yeah!>
"But I'm so good"	→	<Yeah!>
"I'm kind of cocky!"	→	<Roll Call!>

Facilitation Questions:

- What was challenging about this activity?
- What was most memorable? Why?
- How did you come up with your lyrics? Why did you choose the topics to cover that you did?
- How did it feel to be in front of the group?
- What other alternative lyrics or areas were you considering?

SHOE GAME

Number of People:	Between 8-40
Materials:	None
Activity Level:	Low
Risk Level:	Low
Time Required:	10-25 minutes

The group should be in a circle, standing close to one another facing the middle. Everyone should remove their shoes, tie the two shoes together, and place them randomly in a large pile in the middle of the group. If the shoes don't tie, then keep them together as best as possible. Have a volunteer go to the pile of shoes, pick a pair and return to the circle. That person should then make one statement about the owner of the shoes that s/he picked. (i.e. "The owner of these shoes must want to be comfortable because of the padding and soft leather!" The owner of the shoes then will come forward, introduce him/herself and pick out another pair of shoes to introduce. This goes until everyone has had a chance to participate!

Facilitation Questions:

- Why do we do this activity?
- What shoes were most appealing and why did you choose what you did?
- Who got the impression correct and what was way off base?

SNORT

Number of People:	Between 10-35
Materials:	None
Activity Level:	Low
Risk Level:	Low
Time Required:	10-25 minutes

Participants should form circles facing the middle. The object of this activity is for participants to get completely around the circle without laughing. The first person that starts will need to say his/her name and then do some snort (like a pig). The next person in line should then repeat that person's name, snort, say his/her own name, snort and move on to the next person in the circle. The game ends when everyone has gone.

Facilitation Questions:

- Why do we do this activity?
- How difficult was this activity?
- What was most memorable? Why?
- Whose snort was the best and why?

WHOMP'EM

Number of People:	Between 10-30
Materials:	A sponge bat, styrofoam tube, or rolled up newsprint. (The Whomp'-Em Sword)
Activity Level:	Medium
Risk Level:	Low
Time Required:	6-12 minutes

The group is asked to sit in a circle very close together with everyone's legs extended straight in front of them. There should be enough room for an opening in the center so that the "Whomp'Em Master" has room to stand and move around a little. The Whomp'Em master will use the Whomp'Em sword in the game. Someone starts the round by saying the name of a member of the group. The Master must Whomp (hit) the shoes/feet/legs of that person before that person can say another person's name. They cannot repeat a name that has been said in that round already. When the Master succeeds in Whomping someone before they say someone else's name, that person becomes the new master. You may also set a rule that if anyone flinches or moves his/her legs away, they automatically become the Whomp'Em Master in the middle.

Facilitation Questions:

- Why do we do this activity?
- How did you feel about being in the circle, being in the middle?
- How difficult was it to think of names? Why?

ROPES COURSE ACTIVITIES

Ropes Course activities in this book are probably not what you may read in other guides and books! The activities here do not involve zip lines, poles, walls or other permanent fixtures. Although those activities are certainly valuable and are recommended for intensive teambuilding for established groups, the following activities are more like "low ropes" exercises. They are physical, but don't require any specific "ropes course" location in order to facilitate them!

Safety

Safety is vital in any of these activities, as is gauging the level of trust a group may have as well as what will be needed in the future. The facilitator should monitor risky behavior by participants, be aware of the environment where the activity is taking place, and note potential hazards. It is recommended that you examine the physical locations for any of these activities for holes, sticks, rocks, etc. if outdoor, or trip hazards or low clearances for indoors. Check this out before undergoing any of the tasks listed here!

Blindfold safety is another important area to remember. People that are blindfolded are putting their trust in the facilitator and with others in the group to keep them safe. As a facilitator, it is extremely difficult to build trust with someone if s/he bumps her/his head or trips because of something that should have been noted prior to the activity. Check both where people walk as well as up high to keep people's heads safe. Vision is a primary sense we use to navigate in the world and taking this away can be very traumatic and difficult for some people – be sensitive to that!

Spotting

Spotting is assuming a position where you can assist someone that is off-balance or at risk for falling. Proper spotting is <u>not</u> to catch someone or put the spotter at risk of injury himself or herself. To spot someone correctly, you should be aware of and do the following:

- Remove any jewelry, rings, or things that might be sharp from participants and spotters.

- Brace themselves by placing one leg in front of the other, with the back leg far enough back to provide some stability if the spotters were to be pushed backwards. Bend at the knees slightly to provide some flexibility with movement.

- Spotters should have both arms in front of them with palms out and fingers extended.

- If a participant begins to fall in a spotter's direction, they should gently brace that person but should <u>not</u> attempt to catch them. Encourage participants to try and brace themselves in the event of a sudden fall.

- Spotters should be encouraging and provide stability before a fall becomes abrupt or sudden.

For more information on spotting, check out books that specifically deal with spotting and ropes course activities such as, "The Bottomless Bag Revisited!" or "Cowstails and Cobras II." I would encourage any facilitator of traditional ropes course activities to have these in your resource library!

Opting Out

As with many Ropes Course activities, some people may wish to "opt out" of an exercise if they do not feel comfortable. This can be physical exertion, phobias, fears or other reasons. As facilitators, allow people to opt out, but encourage them to challenge themselves to accomplish a task. Do not judge (or allow others to judge) anyone for choosing another role. They may elect to participate by spotting (preventing falls), observing or cheering on the group instead of actively going through the exercise. Remind the group that support is key during many activities and not everyone can be in a "doing" role all of the time!

Remember, facilitating these activities well is the key to success in any ropes course activities!

ALL ABOARD

Number of People:	7-18
Materials:	Some small object (about 2' square) for participants to stand on.
Activity Level:	Medium
Risk Level:	Medium
Time Required:	15-30 minutes

The object of this exercise is for the participants in the group to be completely on the board without touching the ground for a period of 10 seconds. You may also enlarge or decrease the size of the board, depending upon the degree of challenge that you would like for the group. Everyone <u>must</u> have at least one foot on the board, except for those people who may be on shoulders, etc. This exercise is good for facilitation and conversations about communication and group decision-making. Facilitators MUST be aware of safety issues with people being on each other's backs as well as whether the entire group is out of balance on the board. Make sure there is a safe surface surrounding the board and that there are no holes, etc.

Facilitation Questions:

- What was most challenging about this activity?
- Do you feel that you could do more people?
- How was your communication during this exercise?
- Were there ideas that were mentioned that weren't addressed?
- How did you choose your strategy?
- Who were the leaders of this exercise? What role did others play?

BLIND SQUARES

Number of People:	Between 8-30 (More participants requires a longer rope)
Materials:	Blindfolds, long (40' plus) rope
Activity Level:	Medium
Risk Level:	Medium
Time Required:	15-30 minutes

Participants in this game should be blindfolded and told they cannot speak until the facilitators say it is OK to do so. In a separate area that participants haven't seen, there should be a large rope tied into a loop. Once everyone is blindfolded, the facilitators should take a minute and have the rope criss-cross, figure 8, or fold in on itself. Place the rope on the floor for the activity. Once this is complete, the facilitators should begin to lead individuals into the rope room. The facilitators should assist putting people together so that they stand next to the rope, placing each participant at the rope location with both of their hands on the rope. It is a good idea to have participants face opposite directions on the rope and keep people about the same distance from each other on the rope. Once everyone is in place, explain to the group that without being able to see, they are to create some shape by moving or manipulating the group to form a shape (square, triangle, polygon, etc. of facilitator's choosing). The group itself will assess when they feel they are finished with the activity and satisfied with the shape. People may not move their hands along the rope in any way, nor can their hands leave the rope. When ready to begin, explain that people can then talk with each other. When the group has completed the task, they may remove their blindfolds and process the activity to see how they felt they did. Facilitators may also wish to designate some individuals that are allowed to see the activity, but are not allowed to communicate (verbally or non-verbally) as an additional challenge (with or without telling the group of the change!)

Facilitation Questions:

- What was it like being unable to see during this exercise?
- Are you happy with the results of this activity? Why or why not?
- How does this exercise build trust?
- Talk about the clarity of instructions during this challenge.
- Were there times when the group was stuck? How did you overcome them?
- Talk about communication during this exercise – what worked and what didn't.

BUILD YOUR OWN GAME

Number of People:	Between 12-100
Materials Needed:	Assortment of balls, rope, playground equipment or ropes course materials (at least 10 items)
Activity Level:	High
Risk Level:	Low
Time Required:	40-60 minutes

Divide participants into at least three subgroups and give each subgroup a collection of props and materials. The more options you have for each group, the better the imagination could be with the exercise. If participants can find other objects for this activity that weren't given to them, that is fine too. Each group will need to spread out into separate areas. The group's objective is to create a brand new game that all participants can play. There should be plenty of room to play, each group must name the game, and be able to teach the other groups how to play. Give teams a set amount of time to generate their games and then gather the subgroups back together and allow each group to explain the game to everyone. They will then spend 10-15 minutes for each group to play their game with the larger group. Process the activity by talking about teamwork, division of labor, idea generation, consensus, leadership areas and providing for diverse activity levels, etc.

Facilitation Questions:

- What was most difficult about this exercise?
- Talk to me about the creativity involved during this exercise?
- How did you reach decisions in your group?
- How did you deal with time pressure to complete the game?
- What materials did you find you needed? How did you improvise during this exercise?

LOG JAM

Number of People:	Between 10-26
Materials:	A log that is long enough so that everyone can stand on top of it and wide enough so it is relatively easy to stay on top of it (about 9-12 inches)
Activity Level:	High
Risk Level:	Medium
Time Required:	20-30 minutes

Divide the participants into two equal groups (or close to it) and have each line up on the log front to back, facing the other group. Explain that the object of this activity is for each group to get to the other end of the log without falling off of it. People cannot change the order they are currently standing with their team. When completed, the person in front and behind must remain the same throughout the activity. In addition, for an extra challenge, this exercise can be done in complete silence or anyone that falls off the log requires that everyone start again from the beginning. As a facilitator, be aware of safety and stepping issues on this exercise going off the log. If people are falling off the log, they should <u>step down</u> instead of falling!

Facilitation Questions:

- This can often be a challenging activity, how did the group approach this task?
- What strategies were utilized and what were discarded? How did you decide which to use?
- How was the group's communication? Is there anything that you would change if you were to do this exercise again?
- What lessons from this exercise can you carry with you into the future?
- Did someone take the lead? What roles did people play during this exercise? Was it effective or would you change something in the future?

LOG ROLL

Number of People: Between 10-50

Materials: None

Activity Level: High

Risk Level: Medium

Time Required: 5-10 minutes

Ask participants to lie down on their stomachs, shoulder to shoulder with their neighbors, forming a straight line. The person on the end then gets up and rolls over everyone's back until s/he reaches the end. S/he will then lie on his/her stomach, while the next person in the line rolls over everyone as well. The game continues until everyone has rolled. This activity can be a competition between groups as well. Be aware of body issues, keeping one's head safe, and comfort levels of the group with this exercise.

Facilitation Questions:

- What was memorable about this activity?
- What was challenging?

MARS PROBE

Number of People:	Between 5-24
Materials:	Yarn, metal ring, funnel, tennis ball (One string per participant)
Activity Level:	Low
Risk Level:	Medium
Time Required:	12-30 minutes

This exercise should be set up so that pieces of yarn are tied to the ring in the middle. Use the diagram below to set up the materials for this exercise, and you may have up to 24 strings extended out from the center. The yarn should spread out in a circular formation (or a pointy star). Place the ring on a funnel (small end), with a tennis ball in the ring (so that it can fall off easily). The object is for each group member to pick up an end of yarn and pull it tight so that the yarn is stretched and the ball is still in the ring. The participants must then attempt to move the ball over to a bucket (or some other location) and drop the ball into it without the ball hitting the ground. This can be done over several different obstacles courses and terrain to challenge the group.

An alternative method of designing this activity is to have the strings hook up to a center ring with a metal hook connected at the bottom of the ring. Arrange for wooden "probes" (small wood blocks with a closed loop metal hook on the top) to be set up in an area. The teams use the same moving format to walk over, hook each probe, and move it to another location without having the strings or any other part of the probe touch the ground.

Facilitation Questions:
- What was challenging about this activity? What did you enjoy most?
- Communication is a key for this exercise. What was most effective with the group's communication? Least effective?
- Discuss how you coordinated this activity. Was there a 'leader'?
- How were decisions made during this exercise?

PLANE WRECK

Number of People:	Between 6-40
Materials:	Blindfolds for at least half of the group
Activity Level:	Medium
Risk Level:	High
Time Required:	15-40 minutes

Explain that this activity is going to be about trust. The facilitator should give half of the participants a blindfold and ask them to put them on. Those that are terribly uncomfortable with being blindfolded can either try to challenge themselves with the activity or may assume an alternate role – cheerleader, safety coordinator or observer. For the rest of the activity, those that are <u>not</u> blindfolded may not speak. The activity will be complete when every member of the group is again sitting back in this location. Tell the participants that they are the surviving members of a Fantasy Airline plane crash. Everyone must stay together, but the entire group must now try to go to <insert a nearby location> to seek assistance. The group will then carefully travel as a group, relying upon each other for safety and guidance to that new location. Once the group has achieved that location, the facilitator should congratulate the group, but now explain that the group has been attacked by a group of feral ground squirrel. As a result, another challenge hits the group. For example, one more person could be blinded and two members have broken legs and cannot walk (in addition to not being able to see or speak as the case may be). As a group, they must now make it to another nearby location. Once arriving at this last location, congratulate them, but a rescue plane has been flying near the site of the original crash and everyone needs to make it back to the plane. However, a tree has fallen and this creates yet another challenge. Perhaps another person is blinded and one more person has a broken leg. After the group returns to the original location, process the activity for the participants involved.

Facilitation Questions:

- This can be a very challenging activity for a variety of reasons…discuss what it felt like at the beginning of the activity.
- As challenges were added to the group, how did the group adapt to changes?
- Discuss what worked and didn't work with your teamwork during this activity.
- What was the communication used during the group? How was the support of group members? Any feedback that you would provide?
- What lessons can you take with you following this activity?

ROPE WALL

Number of People:	Between 8-32
Materials:	About 10 feet of rope.
Activity Level:	High
Risk Level:	High
Time Required:	12-25 minutes

Divide the group up into two equal halves. One team will be going over the rope while the others will be "spotting" and paying attention to the safety of the other team. Two members of the "spotting" team will have the sole job of holding the rope tight about 4-6 feet above the ground. Ask the group for consensus about the height of the rope and how difficult of a challenge they wish to have. Alternatively, you could tie a rope between two trees or other objects so that it remains tight. The object of this activity is to get everyone from each team over the rope without touching it. Once someone reaches the other side of the "rope," they should take on the role of a spotter for safety. No one is allowed to go under or around the rope. Before people start transferring, talk about safety and spotting each other during the activity. Everyone on the spotting team should follow proper safety procedures. Spotters should try to cushion falls should the need arise. It is important for spotters to take their jobs seriously since the teams will switch once the first team is complete.

After one team is over the rope, the other team should do the same, but they cannot use the help of anyone who has already gone over the wall! Be aware of people's image and size concerns – allowing people to op" out of any exercise and assume alternative roles if they do not feel comfortable participating.

Facilitation Questions:

- How did you feel during this activity?
- What was the trust like for the group during this exercise?
- Talk about a challenge the group faced and how did you overcome it?
- How effective was group communication? What were areas that were effective and not-as-effective? Why?
- What roles did people play during this activity?

THREE PERSON TRUST FALL

Number of People:	Between 3-100 (subgroups of 3)
Materials:	None
Activity Level:	High
Risk Level:	High
Time Required:	4-10 minutes

This is similar to the Two Person Trust Fall activity (see that exercise for more specific instructions on falling, etc.) except that there will be one person on either side. Place the volunteer in the middle of the two people, standing about 2-2 ½ feet from the middle person. Be aware of the safety issues and concerns involving trust falls as well as spotting techniques before you begin the activity. Both of the people on the ends are "catchers" and the middle person is a "faller." When ready, the person in the middle should cross his/her arms in front of his/her chest. Keep their legs and torso as rigidly straight as possible, keeping his/her feet STATIONARY on the ground. When both catchers and the faller are ready, the faller should fall towards one of the catchers, who will then brace and support the person with his/her hand (not near the ground, but merely leaning), pushing him or her back gently to the other catcher on the opposite side. The faller should fall back and forth like a windshield wiper. Note that this activity should not be done at a fast speed! Switch roles after a person has had some time in the middle.

Facilitation Questions:

- Why do we do this activity?
- How did you feel being the person falling? The person in support roles?
- What parallels are there from this activity to working in teams?
- What were your thoughts as the activity was going on?

TRAFFIC JAM

Number of People:	Between 10-60
Materials:	Pieces of paper or markers (one more than the number of people in each group)
Activity Level:	Low
Risk Level:	Low
Time Required:	12-25 minutes

Place the markers on the floor in a straight line. The best markers are those that are sturdy and able to withstand people stepping on them, but paper will suffice. Divide each group into two halves according to the diagram below. The challenge is for the group on either side of the center marker to completely change to the other side by moving one square at a time like in a game of Checkers. Teams must continue to face in their initial direction and may not turn around. Players may move into the vacant spot in front of them or they may "jump" another player by moving to the opposite side of a player <u>from the other group</u>. They <u>cannot</u> jump a player from their own group. Players may <u>not</u> move backwards and two people cannot move at once. Some groups may try to talk out the motions before actually moving, so allow them to do that. If a team gets stuck, they should return to their original positions and begin again, perhaps with new participants in lead positions to increase the challenge.

<u>Start Position</u>

<u>End Position</u>

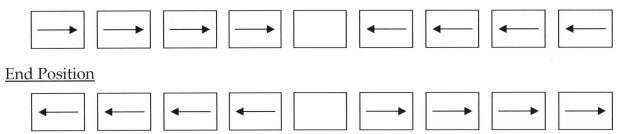

Facilitation Questions:

- How was the group's communication during this exercise?
- What was challenging about this activity?
- How did decisions get made during this exercise?

TRUST WALK

Number of People:	Between 6-60
Materials:	One blindfold per person
Activity Level:	Medium
Risk Level:	High
Time Required:	25-40 minutes

Pairs Version:

Group members should be paired up with someone else for this activity. One person should be blindfolded and the other is able to see. Once participants are ready, the person that can see will be entrusted to lead the blindfolded partner to a different location, going outside, navigating other objects, ramps, branches, etc. The facilitator should prepare the likely routes in advance for safety. Keeping safety in mind is the highest priority in this exercise, as well as every trust activity. Each team should be given about 10 minutes to explore their surroundings. It is also possible to arrange the activity so that you may have one person periodically leaving their partner by themselves (but holding on to something like a tree, fence, sign, etc. for a short period of time). This creates a significant contrast in feeling, and how it is to be alone. Facilitators should then blow a whistle or signal for everyone to begin to return. After returning, switch partners in the group. There are many variations to this exercise. It may be done so that both partners may speak, only the blindfolded person may speak, the walker may speak, neither may speak or even no physical contact can be made with teams.

Group Version:

Every group member in this version should be blindfolded or make a promise not to peek through closed eyes. The leaders of the group will organize the participants in a straight line and all of the participants will join hands together. The leader (who can see-- sometimes a facilitator) will lead the blinded group members around, exploring their surroundings. The key to this activity is that there should be NO TALKING. You can have the group create their own communication methods or use the rules here. For example, if there is an object that needs to be stepped over, the leaders should raise the hand of the group member and the next person will do the same to warn the next person and so on. If there is an object that is at head level, the leaders should lower the arm of the blinded group member, indicating they should duck down and that communication should continue down the line. Note that the leader can pretend there are obstacles that aren't there as well. This activity is done well in the dark, but make sure people feel comfortable with the activity as a whole, keeping trust and safety in mind!

Facilitation Questions:

- What did it feel like to be blindfolded?
- What did it feel like to be leading?
- What responsibility did you have for others? How did you communicate?
- What changed during this exercise for you?

TWO PERSON TRUST FALL

Number of People:	Between 6-150 (in pairs)
Materials:	None
Activity Level:	High
Risk Level:	High
Time Required:	3-8 minutes

Ask participants to find partners of approximately equal height and weight. One partner will designate himself or herself as the "faller" and the other will be the catcher. The participants will be able to switch roles later. The faller's responsibilities are to stay as straight and stiff as possible, do NOT bend at the waist, keep his/her arms folded across his/her chest, and make sure to communicate with the catcher. The catcher's responsibilities are to get in a sturdy stance (one leg in front of the other, braced to support the weight), be aware of what's going on, keep his/her hands below the faller's shoulder blades, use her/his arms as shock absorbers. They should not underestimate the force being generated by the faller. They must also constantly communicate and reassure the faller during the activity. The faller will have his/her back to the catcher. The commands that they should communicate in this activity are that the faller asks the catcher, "Ready?" The catcher should state, "Ready" back to the faller when they are set. The faller then says, "Falling" and waits for the catcher to reply, "Fall Away." The faller should then slowly fall straight back. The catcher will use his/her hands to stop the falling progress of the faller. After three tries, the partners should switch roles.

Facilitation Questions:

- How did you feel during this exercise?
- What fear or challenge did you overcome?
- What was most difficult about this activity?
- How important was communication?

WILLOW IN THE WIND

Number of People:	Between 7-120
Materials:	None
Activity Level:	High
Risk Level:	High
Time Required:	10-20 minutes

This trust fall activity takes trust to a larger group of people than most trust "falls" and often works best if it actually follows a two or three-person trust fall exercise. Use the information in the two or three-person trust fall activities to help as a guide. Each group should stand closely in a circle with their shoulders touching, facing inwards and have a single volunteer faller in the middle. The group can't be too large 8-14 is about right) or there will be too much space between people for the activity to be done safely. That person should have his/her eyes closed, body, torso and legs stiff and straight, feet firmly planted to one spot on the ground in the middle of the group, and arms folded across his/her chest. The rest of the group should stay in a tight circle, each person braced with one leg back and one forward and hands up and ready at chest level to catch the person as they fall. The commands are performed like the two person trust fall and the faller can fall any direction s/he wishes. The rest of the group will gently change the faller's direction by easing their "fall" and <u>gently</u> pushing them in another direction. The middle person will switch after a couple of minutes. Note that the more hands that are on the person in the middle, the safer they will general feel. Ask participants to remain quiet during the activity for greater impact. Remind participants of the safety involved in this activity and that the key is a gentle push, being particularly careful when pushing across the circle.

Facilitation Questions:

- What was most effective about this activity? Least effective?
- What challenged you most personally?
- Would this be easier or more difficult than a two-person fall activity? Why?

ICE BREAKERS

Ice Breakers do exactly that – they break the ice of a group! These activities may or may not have a message or purpose, other than to get a group to know each other, mix, get energized, challenge the group or reach some other objective you set forth. They are best at the beginning of a meeting or gathering, or whenever a group needs to take some time to rejuvenate or find some energy!

A TO Z

Number of People:	Between 6-200
Materials:	None
Activity Level:	Low
Risk Level:	Low
Time Required:	5-10 minutes

Ask participants to get into pairs or groups of three (facilitator choice). The facilitator should come up with some topic or issue related to the group (or any random topic will work as well.) Explain that the participants will need to hold a conversation about that issue with each sentence starting with a specific letter of the alphabet. Each sentence that follows should begin with the next letter and so on. Each group (or the facilitator) should determine which letter to start with and then try to get through all 26 letters within a set period of time (two minutes or so.) Make sure that everyone rotates through and participates in the activity. Alternatively, you may ask that everyone start every sentence with that exact same letter to change things up.

Facilitation Questions:

- What was challenging about this exercise?
- How did you find yourself preparing for this exercise?
- How difficult was it to get through "Q, X, and Z"?
- Could you do better now if you were to do it again? Why?

AMOEBA TAG

Number of People: Between 14-125

Materials: None (Optional: cones to designate tag boundaries)

Activity Level: High

Risk Level: Low

Time Required: 10-20 minutes

Establish boundaries for the game so that there is a large enough space for everyone to run around in. One person should volunteer or be selected to be "it." For the purposes of the game, it is good to have someone that is pretty quick start the activity. That person is now a single-celled organism that has a strong desire to grow and expand. That person will chase the other participants and if s/he tags someone, they then join hands and collectively, the two-person team is the "amoeba" and is "it." If either person touches someone, that next person joins the amoeba. This continues as the amoeba tags additional people until eventually the amoeba has all but one person, who is the winner. If there is a very large number of participants, there can be more than one person designated as "it" at the start of the game, or if the amoeba gets too big, you can alternatively decide that it will "divide" into two separate amoebas.

Facilitation Questions:

- Why do we do this activity?
- How is your energy level? How did it feel to be the amoeba, to be chased by the amoeba(s)?

ARC BALL

Number of People:	Between 14-60
Materials:	One large ball per group
Activity Level:	Medium
Risk Level:	Low
Time Required:	8-20 minutes

Divide participants into two equal teams and ask each group to form a line, front to back, about an arm's length apart. The two teams should face each other at the start but have some distance between them. The ball starts in the front of the team and the object is to pass the ball under legs to the person behind, who then passes the ball over his/her head to the next person, who then passes under the legs, etc. Once the last person has the ball, s/he must run with the ball back to the front of the line and then start again by passing the ball under her/his legs. The first team to return the ball back to the original line up wins.

Facilitation Questions:

- What will you remember about this activity?
- How did you group perform? How did your team communicate?

ASSASSIN

Number of People:	Between 10-80
Materials Needed:	Photos of participants (or names on pieces of paper), water guns
Activity Level:	Low
Risk Level:	Low
Time Required:	Up to Weeks…

This activity is best done outside of meetings or official functions, but where a group will interact over a period of time. The facilitator should have pictures of each of the participants ahead of time if they do not know each other. Each person is then secretly given a picture or name of someone else in the group and either given, or asked to get his/her own water pistol. The object of the game is to collect as many pictures/names by shooting their "target" with water. When a person successfully "assassinates" the person in his/her picture, s/he takes the picture that his/her target had and then s/he tries to "assassinate" that next person. The game continues until everyone has been squirted except for the final person, who is the winner. It is always a good idea for the facilitator or the group to set rules in place about times or places where assassinating is or is not allowed.

Facilitation Questions:
- What stories do you have to share about this exercise?
- Who felt they were skilled at this activity? Who was a sitting duck?

BACK TO BACK

Number of People:	Between 8-300
Materials:	None
Activity Level:	High
Risk Level:	Low
Time Required:	5-15 minutes

Every group member should find a partner of approximately equal height and weight. The partners will start by standing back-to-back and locking arms behind them with their partner. With arms locked at all times and starting from a standing position, the partners should attempt to sit down, kick their legs out so bottoms are sitting on the ground, and then try to stand back up. Once people have completed, get people into groups of four, lock arms and attempt the same task. This can be done until groups of eight, sixteen or even more! This activity would do well to begin a series on trust building or as an energizer. With this activity, please keep in mind the surface of the floor in case of "hard landings!"

Facilitation Questions:

- How did you do during this exercise?
- What might you do differently the next time you did this activity?
- How did trust play a role in this exercise?
- What was different a more people participated in this activity?
- How did you communicate?

BALLOON BLOW OUT

Number of People: Between 5-80

Materials: One balloon per person

Activity Level: Low

Risk Level: Low

Time Required: 4-10 minutes

Explain that everyone in the room is to blow up his or her balloon as full as possible without it popping. Everyone should then hold the end tightly so that no air escapes. The objective is for people to get in a straight line and determine whose balloon will travel the furthest once the balloon is released. You can set the rules so that the balloons can only travel forward or may travel in any direction. This activity can be done also as a competition with elimination rounds, etc.

Facilitation Questions:

- Why do we do this activity?
- Did you have a strategy for this exercise? What was it?
- What was most effective for you? What didn't work as well?
- How could you "think outside the box" during this exercise? Were there things that you could do without breaking any "rules?"

BALLOON TAG

Number of People:	Between 8-50
Materials:	One inflated balloon and a piece of string/yarn per person (3-5 feet each)
Activity Level:	Medium
Risk Level:	Low
Time Required:	4-10 minutes

Ask all participants to tie their string to an inflated and tied balloon. Everyone should tie the balloon to his/her ankle leaving between one to two feet of string between the balloon and ankle. The goal of the activity is for each person to attempt to step on other people's balloons, pop them, while preventing your own balloon from being popped. Once a participant's balloon is popped, s/he is out of the game. The game continues until only one person remains.

Facilitation Questions:

- Did you have a strategy for this exercise? What was it? What was most effective?
- How did this activity affect your energy level?

BANANA RELAY

Number of People:	Between 10-60
Materials:	One banana per group
Activity Level:	Medium
Risk Level:	Medium
Time Required:	8-18 minutes

This activity is very similar to the "Orange Pass" activity in this guide. Gather people in a single group teams or in sub-groups for a competition. Everyone should form a line, front to back with the person next to him or her. The first person in the line will place a banana between his/her knees and s/he must pass it to the next person in line without using any hands. If the banana drops, the team must start over. First team to successfully pass the banana both up and down the line again wins. If the banana is destroyed during the activity, you may want to have back-up bananas or just warn participants that they also have to be gentle since one banana is all you get – no matter the banana's condition!

Facilitation Questions:

- This exercise can produce some embarrassing moments...how did you avoid (or create) contact during this exercise?
- What happened to the bananas?
- What kind of time pressure was there? Did it affect how you played the game?

BARNYARD

Number of People:	Between 8-30
Materials:	One blindfold
Activity Level:	Low
Risk Level:	Low
Time Required:	8-20 minutes

Participants should form a circle facing inward. One volunteer will be placed in the middle and blindfolded. The person in the middle will be spun around a few times to disorient her/him. This person is the "farmer" and the farmer will face towards a person in the outer circle and say the name of some barnyard animal. The person in front of, or closest to the farmer, must imitate that sound as appropriate for the animal. The farmer's task is to guess the person's true identity. The farmer can ask the animal to repeat his/her sound up to three times and the farmer must then guess who the person is. If the farmer guesses it correctly, s/he moves to the outer circle and the animal now becomes the farmer. If the farmer is incorrect, s/he is spun around again and the process starts over. As a facilitator, you may wish to have a backup plan if the farmer fails to guess correctly after three rounds and then do a switching of roles.

Facilitation Questions:

- What clues did you use during this activity?
- How important were using senses other than sight?
- How did you avoid being guessed?

BARNYARD ANIMALS

Number of People:	Between 15-300
Materials:	None
Activity Level:	Low
Risk Level:	Medium
Time Required:	6-15 minutes

Ask participants of the group to think of some barnyard animal that they will wish to become for this activity. You can alternatively give people the option of choosing from a few of the following: cat, dog, cow, chicken, sheep, horse, duck, pig or other animal. People are going to be asked to keep their animal choice to themselves. When you tell them to begin, each person will close his/her eyes and find all the members of the group that have the same animal, using only the animal's own noises as a guide. Once everyone is there, they can open their eyes. The facilitator (and/or a couple of volunteers) should try to be a "spotter" during the activity by making sure people don't get way off line or into walls, and participants should hold their hands in front of their chests as "bumpers" in case of collision. Each participant should move until all of the same animal sounds have found one another. You can also use this exercise with "Sea World Sounds" such as dolphins, whales, jellyfish or other sea creatures that may or may not have recognizable sounds – it is fun to see what people come up with!

Facilitation Questions:

- Why do we do this activity?
- How did you feel doing this exercise?
- What techniques did you use to try to find other animals?

BASKET

Number of People:	Between 6-60
Materials:	Paper and writing instruments
Activity Level:	Low
Risk Level:	Low
Time Required:	10-25 minutes

This activity can be arranged in teams or individually. Write the word "Basket" vertically on a piece of paper and a little further to the right on the page, write the letters upwards or "Teksab" so that the letters line up with "Basket" horizontally (see below). Explain that participants are going to need to form words that begin with the first letter and end with the last letter of the series. For example, "B   T" could be the words "Beet" or "Basket", while "A   E" could be "Apple" or "Appetite" and so on. The longer the word, the better! After a set period of time, ask people to share the words they have created and you may award prizes for the longest words made by the participants or for the total letters used. You might also set a rule that you have to rotate through each letter combination. That way you don't have a group that just works with one combination of letters. You could also set up a scoring system for words that looks like the following:

3-5 letters:	2 points	B	T
6-7 letters:	4 points	A	E
8-9 letters:	7 points	S	K
10 + letters:	10 points	K	S
		E	A
Facilitation Questions:		T	B

- How competitive were you during this activity?
- What techniques did you use to create words? Are there any words you are proud of?

BIRDIE ON A PERCH

Number of People:	Between 15-80
Materials:	None
Activity Level:	High
Risk Level:	Medium
Time Required:	6-15 minutes

This is a very physical activity that involves a lot of contact! First, ask for participants to find a partner. Everyone will need to form two circles, one person on the inner circle and one on the outer circle. The inner circle should stand about an arm's width apart and then make a turn to the left. The outer circle should have the partner about four feet away and facing the opposite direction as the partner. Once the activity begins, each circle should rotate in different directions. When the facilitator says, "Birdie on a Perch," each member of the pair must find the other and hop on the other person's back (like a piggyback). The last pair to do this successfully is out of that round and should sit on the sidelines. The game continues until only one pair remains. Remember, this is a physical activity and talk to participants about safety and not going too far during the course of the activity!

Facilitation Questions:

- This activity is obviously one of high energy. Why are we doing an exercise like this right now?
- What was memorable for you about this exercise?
- Did you and your partner have a strategy for the activity?

BIRTHDAY LINE

Number of People: Between 12-200

Materials: None

Activity Level: Low

Risk Level: Low

Time Required: 1-5 minutes

Explain to participants that this is a non-verbal exercise. Ask the group to form a straight line according to their birthdates. For example, people with January birthdays will be at the beginning of the line, July birthdays in the middle and December dates at the end. There should be no lip-reading or spelling things out with this activity. Once completed, the group can shout out birthdays down the line to verify that everyone was in correct order.

Facilitation Questions:

- What was challenging about this activity?
- What techniques did you use to communicate?
- Were you confident of success? Why?

BITE THE BAG

Number of People:	Between 6-60
Materials:	One full-size paper grocery bag per group
Activity Level:	Medium
Risk Level:	Medium
Time Required:	5-15 minutes

Each team is divided up (groups of no more than 12) and asked to form a circle. The facilitator should put an opened, full-size brown grocery bag face up in the center of the circle. The object of the activity is to have each member bend over and pick up the bag in his/her teeth while standing on one foot, <u>and</u> with both hands held behind his/her back. After the group has gone through and attempted or completed the task, the facilitator should cut about 1-2 inches off the top of the bag and the process repeats with the shorter bag! If a team member touches the floor with his/her raised foot, hands or other part of the body, that person is disqualified (or alternatively, you could give people two chances or more to succeed). After each round, more of the bag is cut off. The last team member who successfully picks up the bag without falling wins! Note that more aggressive participants may get very physical with this activity...spread out and make sure there are no hazards (tables, etc.) in the area.

Facilitation Questions:

- What was your first thought when you were told what the exercise was?
- What did you anticipate would be most challenging for you? Was it?
- What strategies did you use to try to succeed? What didn't work at all for you?

BLACK MAGIC

Number of People:	Between 10-40
Materials:	None
Activity Level:	Low
Risk Level:	Low
Time Required:	12-40 minutes

One person should start as a leader of the activity, but there will need to be at least one other person who knows the "secret" of the game. The leader should explain that s/he has recently been able to tap into a psychic mind-link with the other person in the room (the person who knows the game). Tell the participants that as a group they are going to select some item in the room. The leader will leave the area entirely so that s/he will not hear what the item is. Once the item is selected, the leader will then be brought back into the room. S/he will then guess what that item is among a list of items told to him/her by his/her psychic partner. The partner will go through and begin naming items in the room at random. For example, the partner may say, "Is it this cup?" and if it is not the item, the leader will say, "no." The leader will say no to each item that is NOT the item selected by the participants. The partner knows that the way to communicate the item selected by the group is to name an item that is black in color. The leader will take that as a key that the NEXT item is the one that the group had selected. The game is played so that the leader always knows that the selected item will follow an item mentioned that is black in color. Several rounds should be played until people are able to guess why the leader knows the item. There are no apparent verbal or non-verbal uses as to what the item is! Participants may get frustrated and believe that there is some sort of non-verbal cue, hand signal, etc. Assure people that a true, psychic link has been established and keep the game going. Ask participants that if they figure things out to keep the secret to themselves. You can alter this game to signal anything – it does not have to be black. For example, the group's selected item could be after something that is metal, square, vertical, is wearable or any other differentiating feature.

Facilitation Questions:

- What was frustrating about this activity?
- How did you determine what the "trick" was to the exercise?
- What did it feel like to figure it out early? To be one of the last ones to figure it out?
- Did you share the secret or did you keep it to yourself?

BLIND IDENTIFY

Number of People:	Between 10-30
Materials:	Blindfold
Activity Level:	Low
Risk Level:	Medium
Time Required:	8-15 minutes

Participants should form a circle facing the middle. One person will be a volunteer and blindfolded in the middle of the circle. That person is spun around until they are <u>slightly</u> dizzy. This person will then try to find and identify someone solely by touch (above the neck – start high and work down!) If s/he is successful, then the identified person is then blindfolded and put in the middle. If not successful, then the blindfolded person is spun around in the middle and will try again. This activity is obviously best for groups that are comfortable with touching!

Facilitation Questions:

- What surprised you during this activity?
- How did you recognize someone?

BLINDFOLD LINE-UP

Number of People:	Between 7-40
Materials:	Blindfolds for each person
Activity Level:	Medium
Risk Level:	Medium
Time Required:	5-10 minutes

Ask everyone to put on blindfolds or close their eyes (honor system). For safety reasons in this exercise, participants will need to cross their hands in front of their chests and move slowly (in case of collisions). Ask the group to mill around the room without talking until the facilitator says to stop (about 15-30 seconds). Ask for everyone to lower their hands, keep eyes closed, and wait where they stand, keeping quiet. The leader will tap each person on the shoulder and give each person a number (sequential). When everyone has a number, ask the participants raise their hands again and line themselves up by number without talking or opening their eyes. Once everyone is in a line, ask them to count off and see how the group performed.

Facilitation Questions:

- How was it being blindfolded?
- How did you make attempts to communicate?
- Was there a frustrating part in the activity and if so, how did you work through it?

BODY ENGLISH

Number of People:	Between 6-70
Materials:	None
Activity Level:	Medium
Risk Level:	Low
Time Required:	5-10 minutes

The object of this exercise is for small groups of participants to use their bodies to clearly spell words out to the other groups. Divide participants into subgroups and ask them to get together to plan and spell out a word (from a list that you can provide or make up) using only their bodies. No hand signs or signals are allowed. The other group(s) must figure out what they are spelling. Start with single words or maybe move to phrases as the groups get better at spelling in this fashion. The size of the words depends upon the size of the subgroups. In addition, this exercise can be a competition with teams buzzing in to guess the words being created. Another challenge is to not allow groups to speak at all while planning and creating the words with their bodies.

Facilitation Questions:

- How did the group use creativity in this exercise?
- Were there words that you thought were something else?

BRAIN BENDERS

Number of People:	Between 8-80
Materials Needed:	Copies of Brain Bender Examples or make up your own.
Activity Level:	Low
Risk Level:	Low
Time Required:	10-20 minutes

Divide participants into small groups (2-6 people) and explain that they will need to think creatively while encouraging full participation in the exercise. Each group will be given a copy of the brain benders page face down and asked to determine the answer to each one. Give teams 4-5 minutes to complete the list to the best of their abilities. After the allotted time is up, groups should share their answers. Prizes can be awarded to winning teams for a competitive component to the exercise.

Solutions for benders on next page (starting from upper left and moving left to right):

- Sitting on top of the world
- You ought to be in pictures
- You're under arrest
- No excuse for it
- Pay through the nose
- Cyclones
- Mother-in-law
- Right under your nose
- Take you out to lunch
- Forget it
- Deep sea fishing
- Play on words
- 3 square meals a day
- Big man on campus
- Unfinished business
- Back seat driver

Facilitation Questions:

- Which were the easiest and which were most difficult?
- How did you try to solve the benders?
- How did collaboration help you in this exercise? Was competition a factor?

Newstrom and Scannell, *Still More Games Trainers Play*, © 1991, The McGraw-Hill Companies. Material reproduced and adapted with permission of the McGraw-Hill Companies.

sitting world	**PICT RES**	arrest you're	NOXQQIVIT
P **NOANO** **Y**	**cy** **cy**	POLMOMICE	NO NO CORRECT
L NCH L NCH	GET IT GET IT GET IT GET IT	FISHING c	**KING** **LEAR** **WORDS**
ME ME ME AL AL AL Day	**MAN** campus	**BUSINES**	**REVIRDTAES**

BUZZ

Number of People:	Between 10-40
Materials:	None
Activity Level:	Low
Risk Level:	Low
Time Required:	8-15 minutes

Ask people to form a circle (or subgroups.) Explain that in this activity everyone is going to need to think about numbers. Specifically, think of numbers that are multiples of 4 as well as numbers that contain "4" in them (such as 14). Everyone will go around the circle and begin counting up out loud starting from "1". Whenever anyone reaches a number that is a multiple of 4, they are to say, "Buzz" instead of that number. In addition, whenever anyone reaches a number that has a 4 in it, they should say "Buzzteen" for 14 or "Twenty Buzz" for 24. Forty-four would be "Buzzy Buzz". Play goes around the circle as quickly as possible. If a person gets the number incorrect, buzzes inappropriately or other rule infraction, s/he is out for the remainder of the game can try to distract the remaining members of the game.

Facilitation Questions:
- What was challenging about this activity?
- How were you able to concentrate on the numbers?

CALLS OF THE NIGHT

Number of People:	Between 6-24
Materials:	One ball about the size of a volleyball
Activity Level:	Low
Risk Level:	Low
Time Required:	12-20 minutes

Participants in this activity should sit in a perfect circle facing the middle with their legs out in a V-shape, feet touching the feet of the people next to them. Explain that each participant will need to go around the circle and create some sound that you might find at night. (i.e. dog howling, crickets, cats meow, yelling neighbor, owl's hoot, etc.) Everyone will need to close their eyes for this activity or the facilitator can really darken the room. Each player has his/her sound as his/her personal signal. The first player will have the ball, will make his/her sound and then the sound of the person to whom they want to roll the ball. The sound that is "called" replies so that the first person knows where to direct the ball. The first player then rolls the ball. If the intended player receives the ball, s/he makes his/her sound loudly and everyone else rejoices by making their sounds. If the intended player misses, the ball goes back to the first player to try someone else. Remind everyone that this activity is done entirely with eyes closed!

Facilitation Questions:

- What were your impressions of this activity?
- How did it feel to let down your guard and be an animal?
- How might letting your guard down be important for this group?

CATCH ME IF YOU CAN

Number of People:	Between 6-200
Materials:	None
Activity Level:	Low
Risk Level:	Low
Time Required:	4-10 minutes

Players should be paired up and divided into two lines facing each other. Participants should be given about 30 seconds to look at their partners and take in all the details of that individual. The leader then instructs the two lines to turn away from the center and not look at their partners. One or both lines (facilitator's choice) has another 15 seconds to change something about their appearance (change watch to a different arm, unbutton a button, remove a belt, etc.) The change should be discrete, but visible to the partner. The players are then to turn to face each other and they then have 30 seconds to discover the physical changes that have been made. You can do this activity a few different times, giving participants time to think of what changes they could make.

Facilitation Questions:

- Why do we do this activity?
- What does this exercise have to say about observation?
- How closely did you really notice your partner?

CHALKBOARD SENTENCES

Number of People:	Between 12-48
Materials:	Space to write (butcher paper or dry erase board), writing instrument for each group
Activity Level:	Low
Risk Level:	Low
Time Required:	10-18 minutes

Divide participants into equal teams (2-4 teams work best) for this competitive activity. Everyone will create sentences as a team and each team member has to contribute a word to that sentence. If there are uneven teams, then one person on the team(s) with fewest people will have to go twice. Each team should line up 10 feet from the board and the first person of each team should receive a writing instrument. When the facilitator says to begin, the first person will go to the board and write down a word (it must be legible!), run back, give the marker to the next player, and then go to the back of the line. That next person will go up and add a word to the board, give the marker to the next person and so on. Team members may not talk to others during this activity or pre-plan what sentences are going to say. The sentence that is created must contain the same number of words as are members of the team or some number set by the facilitator. Players may not add words in between words that are already written. The first team to complete a rational and logical sentence gets a point. You may create new rules to make it more challenging such as "words that end in vowels only" or "words that start with the letters S, T, and H only." Alternatively, you can give some parameter to the sentence that can tie into future learning. You might choose a topic that relates to what you are covering, relating to team dynamics, or some other area of importance.

Facilitation Questions:

- What was challenging about this exercise?
- How did people support each other during this exercise?
- If you could strategize as a team, how might you approach this activity differently in the future?
- How was communication important for this activity?

CHARLIE'S ANGELS

Number of People: Between 12-45

Materials: None

Activity Level: Low

Risk Level: Low

Time Required: 15-25 minutes

All participants will need to form a circle facing inwards about two feet apart from their neighbors. The facilitator becomes "Charlie" and will start off the game. Each participant will need to learn the motions of this game, so the leader should be very familiar with the activity. It works best if there are another three people that know the formations as well to demonstrate to the group. If not, then the facilitator can show them. In this game, the facilitator will point to someone in the circle of participants. Charlie will then count to eight as quickly or slowly as they would like (although slower is better while people are learning the game.) The person pointed to, and the people on his/her immediate left and right have to complete the motion before the center person counts to eight. If <u>any</u> one of the people is slow, does the wrong motion or doesn't move at all, s/he is now the person in the middle. In the event that more than one person does something incorrectly or slow, the person originally pointed to defaults to become Charlie. The following are the motions that can be used in this activity:

- "Fire Hydrant" – the person in the middle stands with hands together, raised in the air while the people on either side must turn and "lift their legs" towards the person in the middle.
- "Charlie's Angels" – the person in the middle must stand with his/her hands in a gun motion and pointing in the air. The people on either side need to turn away from the center person and make the same gun motions. Facial expressions are appreciated!
- "Elephant" – the person in the middle must grab his/her opposite ear with one hand and stick the other hand through that opening like an elephant's trunk. The people on either side must make their arms into a giant "C" to simulate big ears on the person in the middle.
- "Mosquito" – the person in the middle must put his/her hand (palm inward) up to his/her nose and stick the index finger of the other hand through the fingers it to simulate a mosquito's nose. The people on the sides must turn away from the center person and simulate flapping wings very quickly with their hands.

- "Alligator" – the person in the middle must make both of his/her arms move in a chopping mouth motion. The people on the sides must move behind the middle person, forming a train as the "tail" behind the center person, wiggling their behinds.
- "Flight Attendant" – the person in the middle must simulate putting on the oxygen mask (as in an airplane's safety procedures) while the people on either side must simulate pointing out the emergency exit doors on an airplane.
- "Chia Pet" – the person in the middle must get on his/her hands and knees while the people on either side must put their hands in the center person's hair and with those hands, make a motion as if it was growing while saying "Cha Cha Cha Chia".
- "Luau" – the person in the middle must get on her/his hands and knees and mimic having a large apple in his/her mouth while the persons on either side must make hula motions with their bodies.
- "Cow" – the person in the middle puts his/her arms out, extends them in front of him/her and points his/her thumbs down. The people on the sides must grab a thumb and make milking motions.
- "Hear No Evil" – the person in the middle must make a motion by covering eyes, the person on the middle's right must cover his/her ears and the person on the left side must cover his/her mouth. The appearance should appear as a "Hear no evil, see no evil, and speak no evil" from an observer's point of view.

Feel free to make up other motions that you feel work well, but remember that the activity becomes significantly more difficult with the more formations you create.

Facilitation Questions:

- How did this exercise relate to "thinking on your feet?"
- What were the hardest to remember? The easiest?
- Which of the characters were you dreading the most?

CHOCALOTASCHNIZZEL

Number of People:	Between 8-30 (At least 2 groups)
Materials:	Large chocolate bar per group wrapped in newspaper, tape, aluminum foil, or other wraps; plastic knife & fork per group; mittens, hat, scarf and other clothing for each group; one die per group
Activity Level:	Medium
Risk Level:	Low
Time Required:	12-20 minutes

Prior to the activity, the facilitator should have thoroughly prepared the wrapped chocolate bars in advance. The bars should be wrapped in layers of various materials available and listed above to provide a challenge to the group. Divide participants into subgroups and ask them to sit in a circle. Explain that they will be doing a group activity that is high-speed and has a treat at the end. One person will start by rolling the die and the person to the left will grab the die and roll it, going around the circle. Whenever anyone rolls a six, the person who rolled it has to say, "Chocalotaschnizzel" and then put on all of the clothing. They will then take the thoroughly wrapped chocolate bar and attempt to cut into it using only the plastic fork and knife. In the meantime, the other people in the circle have to continue to roll the die. Once any other member of the group rolls a six, s/he says "Chocalotaschnizzel," and now has to put on the clothing (as the first person removes it), and they resume trying to cut into the package. The game ends when the package is opened and everyone on each group can share the chocolate bar. As a note to the facilitator, the chocolate bars sometimes get mangled in this activity, so you may want to have back-up chocolate bars for people to eat.

Facilitation Questions:

- What was challenging about this exercise?
- How did the fast pace of the game influence the activity?
- How did teams coordinate trading clothing?

CHUBBY BUNNY

Number of People: Between 4-30

Materials: Lots of Jumbo marshmallows, garbage cans

Activity Level: Low

Risk Level: Medium

Time Required: 6-15 minutes

The activity starts with everyone who wishes to play placing a marshmallow in his/her mouth and saying the words, "Chubby Bunny." Participants will continue to add marshmallows, one at a time and, without swallowing, repeat the line, "Chubby Bunny". The game continues until the last person to do so successfully without spitting out marshmallows wins. Having garbage cans available for people to spit out marshmallows is also a very good idea.

Facilitation Questions:

- Who was the funniest during this activity? Why?

CLAM FREE

Number of People:	Between 16-60
Materials:	One nerf ball or soft object (cones for marking playing area are optional)
Activity Level:	High
Risk Level:	Low
Time Required:	12-20 minutes

Define the boundaries of the playing field to begin – appropriate size to the number of participants. One person should volunteer to be the "nuclear reactor" and given the nerf ball. The rest of the participants are clams and they should be happy clams. The object of the game is for the nuclear reactor to contaminate all of the clams by tagging them with the nerf ball's "toxic sludge." The nuclear reactor can throw the ball or tag them with it in his/her hand for it to be effective. Of course, clams no longer can be happy if they are contaminated, so they want to avoid this at all costs! If a clam is tagged and therefore contaminated, s/he must sit on the ground and repeatedly say in a high-pitched voice, "Help me! Help me! Help me!" The contaminated clams, however, can be cleaned of their sludge status if two clean, mobile clams (or more if you desire) manage to link hands around the contaminated clam, lower their hands around the clam and then raise them high and yell, "Clam Free!" The tagged clam is now clean and free to move about. The activity continues until all the clams are contaminated or until the group gets tired. Facilitators may wish to have extra balls available if one gets far off course or you may wish to have more than one nuclear reactor.

Facilitation Questions:

- Why do we do this activity?
- How helpless were you when you were tagged?

Ultimate Icebreaker & Teambuilder Guide © 2007

CLAPPING CLUES

Number of People: Between 6-60

Materials: None

Activity Level: Low

Risk Level: Low

Time Required: 10-20 minutes

One participant will be asked to leave the room and should be unable to see/hear the rest of the participants. The remaining group will secretly designate an object in the room as the "target". The person that left will then be called back into the room. That person must find the object without any verbal hints from the group…only by applause. When the person is close to the object, the applause is loud and enthusiastic, but when the person is far away, the applause is weak and quiet. The exercise continues for a few rounds and for a few objects with new people each time. The person doing the searching could get a standing ovation when s/he finds the item.

Facilitation Questions:

- Did you feel supported or not while in the middle?
- What was challenging about this exercise?

CLOTHESPIN TAG

Number of People: Between 8-50

Materials: 4 clothespins per participant

Activity Level: Medium

Risk Level: Low

Time Required: 5-12 minutes

Each player should receive four clothespins. The object of the game is to have each player get rid of his/her pins by attaching them to other players' clothing (not the people themselves). Participants must remain within the defined boundaries for the game. In addition, the four pins must be placed on four separate players. Once someone has gotten rid of his/her pins, the game stops. This game can be played several times.

Facilitation Questions:

- Why do we do an activity like this within the group?

COLOR, CAR, CHARACTER

Number of People:	Between 10-40
Materials:	None
Activity Level:	Low
Risk Level:	Low
Time Required:	12-30 minutes

Ask participants to form a circle and sit down. Participants will have a couple of minutes to think about a type of car, a color and a fictional character that best describes his/her personality. After selecting, each person should give a brief explanation as to why s/he chose those particular items. The activity continues until everyone has shared.

Facilitation Questions:

- Why did you choose the car you did?
- What parts of your personality were most difficult to describe?
- Why did you choose the fictional character that you did?
- Do you feel that you know people a little better now than you did before?

COMIC STRIP CHAOS

Number of People: Between 20-100

Materials: Cut comic strips into individual frames (one per person
                     playing), tape, and container to put them in

Activity Level: Low

Risk Level: Low

Time Required: 4-8 minutes

Each participant should take a comic strip frame at random. The facilitator should verify that there are an equal number of frames as there are participants in the activity. After the entire group has selected one, the participants should search for others in the room that shares the same comic sequence. It is a good idea to mix multiple days of the same comic to make things more difficult for people. After they have found everyone with the comic sequence, they must arrange themselves in chronological order to form the comic strip. Upon completing the sequence, the group sits together. They can then share the comic with others, etc. It is great way to break a large group into smaller groups as well. Use Sunday comics for larger groups or dailies for small groups/triads.

Facilitation Questions:
- What did you think of your comic?
- What strategy did you use to find your partners?

CONFUSION BINGO

Number of People: Between 10-100

Materials: Writing instruments and copies of Confusion Bingo cards

Activity Level: Medium

Risk Level: Medium

Time Required: 8-15 minutes

Similar to "Person Bingo" in that everyone should have a pre-made bingo card and something to write with. Ask participants to not read what is on their bingo cards before the activity begins. Once the game starts, everyone must move, interact and mingle with each other while trying to get other players to initial their bingo cards. In Confusion Bingo, each box on the bingo card represents some action or activity that another person (or persons) must do in order to have the card initialed. There should be a good mix of silly, physical and light activities for people to participate in. Create your own or use the examples provided. The goal of the activity is that each participant should try to completely fill the bingo card. Depending upon the number of people participating, each person may only have one or two items on the card initialed by the same person. This will require each person to meet more people in the group. The facilitator can alternatively have a prize or other goodies available for people when they finish their cards. The cards can be in any size you wish, from a three by three or four by four square card on up to a six by six card or even larger, but remember that people may get physically tired if they have to do so many stunts!

Facilitation Questions:

- What were you willing (or not willing) to do in this activity?
- How is embarrassment good for a group? What about shared experiences?
- Any surprises from this exercise?

Confusion Bingo

Get a man to do 5 jumping jacks and sign here.	Get a woman to stand on one foot with arms outstretched for 20 seconds and sign here.	Ask someone to swing their hips left to right 10 times and sign here.	Get someone to say the alphabet backwards to you and have them sign here.
Ask someone to act like a chicken for 15 seconds and have them sign here.	Create a secret handshake with someone and then 2 minutes later, come back, repeat it, and have them sign here.	Ask someone to count to 10 in a language other than English and sign here.	Ask someone to do a "Pulp Fiction" dance with you and sign here.
Find someone to do three consecutive somersaults and sign here.	Ask someone to give their best attempt at a loud yodel and sign here.	Ask someone to share their "most embarrassing moment" with you and sign here.	Ask someone to go up to an unexpecting person in the group and give them a big hug, then sign here.
Ask someone to show you their navel and have them sign here.	Play "Ring Around the Rosy" with 2 other people and have them sign here.	Ask someone to give you the names of all 7 of the Seven Dwarfs and sign here.	Have someone spin around 8 complete times in a circle and while they are still dizzy, sign here.

COUNT OFF

Number of People:	Between 8-25
Materials:	None
Activity Level:	Low
Risk Level:	Low
Time Required:	5-8 minutes

This is a simple game that actually is more difficult than it seems. Ask everyone to get into a circle and face the outside of the ring. The objective of the game is for each group to count up to XX (the number of players.) They will do so collectively without any pre-planning as to who is going to say what number. Players may only say one number each and once they're done, they must sit silently. No verbal or non-verbal signals are allowed. The group must do the activity without any two people saying the number simultaneously or saying the same number twice. If this occurs, the group must again start at one and begin again. Process the activity in terms of difficulty in communication, need for pre-planning, etc.

Facilitation Questions:

- What was your first impression of this exercise? Was it going to be easy or difficult?
- How did you know when to speak a number or wait?
- What does this say about communication?

DEAD FISH

Number of People:	Between 8-50
Materials:	None
Activity Level:	Low
Risk Level:	Low
Time Required:	4-10 minutes

Ask all the participants to get into a comfortable position on the ground or floor that they can sustain for a long period of time. Once everyone has settled, the leader will count down from ten to zero. At zero, the game will begin. Once the game has begun, nobody is allowed to talk or move, with the exception of the eyes and chest for breathing. If the leader (and ONLY the leader) should notice anyone talk, laugh or move, then s/he will verbally remove that person from the game. Anyone removed from playing may then persuade others to talk or move, but may not physically touch players still in the game. The winner is the last person remaining who then becomes the leader of the next game.

Facilitation Questions:

- What provoked you to move or talk?
- Who were the bad influences with this exercise?
- For those of you who were left until the end, how did you focus on the task?
- What was the worst distraction in this activity?

Ultimate Icebreaker & Teambuilder Guide © 2007

DETECTIVE

Number of People:	Between 12-50
Materials:	None
Activity Level:	Low
Risk Level:	Low
Time Required:	8-15 minutes

This is a game of "Hide and Seek" but done in the open! Before the actual game begins, have everyone circulate around the room in any direction. Explain to the participants, "Whenever you see an empty space open up in the room, you should move quickly to try and fill in that empty space. As other spaces open up, you then move to fill those, etc." Everyone should be moving silently. After a few minutes of walking around, give instructions to the participants, "You are detectives. Select someone in the room to observe, but <u>don't let them know who it is</u>. As you walk around the room, make sure that you keep that person in sight at all times, but do <u>not</u> let that person know you are watching them! Don't be obvious!" Let everyone wander around and shadow each other for a few minutes and remind people not to talk. It may be good for participants if they make it difficult to be seen by hiding in and out of others in the group. Players have to remember to keep looking at the person they are observing. Remind players that because they are self-selecting people to watch that not everyone playing may have someone watching them and others may have more than one! There are two ways to end the activity. You can ask participants to "Follow your person around no matter where they go." Players may eventually form into some sort of line. You may also ask them after awhile if they correctly identified their detectives! Alternatively, you can ask players to stop and guess out loud who is watching them!

Facilitation Questions:

- Why do we do this activity?
- What strategies did you use during this exercise?
- What was most memorable?

DIZZY BAT

Number of People: Between 8-60 in teams of at least 4

Materials: One plastic bat (or similar) per team

Activity Level: High

Risk Level: Medium

Time Required: 6-15 minutes

Participants should be formed into teams. Place a bat on the ground for each team that is the same distance away. When ready, the first person in line must run to the bat, stand it up, place one end on the ground, bend over so his/her forehead is on the bat and spin around the bat eight times. Leaving the bat behind, that person must then run back towards the group and tag the next person in line, who then runs to the bat to do the same thing. The entire group must complete the task. The first team that is done, wins. Be aware that people will likely have a difficult time going in a straight line after spinning and should be aware to not trip on themselves or run into other players!

Facilitation Questions:
- Why do we do this activity?
- How did competition affect this activity? How might competition affect a group or a team?
- Did you find people encouraging or not helpful while you were completing the task?

DO YOU LOVE YOUR NEIGHBOR?

Number of People:	Between 14-80
Materials:	None
Activity Level:	Medium
Risk Level:	Low
Time Required:	10-20 minutes

Ask participants to form a circle, standing about two feet apart from each other, facing the middle. Everyone should remove their shoes and place them immediately behind them in the circle to mark their location. One person will begin play in the middle of the circle, removing his/her shoes from the circle so that there is one less set of shoes than people playing. The middle person can then say to someone in the outer circle, "<person's name>, do you love your neighbor?" The individual pointed out should say, "Yes, I love my neighbors <left person> and <right person>, but I REALLY love people that <name some trait> (are wearing green, are from Oregon, have been out of the country, etc.). This trait MUST be something that is true for the middle person! Now, all members of the group that fit that characteristic must move and find a new spot in the circle at least three spaces away from where they were standing. The person with no space (last person remaining) becomes the caller in the middle. When asked if they love their neighbors, the person pointed to can also say, "No, I don't" in which case the two "neighbors" on either side of him/her must switch places with one another, and the last person to their space becomes the caller. To add to the activity, you can alternatively add penalties for being in the middle three, four, five or more times by asking the middle person to do something embarrassing such as sing "I'm a little teapot" or butt-spell something for the group. This activity can also be done such that if someone says, "No, I don't" then <u>everyone</u> participating in the activity must switch places.

Facilitation Questions:
- Why do we do this activity?
- What surprised you about people here?
- What was your biggest fear in this exercise and why?
- Who did you make a connection with?

DRIP, DRIP, DROP

Number of People:	Between 15-40
Materials:	A bucket of water (about 1-2 gallons), water outlet
Activity Level:	High
Risk Level:	High
Time Required:	10-20 minutes

This activity plays similarly to a game of "Duck, Duck, Goose" except for the addition of a lot of water! As a result, this activity probably needs to be done outdoors. Participants should sit in a circle facing inwards with their eyes closed. One person will be selected to start the activity and given a bucket of water. That person will take the bucket of water and begin to walk around the circle, dipping his or her hand in the bucket and saying the word, "Drip." At the same time, s/he should sprinkle a <u>little</u> water from his/her fingertips at the person they are passing. This should continue until s/he reaches a "target" and instead of sprinkling water on that person, s/he should dump the bucket of water on them and say, "Drop." The "dumper" should begin to run around the circle two times, being chased by the wet target. If the target catches the dumper, then the target gets to become the dumper. If the dumper is able to go around the circle two times without being touched and sit down in the target's spot, s/he is able to again dump water on someone for the next round. Be aware of safety issues with running on potentially wet surfaces and alternatively you may use a cup of water instead of a bucket. The game continues until everyone is resoundingly wet.

Facilitation Questions:
- Why do we do this activity?
- How does energy level affect the group?
- What were your thoughts when someone walked behind you in the circle?

DUCKY WUCKY

Number of People: Between 10-40

Materials: Blindfold

Activity Level: Low

Risk Level: Medium

Time Required: 8-15 minutes

Ask participants to form a circle facing the center. One volunteer should be taken out of the circle, moved to the middle and be blindfolded. The people in the circle must sit on the ground comfortably. The person in the middle will be blindfolded and spun around 7 times to be disoriented. The blindfolded person will then slowly crawl his/her way to the outside circle and sit on a person's leg. Once sitting, the blindfolded person will say, "Ducky Wucky." The sitting person will reply with a simple, "Quack." The blindfolded person can say "Ducky Wucky" up to three times in order to try to determine who the person is. The blindfolded person has two guesses to try to figure out who the sitting person is. If s/he is successful, the sitting person goes to the middle. If not, the blindfolded person goes to the middle to try again. If the blindfolded person isn't successful after two different people, a new person can be found and roles may be switched.

Facilitation Questions:
- Why do we do this activity?
- What was most memorable?
- What cues did you use to be successful? How did you hide your identity?

ELBOW TAG

Number of People: Between 14-36

Materials: None (Optional: cones to mark activity boundaries)

Activity Level: High

Risk Level: Medium

Time Required: 12-20 minutes

Ask participants to find a partner and link one arm linked with each other's elbow, facing the same direction. The pairs should spread out around the designated playing area and two individuals are chosen to be "it". One is the chaser and one is to be chased. Once the game begins, the person being chased will run around the area to some other pair of people and hook elbows with another person (facing either direction). The third person in the group on the far side is now the one being chased and should run off. The chaser must then chase after this new player. If at any time chaser tags the person being chased, the person that was being chased spins around three times and becomes the new chaser. The chaser is now the one being chased. The game continues until completed, but you may want to have a time limit to prevent overly tired chasers and to allow continued participation from the group. Also note that people should be careful running as well as violent arm linking at a full sprint for safety reasons.

Facilitation Questions:

- What strategies did you use during this game?
- When might this game be applicable for a group?

ELVES, GIANTS, & CHICKENS

Number of People: Between 15-250

Materials: None

Activity Level: Medium

Risk Level: Low

Time Required: 8-12 minutes

Participants should know how to play the game "Rock, Paper, Scissors" in order to successfully do this activity! Everyone will initially start off as a "chicken" in this game, and will wander around to others by squatting and have his/her arms make wing motions. The facilitator should ask participants to loudly say what they are so that others may hear. People should repeat out loud, "I'm a chicken, I'm a chicken…" or "I'm an elf, I'm an elf" so that others of their species can find them! When the player (as a chicken) comes up to another chicken, they play a game of "Rock, Paper, Scissors." Once one person wins, that person is now promoted to an "elf", while the losing player remains a chicken. Elves should walk hunched over with hands sticking in the air near their ears. Chickens can only play with other chickens, elves with other elves, etc. When two elves play against each other, the winner becomes a giant and thus, giants can only play other giants. Giants must walk around, pretending to be huge in size with arms extended high in the air. If at any time, however, an elf or giant loses his/her game of "Rock, Paper, Scissors," s/he is demoted to be a chicken again. Once a giant has successfully beaten another giant, s/he has the option to continue playing as a giant or become an observer of the activity.

Facilitation Questions:

- Why do we do this activity?
- What was a memorable moment from this activity and with whom?
- Who was successful at this activity? Who wasn't? Why?

EVOLUTION

Number of People:	Between 16-50
Materials:	None
Activity Level:	Low
Risk Level:	Low
Time Required:	10-20 minutes

The facilitator should choose an "Evolver" before the game begins. Explain to the participants that the Evolver can change people into animals simply by whispering to them. Everyone else is allowed to communicate as well, but only in a whisper. Ask people to mill about as if at a party. Encourage people to shake hands and whisper to others in the group. At some point, the Evolver says quietly to another player, "You are a turtle (cow, duck, bird, hippopotamus, other animal.)" The player whispered to should count to ten seconds silently to him/herself and then slowly turn into that animal. No other player is allowed to use the phrase, "You're a…" except the Evolver. Gradually players will turn into the various animals. If a player thinks that s/he knows the identity of the "Evolver," then s/he should raise his/her hand and yell, "I accuse!" Everyone freezes in place at that point and the player points to the person that s/he thinks is the Evolver and says, "You are the Evolver!" If correct, then the Evolver becomes that animal, but if the accusation is incorrect, the accuser becomes that animal and the game continues. When in animal form, players should be able to talk but use a cow-like (or their appropriate animal) "accents." They must walk like that animal, etc. The activity continues until a set period of time or a few rounds have taken place.

Facilitation Questions:
- What was a funny or memorable moment from this activity?
- What cues did you use to suspect someone was the Evolver?
- What ideas would make this game more challenging to the group?

FAMOUS PAIRS

Number of People:	Between 16-80
Materials:	Note cards with famous pairs, tape
Activity Level:	Low
Risk Level:	Low
Time Required:	12-20 minutes

Each participant should receive a note card taped to his/her back so that s/he is unable to see or read what is taped there. The famous pairs are people in society, media or entertainment that go together (Fred Flintstone & Wilma Flintstone, Lucille Ball & Desi Arnaz, etc.) You may use the example sheets created on the next pages (or create your own contemporary list since things change all the time!) The object of the game is for each participant to try to guess the name on his/her back. Players can only ask yes/no questions and only one/two/three (facilitator choice) questions to a single individual in the room before they have to move on to someone else. Once someone determines who the note card name is, s/he should find that card's partner If the partner is found, but hasn't figured out who s/he is yet, then wait until s/he figures it out before introductions take place.

Facilitation Questions:
- Who had a difficult time at this activity? Who had it easy? What made it so?
- What questions did you ask that were most revealing?

Newstrom and Scannell, *Still More Games Trainers Play*, © 1991, The McGraw-Hill Companies. Material reproduced and adapted with permission of the McGraw-Hill Companies.

Fred Flintstone	Wilma Flintstone
Jack Dawson	Rose
Batman	Robin
Monica	Chandler
Will Truman	Grace Adler
Marge Simpson	Homer Simpson
Bill Clinton	Monica Lewinsky

George W. Bush	Laura Bush
Scooby Doo	Shaggy
Mickey Mouse	Minnie Mouse
George Washington	Martha Washington
Luke Skywalker	Princess Leia
Brad Pitt	Angelina Jolie
Agent Mulder	Agent Sculley

Bugs Bunny	Daffy Duck
Captain Kirk	Mr. Spock
Ginger Rogers	Fred Astaire
Moe	Curly
Harry Potter	Lord Voldemort
Frodo	Aragorn
Peter Parker	Mary Jane

Garfield	Odie
Dorothy	Wicked Witch of West
Siegfried	Roy
Superman	Lois Lane
Mona Lisa	Leonardo Da Vinci
Bill Cosby	Jell-O
Ozzy Osbourne	Sharon Osbourne

Meredith Viera	Matt Lauer
Lone Ranger	Tonto
Regis Philbin	Kelly Ripa
Romeo	Juliet
Ronald Reagan	Nancy Reagan
Sleeping Beauty	Prince Charming
Prince Charles	Princess Diana

Snoopy	Charlie Brown
Zeus	Hera
Martin Luther King Jr.	Coretta Scott King
Simba	Mufasa
Aladdin	Jasmine
Beauty	Beast
Starsky	Hutch

Godzilla	Moth-ra
Sonny Bono	Cher
Mike Brady	Carol Brady
Six Million Dollar Man	Bionic Woman
Gilligan	The Skipper
Lewis	Clark
Adam	Eve

Barbie	Ken
John Lennon	Yoko Ono
Ashton Kutcher	Demi Moore
Lucille Ball	Desi Arnaz
Lancelot	King Arthur
Franklin Roosevelt	Eleanor Roosevelt
Gomez Addams	Morticia Addams

Whitney Houston	Bobby Brown
Hansel	Gretel
Pamela Anderson	Tommy Lee
Bert	Ernie
JFK	Jackie Kennedy
Shrek	Donkey
3 Little Pigs	Big Bad Wolf

Jessica Simpson	Nick Lachey
Ben Stiller	Owen Wilson
Pinky	The Brain
Ren	Stimpy
Faith Hill	Tim McGraw
Beyonce	Jay-Z
Will Smith	Jada Pinkett-Smith

John Travolta	Olivia Newton-John
Tom Cruise	Katie Holmes
Neo	Morpheus
Kenny	Cartman

Ultimate Icebreaker & Teambuilder Guide © 2007

FIVE THINGS

Number of People: Between 6-75

Materials: Construction paper, scissors, pens for participants, tape

Activity Level: Low

Risk Level: Low

Time Required: 20-30 minutes

This exercise is very visual and can remind you of things that you may have done in grade school! Ask everyone to trace on paper one of their hands using a pen. Use the scissors to cut out his/her hand. The facilitator should come up with a question that has the potential to have five answers. For example, ask participants to come up with "Five things that you want people to know about yourself," or "Five things you love about your job." Ask participants to write those five things on the fingers of their hands and their names on the palm. Depending upon the group size, you can ask people to share their five things within the group, in small groups or you can arrange to post the hands somewhere for people to see.

Facilitation Questions:

- How did you choose your five things?
- What did you learn about others here in the room? What would you want to learn more about?
- How effective was this exercise in getting to know people?

FLOUR GAME

Number of People:	Between 6-24
Materials:	Flour, bowl, pan (cookie sheet), dime, knife
Activity Level:	Low
Risk Level:	Medium
Time Required:	15-30 minutes

The facilitator should fill a bowl completely full of flour. Place the pan over the top of the bowl, then gently flip the bowl, and pan over while holding the two together. Smoothly and carefully, lift the bowl off of the pan, leaving a mound of flour (if it cracks then try again.) Gently place a dime on top of the mound. The objective of the game is for participants to slice into the mound of flour without the dime falling. The person who makes the cut that results in the dime falling has to dig through the flour to find the dime with just their mouth. Alternatively, you can have some other fun, gross or disgusting task when the dime falls. Also, you could ask participants to say some fact about him/herself prior to each cut made in the flour. This activity may or may not require multiple dimes and large amount of flour, depending upon the group.

Facilitation Questions:
- What was challenging about this activity?
- What strategies did you use?
- How did you communicate with this activity? Was it successful?

FOLLOW THE LEADER

Number of People: Between 10-50

Materials: None

Activity Level: High

Risk Level: Low

Time Required: 10-18 minutes

This is the standard children's game that actually works well with any energetic group! Assign or ask for a volunteer to lead the group. That person should take off and go over, around, and under things in the general area (outside is better). The rest of the participants should exactly follow the route taken by the leader. After about one minute, the leader should yell, "switch" and move to the back of the line, causing a new leader to move forward! This can continue until everyone has been a leader or gets tired. The game ends once the group returns to the starting point.

Facilitation Questions:

- Why do we do this activity?
- How are some children's games good for adults too?

FREEZE TAG

Number of People: Between 15-150

Materials: None (Optional cones to mark activity boundaries)

Activity Level: High

Risk Level: Medium

Time Required: 10-18 minutes

This is a standard game of tag, but once a person is tagged, s/he is frozen in place with his/her legs spread apart in an upside-down "V" shape. The only way to be "unfrozen" is to have another player crawl under and through the legs. The game can be made more difficult by having more than one person being "it" or requiring two people to crawl under legs to unfreeze someone. Be aware of safety concerns and designate a set playing field with "out of bounds".

Facilitation Questions:

- Why do we do this activity?
- How do children's outdoor games influence team development even now?

GROUP STORY

Number of People:	Between 4-40
Materials:	None
Activity Level:	Low
Risk Level:	Low
Time Required:	6-12 minutes

This exercise will ask participants to work in teams to create a story. This story will be started out by the facilitator but continued by the participants. An example of the start of a story could be, "Once upon a time in a land far, far away there lived a vicious troll…" Each participant will then go around the circle and give the next sentence to the story. The next person will provide the subsequent sentence and so on. You can ask that everyone contribute one or more sentences in the circle, depending upon the number of people in the group. There should be a definite beginning, middle, climax and end to the story.

Facilitation Questions:

- Why did you decide to take the story the direction you did?
- What does this exercise say about creativity in the group?
- How did you feel making your sentence?

GUARD THE BONE

Number of People:	Between 8-30 in groups of four
Materials:	One towel or shirt per group
Activity Level:	Medium
Risk Level:	Low
Time Required:	6-15 minutes

One person becomes the "dog" in the group and gets on his/her hands and knees. The other players should form a small circle sitting around the dog. Each group needs a towel/shirt/other object placed under the dog. The dog must protect that object from others trying to take it. The other players, also on their hands and knees, must try to get the item from the dog without being touched. If someone is successful, s/he becomes the dog. If the dog tags someone before s/he gets the towel, the tagged person is "out" until the next game.

Facilitation Questions:

- Why do we do this activity?
- Was there teamwork involved in this activity? How so?

HA!

Number of People:	Between 10-30
Materials:	None
Activity Level:	Medium
Risk Level:	Medium
Time Required:	8-12 minutes

Ask all participants to lie on the ground or the floor, positioning themselves so that one person's head lies on another person's stomach and so on, forming a chain of people. One of the people on an end will start. That person should start by saying, "HA!" The next person in the chain goes next and says, "HA HA!" With each subsequent person, add one more "HA!" so that if there are 30 people. The last person will then say 30 "HA's!" The object is to get through the group of people without having anyone actually laugh. If people laugh, they have to start again. You could also arrange participants to form a complete circle lying down for this activity if the group isn't as familiar with each other.

Facilitation Questions:

- Who had the most difficulty with this exercise? Who did you expect to not do well?
- What challenged you?

HEIGHT LINE

Number of People:	Between 10-60
Materials:	Blindfolds (or closing eyes)
Activity Level:	Low
Risk Level:	Low
Time Required:	4-8 minutes

The object of this activity is for participants to line up by height without being able to see. Players should put their arms up folded across their chests and move slowly so that no collisions will occur. The facilitator may choose the group to arrange by touch or by saying their height out loud (or some other creative method). This activity can even be more challenging if you explain words that participants cannot use such as "five" "inches" or "six". At the conclusion of the activity, ask each person to go down the line and say their height or the facilitator can visually check the heights of the line.

Facilitation Questions:

- What was challenging about this exercise?
- How would this activity been different if you could strategize before beginning?

HOG CALL

Number of People:	Between 20-200
Materials:	None
Activity Level:	Low
Risk Level:	Medium
Time Required:	4-8 minutes

Break the group into pairs. Each pair must choose two things: a machine and an animal. The members of the group must decide who is which and think of a specific machine or animal they would be, sharing it with their partner. The facilitator should then place animals and machines at opposite sides of the room. Everyone must close their eyes and by making only the noise of their respective animal or machine, they must find their partner. Remind people to be careful and move slowly with arms up across their chests as "bumpers." When they find their partner, they can open their eyes and wait until everyone else is done.

Facilitation Questions:

- What was funniest or most enjoyable about this activity?
- Who had a difficult animal or machine? What made it so?

HOW YOU DOIN'?

Number of People: Between 15-70

Materials: None

Activity Level: Low

Risk Level: Medium

Time Required: 8-12 minutes

Ask participants to close their eyes and get into a circle facing inwards (shoulder to shoulder.) Ask people to count off and remember their numbers. With eyes still closed, ask each person to shake hands with the person to their left and ask them, "How YOU doin'?" (Think Joey from *Friends*) The person should answer, "Just fine, thanks." Ask the participants to do this three or four times. Then ask the group (with eyes still closed and with their hands crossed in front of their chests for safety) to <u>slowly</u> begin to wander around until they are thoroughly mixed up. Then ask the group to return to their sequential order, with their eyes closed – all they can say is "How YOU doin'?" and "Just fine, thanks."

Facilitation Questions:

- How did you feel doing this activity?
- What were you expecting prior to closing your eyes?

HULA HOOP RELAY

Number of People:	Between 9-50
Materials:	One hula-hoop (per group)
Activity Level:	Medium
Risk Level:	Low
Time Required:	8-15 minutes

Ask all of the participants to form a circle and join hands. The facilitator will break the circle and place the hula-hoop looping around the arms of two people, who re-join their hands. The idea is to pass the hula-hoop completely around the circle without anyone breaking their link of hands.

Facilitation Questions:

- Why do we do this activity?
- What strategies did you use to try to be successful?
- What parts of the body were most challenging?

HUM THAT TUNE

Number of People:	Between 15-300
Materials:	Pieces of paper with a nursery rhyme or song on it – one piece per participant
Activity Level:	Low
Risk Level:	Low
Time Required:	4-8 minutes

This exercise is good if you are going to divide people into groups. Each participant should receive a piece of paper with the name of a nursery rhyme or other song (i.e. "Row your Boat" or "Twinkle, Twinkle" or "Stop, in the Name of Love" or other familiar tune). When the facilitator signals, all of the people who have a specific song must hum that tune and find everyone else with the same song. Everyone forms into that group. This exercise can also be done with eyes closed. Use the same number of songs or as groups that you wish to divide people in to.

Facilitation Questions:

- Was there any affinity to the song you chose?
- What techniques did you use to get with your group?

HUMAN KNOT

Number of People: Between 6-40

Materials: None

Activity Level: High

Risk Level: Medium

Time Required: 12-25 minutes

Ask the participants to get together into a circle facing the middle. People should get as close as they can to their neighbors. The facilitator will then ask everyone to take his/her right hand and extend it into the middle of the circle and grab the hand of someone else in the circle. The group members then should take their left hand and do the same, but not grab the same person. Without letting go of the hands, the team has to untangle themselves until a circle is formed. This is a very physical exercise that will challenge group problem solving. If a group is having a difficult time, and with the group's consensus, you can be a set of shears and "cut" one of the tangled hands and allow the group to continue. Realize that some knots may not be solvable or have two separate circles as well. As an alternative way to challenge the group, you can ask everyone to do the activity without talking.

Facilitation Questions:

- Who was the leader of your group during this exercise?
- How did you deal with difficulties or getting "stuck"?
- How was the group's communication during this activity?
- What group roles did people have during this exercise?

HUMAN TACO (OR BURGER)

Number of People:	Between 20-300
Materials:	Tape, pieces of paper with a taco (or burger) ingredient on it (See list on next page)
Activity Level:	Low
Risk Level:	Low
Time Required:	8-20 minutes

To begin, facilitators should tape a piece of paper to participant's backs so that they cannot see it. When distributing the pieces of paper, make sure that there is enough for everyone. When everyone is ready to start, each player will begin to mingle around. Each person will ask yes/no questions to determine what the ingredient is that they have on their back. See the examples that follow for cards that have taco ingredients on it. They can only ask one yes/no question to any one person. Once they have determined their ingredient they must form a complete taco with other participants in order. Explain that the correct order of ingredients for a taco will be: shell, meat, cheese, lettuce, tomato, salsa, guacamole, and sour cream. Having a sign or poster with the order of ingredients will be helpful as well. This game can be done with hamburger ingredients of your choice as well. Remind people that leftovers are always good (people without a whole taco) and ask them to join a complete taco as "extra cheese," etc. This exercise works well to break people up into smaller groups for further activities.

Facilitation Questions:
- Why do we do this activity?
- What questions did you ask to determine what you were?
- How does this exercise work in group situations?

TACO SHELL	GROUND BEEF
CHEESE	LETTUCE
SALSA	GUACAMOLE
SOUR CREAM	TOMATO

HUMAN TWISTER

Number of People:	Between 6-40
Materials:	Two different colored slips of paper (3x5 note card size) per person & rolls of tape
Activity Level:	Low
Risk Level:	Medium
Time Required:	8-15 minutes

Provide each participant with two different colored slips of paper and tape. Depending upon the size of the group, use a total of four to six colors – larger groups should have the fewest colors. Ask players to tape the card to two places on their bodies. Remind participants to place paper on places where they are OK with and it is appropriate to touch! When everyone has taped on their cards, challenge the group to line up, matching and touching their cards to someone else's of the same color. Alternatively, you can create a spinner and encourage people to do "left hand green" or "right leg blue" and challenge people to get tied up into complete knots!

Facilitation Questions:

- Why do we do this activity?
- What role does touch play (or not play) within a team?

I LOVE YOU BABY, BUT I JUST CAN'T SMILE

Number of People: Between 10-45

Materials: None

Activity Level: Low

Risk Level: Low

Time Required: 6-12 minutes

Ask the participants to form a circle facing the middle. One person is going to be "it" and will approach someone else in the circle and will say, "I love you, baby." The player in the circle must respond by saying, "I love you baby, but I just can't smile." If that player smiles while speaking these words, s/he becomes "it." If the player doesn't smile, "it" must approach someone else and try again until they can make someone smile. No one is allowed to touch anyone else during the activity to try to make someone smile, but anything else is fair play.

Facilitation Questions:

- Who was most successful at this exercise and why?
- What techniques were used to make people smile?

ICE CUBES

Number of People:	Between 6-60 in teams
Materials:	Collection of similar-sized ice cubes
Activity Level:	Medium
Risk Level:	Medium
Time Required:	8-20 minutes

Start this activity by dividing participants into equal teams. When everyone is ready to begin, explain that the object is for each team to get their ice cube and melt it as quickly as possible. Only one person may touch a cube at a time. Players can rub it between hands, against clothes or other areas, but may not put it in their mouths. While they are trying to melt the cube, it should be passed around the team frequently so that no one player should keep it for more than a few seconds at a time. The facilitator may be a neutral observer and determine when to switch the ice cubes. Players must also try to keep the cube off the ground or they must start with a fresh cube! The first team to melt the cube wins.

Facilitation Questions:

- What did people do to be successful?
- How does time pressure influence how you complete a task? Would this have been easier if more time was given? How so?

I'M THINKING OF SOMEONE

Number of People:	Between 10-45
Materials:	None
Activity Level:	Low
Risk Level:	Low
Time Required:	10-20 minutes

This activity can frustrate people as they try to determine the secret of the game. The facilitator (who knows the activity) should start this activity by looking at the participants and say the following phrase, "I'm thinking of someone and that someone is…" At that point, the facilitator should entertain guesses from the group as to who s/he is thinking of in the room. In reality, the person who the leader is thinking of is the FIRST person who speaks (or makes a noise if you prefer) following the end of the statement. It may take the group some time to figure out the game so be patient and encouraging. After someone guesses either correctly or incorrectly, acknowledge who the real person was. Repeat the phrase again and now the next person who speaks is the person who is being thought of, etc. The game continues until everyone figures it out.

Facilitation Questions:
- What clues and cues did you use to figure out the game?
- How did it feel to be one of the people to first figure it out? Last people?
- How did people collaborate or assist others? What support was given?

IMAGINARY DOUGH

Number of People: Between 6-50

Materials: None

Activity Level: Low

Risk Level: Low

Time Required: 10-25 minutes

Arrange participants into subgroups and ask them to sit in a circle. Arrange for a volunteer in each subgroup and explain that s/he will be taking a chunk of "dough" out of an imaginary ball of dough in the middle of each circle. That person will need to come up with some ordinary object and attempt to sculpt it out of the imaginary dough. The people in the circle will need to try to guess what that object is. Alternatively, the facilitator can prepare slips of paper that have objects on them and hand them out to groups for the activity.

Facilitation Questions:

- How did you decide what object you were going to use?
- What did you do to convey your object to the group?

KEEP IT UP

Number of People: Between 6-20

Materials: One inflatable beach ball

Activity Level: Medium

Risk Level: Low

Time Required: 6-15 minutes

Arrange participants into a circle with about 10 feet from other people on either side. (You may also arrange participants to form a filled circle equidistant apart from each other.) Explain to players that their objective is going to be to keep the ball up in the air as long as they can. Team members may not catch the balls, nor can they have their feet leave their current spot in the circle. Once the ball hits the ground, the game starts again. Teams can set goals for themselves to try and beat, etc. This exercise is even more challenging if it is windy.

Facilitation Questions:

- What goals did you set for this activity?
- What strategies did you have or come up with to be successful?
- How was the group's communication during this exercise?

KILLER

Number of People:	Between 16-50
Materials:	None
Activity Level:	Low
Risk Level:	Low
Time Required:	10-20 minutes

This activity doesn't involve actual murder, but is actually similar to the activity "Stinger." Everyone will start by sitting closely together with their heads down, eyes closed and both arms raised with thumbs up. The facilitator will go around the room and squeeze the thump of one person. That person is now the killer. With eyes still closed, the leader will squeeze the thumb of another group member twice. That person then becomes the sheriff. These two people must keep quiet about their roles. Once the two people have been established, everyone should stand and open their eyes. Only those selected will know who the sheriff or killer is. Everyone will begin walking around, making eye contact with everyone else. The object of the game is for the killer to kill everyone without getting caught. The killer does this by winking one eye at someone. If the killer winks at someone, that person is "dead." The person winked at must let 15 seconds pass and then will drop "dead" to the floor in dramatic fashion. Anyone can be killed (including the sheriff), but only the sheriff can guess who the killer is. If the killer winks at the sheriff before the sheriff guesses correctly, the sheriff should silently count to 15 and fall down dead without guessing…allowing the killer to finish off the participants. If the sheriff does guess correctly, s/he wins. If s/he guesses incorrectly, the sheriff immediately dies and the killer wins.

Facilitation Questions:
- What was frustrating about this exercise?
- What did you see happen?

LAP SIT

Number of People:	Between 6-300
Materials:	None
Activity Level:	Medium
Risk Level:	Medium
Time Required:	6-10 minutes

The group should start in a tight circle, facing the center and standing shoulder-to-shoulder. Ask everyone to then turn to their right and take enough steps to the left so that people are right up against the person ahead and behind them, forming a very tight circle. With hands on the shoulders of the people in front of them, the group will gently go down and sit on lap of the person behind them. Once everyone is sitting down the facilitator can then choose to challenge the group to try to walk in that formation, communicating each foot to lift and move as a group. This is a dynamic activity that will give the group a sense of accomplishment.

Facilitation Questions:

- You were challenged during this activity, how did you try to meet that challenge?
- What role does challenge play within a group?
- How did you work to succeed?

LIFE SAVER RELAY

Number of People:	Between 12-50
Materials:	Toothpicks and Lifesaver-like candies with holes in the middle
Activity Level:	Low
Risk Level:	Medium
Time Required:	5-10 minutes

In this game, each participant should receive a toothpick. At the start of the activity, s/he will place it between his/her teeth. The first person in the line will be given a lifesaver candy to place over the toothpick. When the facilitator indicates, the lifesaver must be passed to the next person in line from one toothpick to another without using any hands. If the lifesaver drops, a new lifesaver will be given to the first person in the line and the group must start again. Remember to be careful with poking each other with the toothpicks!

Facilitation Questions:

- What were you thinking about while doing this exercise?
- What were memorable moments during this activity?

Ultimate Icebreaker & Teambuilder Guide © 2007

LINE RELAY

Number of People: Between 10-60

Materials: None

Activity Level: High

Risk Level: Low

Time Required: 6-12 minutes

Divide participants into equal groups and designate a starting line and a finish line. When the signal is given, the first person in each line will lay down parallel to the starting line with arms spread out to his/her side. The next person in the line jumps over the first person and lies down, spreading his/her arms as well with fingers touching. This continues until the whole team is over the finish line. If a person is lying down and the group still has to get to the finish line, the person farthest away will get up and jump over to get to the final spot. Once a team member extends over the end line, they can stand up and cheer the remaining participants on.

Facilitation Questions:

- What rules were clear and which could have been broken?
- How were groups pushed to succeed? What did that feel like?
- What was challenging about this exercise?

LIST STORIES

Number of People:	Between 6-36 in pairs
Materials:	Large sheets of paper, markers, writing paper and pencils
Activity Level:	Low
Risk Level:	Low
Time Required:	10-20 minutes

Prior to the start of the activity, divide participants into pairs and give each pair paper and something to write with. As a large group, ask the participants to list 10 items of some designated category (candy bars, types of cars, trees, flowers, donuts, etc.) Explain to everyone that they are going to create a story using that list of ten things they just brainstormed. The stories need to make sense and should have a clear beginning, middle and end. Groups should use their creativity! Give them about 4-5 minutes to complete the task and then the pairs will need to read their stories to the rest of the group.

Facilitation Questions:

- Why did you take your story in the direction you did?
- How did you work in the group? How were your communications and decision making processes?
- Any changes or things you would do differently when working in the future?

LOLLIPOP

Number of People:	Between 4-30
Materials:	One "Dum-Dum" or "Tootsie" lollipop per person
Activity Level:	Low
Risk Level:	Low
Time Required:	15-40 minutes

This is a sharing activity best for groups that will get to know each other. Allow each person to take a lollipop of his/her choice. For every letter that appears in the name of the flavor that was chosen, that person has to share one thing about him/herself to the group. Continue with the activity until everyone has had a chance to share. Once a person has gone, they can eat their lollipop!

Facilitation Questions:

- What prompted you to choose your particular lollipop?
- What did you learn about the others here?
- Why did you elect to share what you did?
- How is this exercise important for new groups?

M&M GAME

Number of People:	Between 4-30
Materials:	One big bag of M&Ms (or other candy)
Activity Level:	Low
Risk Level:	Low
Time Required:	15-40 minutes

Ask people to sit in a circle, facing the middle for this activity. Each person should be allowed to take some M&Ms but can NOT eat them until they are told to do so. Once the bag has been passed around the circle of people and everyone has M&Ms, explain that for every M&M that they took, they will have to share one thing about themselves to the group. Once they have gotten done sharing, they can eat their M&Ms. The facilitator can alternatively say that each color represents something specific to share (red means something about family, blue about hobbies, etc.)

Facilitation Questions:

- Why do we do this activity?
- What did you learn about others through this activity?
- Why did you take the number of M&M's that you did?

M&M SWAP

Number of People:	Between 5-50
Materials:	One plastic spoon per participant and a big bag of M&Ms (or similar candy)
Activity Level:	Medium
Risk Level:	Low
Time Required:	8-15 minutes

Arrange the group in teams for competition, or ask everyone stand in a circle for cooperative play in small groups. Each pair should receive a plastic spoon and the first player to start should be given 4-5 M&Ms to hold in his/her spoon. Each participant must put the spoon in their mouths, holding the handle between their teeth with the scoop of the spoon facing up. The object of the activity is to pass the M&Ms from the first person to the next and so on, without using any hands and without dropping any M&Ms! Dropping M&Ms means starting back at the beginning. Alternatively, you may say that at least X number of M&M's must remain at the end for the activity to be successful. People can then have some M&M's as snacks at the end.

Facilitation Questions:

- What was challenging about this activity? What did you enjoy most?
- How did it feel to have pressure to not drop the M&M's?
- Did you feel part of a team? What roles did people play when not actively working?

MACHINE GAME

Number of People: Between 10-120

Materials: None

Activity Level: Medium

Risk Level: Low

Time Required: 10-20 minutes

The object of the exercise is for each group to create a machine using only the people in the group as "material." The facilitator can either have pre-made machines given to each group or can ask each group to create their own machine. Each person must be some part of the machine and either have a motion and/or noise. The group members will then put together the motions and sounds to complete the machine. Each group should have about five minutes to prepare and then present their machine to the rest of the group. The audience should try to guess what the machine is. Examples of machines include: typewriter, washing machines, motorcycles, blenders, toasters, cars, tractors, jet skis, copy machines and much more.

Facilitation Questions:

- How did the group determine the make-up of the machine?
- How did communication play a role in decision-making?
- Did everyone feel that their voices and ideas were heard? Why or why not?

MAFIA

Number of People: Between 8-25

Materials: One deck of playing cards with cards removed (see below)

Activity Level: Low

Risk Level: Low

Time Required: 20 minutes (+)

This game is one you often have to play only more than once! One person familiar with the rules of the game should be the narrator. The game setup requires that the group of people sit in a circle where everyone can see each other. The back-story for the activity is that the small group of participants has been infiltrated by the mafia. For the activity, these mafia are going to try and pick off and eliminate other participants. The object for the activity is that the mafia needs to try to eliminate everyone else before the townspeople (non-mafia) vote out and discover the mafia. From a standard deck of playing cards, hand out one card per participant and ask them to keep their card a secret. Include in these cards 4 Kings, 1 Queen and 1 Ace….the remaining can be any card or suit. There should be one card in the deck for each participant. (You can also adapt the number of each character to change the nature of the game.) The king represents who is mafia, the queen is the "doctor" and the ace is the "detective." The doctor's role is to try and "save" people that have been selected by the mafia to be eliminated. The detective is trying to determine separately who the members of the mafia actually are and gets help from the narrator. Tell participants to keep their cards <u>absolutely secret</u> – they can't be shown to anyone and no one can reveal or hint if they are a detective, doctor, mafia member or townsperson!

The narrator is responsible for keeping the activity going and the order of the game is as follows:

1.   Everyone closes their eyes.
2.   The mafia (king cards) wake up and the mafia silently decide who to eliminate by a consensus. The mafia then closes their eyes.
3.   The doctor (queen card) is asked to wake up and point to person that s/he wishes to try to save/protect from the mafia. It can even be him/herself. The doctor then closes his/her eyes.
4.   The detective wakes up and points at someone in the circle. The facilitator nods "yes" or shakes head "no" with the answer as to whether someone is a member of the mafia or not. The detective the closes his/her eyes.

5. The narrator wakes everyone up and explains results…who was selected for termination and whether the doctor saved him/her.

6. Everyone can now try to make accusations about who is mafia.

7. The group decides upon up to 3-4 names. Those people are allowed one minute each to defend him/herself.

8. The group votes on someone to kick out of town. If a majority of votes goes to one person, then that person is voted out. S/he then shows everyone his/her card. If not, then the townspeople can't decide and the activity moves on.

9. Process repeats at #1.

The actual play of the game might resemble below (subject to narrator's change):

"It's a beautiful spring day in the town of Springfield….the birds are chirping, the sun is shining, but a dark shadow has entered our peaceful town today. The mafia has come to town! Everyone now needs to close their eyes and put their heads down in complete silence!" *When everyone has done so, the facilitator should then say,* "Mafia members (and ONLY mafia members), please quietly open your eyes and look at the other members of the mafia in town." *The 4 mafias will open their eyes and make eye contact with each other.* "OK, mafia members, you need to decide who you wish to have wear 'cement shoes' and leave the game." *Decisions on who is taken out must be unanimous and done in silence. Pointing is the most obvious way that this takes place during the game. Once someone is selected, the facilitator should say,* "OK, close your eyes mafia members. Doctor, now you have the ability to save one person in this room from the mafia. At this time, doctor, open your eyes and silently decide who you wish to save from elimination." *The doctor will make a decision about who to save and point that person out.* "OK, close your eyes. Detective, please open your eyes. You can point at someone and I will nod yes or shake my head no to let you know if that person is mafia. Please do so now." *The facilitator should know who the mafia members are and truthfully nod or shake his/her head to whether or not the pointed person is a mafia member.* "OK, detective, close your eyes."

Play continues on as follows: "Well, good morning everyone. Everyone can open your eyes. You awaken to the sound of your alarm clock buzzing at you and the normally peaceful town of Springfield has been wracked with tragedy! An echoing scream pierces the town as you realize that XX (person selected by mafia) has been killed by a pack of wild, feral chickens! (Insert some random or funny demise here). Now, the question is, who here are members of the mafia and are responsible? You have the opportunity to vote one of the alleged perpetrators out of town in an effort to make Springfield mafia-free."

Participants should all be allowed to talk and state their case about what they saw, heard, believe, interpreted with body language, smelled, guessed or whatever to believe that someone is or is not a mafia member. Mafia members should try to lie, deceive or cajole others into selecting innocent people to be voted out of town. They should do anything to stay in the game! A discussion should take place for a few minutes among participants until the narrator asks the group who they wish to try to vote out of town. The narrator should take about 3-4 names only (often the first ones said or the loudest, most convincing people). The narrator should then explain that the accused can now take a minute to state their case. Following the accuser can take time to make his/her case as well. Proceed then on to the next person accused, etc. After everyone has had a chance to speak, the facilitator should hold a vote. Everyone playing the game can vote, including mafia! Only a person with a MAJORITY of votes (not merely a plurality) can be voted out. If a person is voted off, they reveal their card to the rest of everyone at that time. Doctors, mafia and detectives can be voted out of the town! The person voted off is out of the game and cannot contribute to discussion or voting from this point forward.

During the play of the game, if the doctor points out someone that is not to be eliminating the mafia, then nothing happens. If the doctor DOES save the person who the mafia selected, the facilitator should say something similar to: "and a miraculous situation has occurred. Just when the mafia were about to push XX off of a bridge, a truck carrying fluffy pillows was driving by and caught XX, bringing him/her to safety." The detective may also be correct is selecting someone as mafia. S/he may argue their case, but never can s/he mention that they KNOW the truth about someone being mafia. S/he must be discreet and cannot state or allude that s/he are the detective. Others playing may be able to guess who the doctor or detective are, but cannot be confirmed by the players themselves!

Play continues with multiple rounds until either the last people remaining are mafia or all of the mafia has been voted out of the game by the townspeople.

You can find more on this game and variations by going to Wikipedia at: http://en.wikipedia.org/wiki/Mafia_(game)

Facilitation Questions:
- What did you think of this activity?
- What were some of the most memorable moments about this exercise?
- How did you deceive others?
- What cues did you use to see if people were lying?

MAKE A DATE

Number of People:	Between 8-50
Materials:	One paper plate and writing instrument per person
Activity Level:	Low
Risk Level:	Low
Time Required:	12-20 minutes

Each participant should have a paper plate and something to write with for this activity. Ask everyone to draw the face of a clock on their plate with a small horizontal line next to each number (no digital clocks!) Alternatively, if there are fewer people, you can ask people to divide their plates into four, six or eight different quadrants. Once done, ask each person to walk around and find a "date" for each hour and write that person's name on the line by the hour. Gender should not be an issue for the dates! The catch is that no one doing the exercise can make a "date" with more than one person per hour. Remember that each pair has to have the same time available in order for the date or occur or a new partner must be found.

After everyone has made their dates, explain that it is now 12 o'clock (or quadrant #1) and everyone should go and find their dates. Allow 1-3 minutes for each pair to meet at each time on the clock. After time is up, speed forward time to the next hour and find your next date. The facilitator can provide a question for discussion for each hour and each date so people have a chance to get to know each other.

Facilitation Questions:

- Why do we do this activity?
- What did you learn about others in this activity?
- How was the clock organization of the activity? How did you find success as a group?

MAN OVERBOARD

Number of People:	Between 12-125
Materials:	None
Activity Level:	Medium
Risk Level:	Medium
Time Required:	20-30 minutes

The facilitator of the game is the "Captain" of the ship and everyone else is a crewmember. In the facilitator's best pirate or captain voice, explain the instructions to the crew and the nautical directions of the ship. (Starboard = right, Port = left, Stern = back, Bow = front). Test the group on the directions so that everyone knows what they are. The following are different instructions that the captain can give to the crew:

- "Attention on Deck" – Everyone comes to the middle of the ship and forms lines in front of the captain
- "Man a ___ person lifeboat!" - Everyone must find the correct number of partners and sit down with legs in a "V" shape around the person in front of them. Everyone in the group will begin rowing. The number of people is up to the captain. Leftover players can form their own small group, pretend to drown in the water, go down with the ship, or some other task.
- "Man Overboard" – Everyone must grab a partner and act as if s/he is rescuing a drowning victim.
- "Man your Cannon!" – Everyone grabs a partner…one person is in a wheelbarrow position making cannon noises, while the other grabs and lifts his/her legs.
- "Scrub the Port Deck" – Everyone gets on hands and knees and scrubs the floor on the left side of the ship – or other side that you name.
- "Mop the Stern Deck" – Everyone pretends to mop the floor at the back of the boat.
- "Everyone at the Periscope!" Everyone must lie on their backs and lift their legs in the air.
- "Ride the Dolphin" – Everyone grabs a partner, one partner riding on the back of the other.
- "Pirates are coming!" - Everyone gets out binoculars and begins looking for the pirates.

- "Hail the coast guard" – Everyone finds a partner. One person gets on hands and knees and the other person puts his/her foot on the other's back, has one hand on his/her hip, and yells at the others, "Hey Sailor."
- "The Captain is coming!" – Everyone stands at attention for the captain.

During this activity, it is good to introduce 3 or 4 different commands and slowly add others into the game. Once people are familiar with the commands, as part of the game, the captain can issue demerits for people that are the last to do the commands. Once someone receives three, s/he is eliminated from the game.

Facilitation Questions:

- How did partners know their roles during this activity?
- Once you had done one of them more than once, how did that affect expectations?
- How can you relate aspects of this exercise to "real life" situations?

MIRROR, MIRROR

Number of People: Between 8-30

Materials: Index cards, writing instruments

Activity Level: Low

Risk Level: Low

Time Required: 6-15 minutes

The facilitator will give each participant one index card and instructions to write on the card the name of a famous person that s/he has been told s/he looks or sounds like. Everyone should keep their responses secret, put them into a hat or bowl, and have a player pick a card at random. That person should read the card out loud while the rest of the group must try to guess the group member that wrote that name on the card.

Facilitation Questions:

- Who here looks the <u>most</u> like their celebrity? Why?
- Were there other celebrities that didn't appear on the list that fit for people?

MRS. MUMBLES

Number of People:	Between 8-40
Materials:	None
Activity Level:	Low
Risk Level:	Low
Time Required:	10-18 minutes

The group will sit close together in a circle facing the middle for this activity. The object of this game is to get the conversation moving quickly, but <u>without the people speaking showing their teeth</u>. The pattern of the conversation looks like below:

Facilitator to 2nd person:	"Is Mrs. Mumbles home?"
2nd person to Facilitator:	"Who?"
Facilitator to 2nd person:	"Mrs. Mumbles."
2nd person to Facilitator:	"I don't know, let me ask my neighbor."
2nd person to 3rd person:	"Is Mrs. Mumbles home?
3rd person to 2nd person:	"Who?"
2nd person to Facilitator:	"Who?"
Facilitator to 2nd person:	"Mrs. Mumbles."
2nd person to 3rd person:	"Mrs. Mumbles."
3rd person to 2nd person:	"I don't know, let me ask my neighbor."

The third will then turn to the fourth person and the chain continues. If the facilitator wishes to make this more difficult, send the same two messages in opposite directions at the same time.

Facilitation Questions:
- How did you feel doing this exercise?
- What role can silliness play on a team?

Ultimate Icebreaker & Teambuilder Guide © 2007

MUSICAL INTERPRETATION

Number of People:	Between 10-200
Materials Needed:	Music and music player, wide variety of music
Activity Level:	Medium
Risk Level:	Low
Time Required:	5-10 minutes

Group members should spread out and find sufficient room in which to stand and have a clear area in which to move. The facilitator should ask people to stand with their eyes closed and relax, allowing them to do this for a minute or so. Explain that in a minute the music will begin and they are going to need to keep their eyes closed (we will know if they're opened because people might laugh.) Participants should feel free to move their bodies in whatever way they wish to interpret the music that is played, keeping in mind that others are in the general vicinity and not run into each other. The theme from *Star Wars*, Enya, other instrumental selections as well as contemporary hits would be appropriate. When some music ends, move on to the next piece. The facilitators may also secretly record on video the exercise to use for blackmail and humor value at some later day and time.

Facilitation Questions:

- Who felt inhibited during this exercise? Who felt like they couldn't do everything they wanted to because people were watching?
- What does music do to inspire you?

MY FAVORITE PLACE

Number of People:	Between 5-30
Materials:	Paper, crayons, pencils or markers – have a wide variety of colors available
Activity Level:	Low
Risk Level:	Low
Time Required:	15-25 minutes

Explain to participants that they are about to begin a creative exercise. Ask them to sit back and to visualize a special place for them – real or imaginary are both fine. Using the writing materials provided, ask them to spend some time drawing their special place. Explain that artistic talent is not required and the drawing can be abstract, concrete, stick figure, detailed or general in design – just draw something that is "right" for them. Give participants a set period of time in which to complete their drawings. Depending upon the size of the group, ask participants to share their special place and its meaning with the group or subgroups.

Facilitation Questions:

- How did you artistic ability (or perceived last thereof) affect your vision?
- What made your favorite place most memorable for you?
- Is your special place a public or private place (for you only or can people come with you?) Why?
- What does this place mean to you?

NUMBER GROUPS

Number of People:	Between 15-300
Materials:	None
Activity Level:	Low
Risk Level:	Low
Time Required:	3-8 minutes

Participants should have space to move around in for this exercise. The facilitator should explain that in this activity, the object is for people to form groups as quickly as possible. The facilitator will call out a number and everyone must work together to get into groups of exactly that number. Those people left over can be "out" for the rest of the activity, or can wait for the next number to participate again. It is possible to be tricky when doing this exercise! For example, you could explain that you want groups of "the square root of 9," groups of "multiples of three" (which could be 3, 6, 9, etc.) or "prime numbers."

Facilitation Questions:

- Who had an easy time with this exercise? A difficult time? Why?
- How did people communicate their needs during this exercise?
- Why might we use this to divide people into groups?

OOO, AAAAH, OOOH!

Number of People:	Between 9-32
Materials:	None
Activity Level:	Low
Risk Level:	Low
Time Required:	8-15 minutes

Ask participants to form a close circle nearly shoulder-to-shoulder. The object of this game is to be among the last people playing after others have been eliminated. The facilitator should show the three hand signals and accompanying sounds used in the game. The first is the "Oooo!" signal which is a military salute to the forehead with the fingers pointing towards the person on the left or right (either hand works for this activity). The second is "Aaah!" and that is the same gesture of salute, but held at chest level pointing fingers in either direction. The last is "Oh!" (pronounced like the "oa" in "boat") and has two hands, palms together that are then pointed out across the circle to another player. The gestures are now set and the activity requires it remain in the order mentioned above. Using the simultaneous sound and gesture, one person will start with the first gesture and point to the person on his/her left or right. The person s/he is pointing to must do the second combination, pointing to the left or right person (it is ok to go back to the original person too!). The last person will do the final gesture and sound and point to anyone s/he wishes with a loud, guttural "Oh!" sound. That person then starts the cycle over again with the salute. The game is supposed to be fast-paced once people get it figured out. You may also wish to do a practice round. If anyone delays, uses the wrong gesture/sound or is out of turn, s/he is 'out' and removed from the circle. When someone goofs up, the entire circle can yell out loud, "Yoooooooou're outta here!" The person to the immediate right of the "out" person starts the game again quickly. Those people that have been bounced out of the game are allowed to try to make noises and do anything (other than touching) to distract the circle members into goofing up. The game ends when only three people remain. The facilitator may wish to consolidate the group as hands become removed from the game and ask people to again overlap hands with neighbors.

Facilitation Questions:

- What was memorable about this activity? What was most distracting?
- What factor of the game made people mess up the most? How would you avoid that in the future?

ORANGE PASS

Number of People: Between 7-50

Materials: One orange per group (and maybe a couple of extras)

Activity Level: Medium

Risk Level: Medium

Time Required: 6-12 minutes

Arrange the groups to form a line all facing the same direction, front to back. The first person in each line should be given an orange and told that s/he must take the orange and hold it between his/her chin and neck and pass it that way to the next person. That person will pass it to the next person and so on. If the orange drops, or is touched by hands then the group must start again. No one can use other parts of their body such as hands, arms or legs. Oranges can get squishy, so be aware of that with the exercise in case replacement oranges are needed.

Facilitation Questions:

- What was a really funny moment?
- How did competition affect this exercise? What does that say about this group?
- What do gender roles say about this activity?

ORCHESTRA

Number of People:	Between 10-200
Materials:	None
Activity Level:	Low
Risk Level:	Low
Time Required:	6-10 minutes

Arrange participants into subgroups and designate each group to a specific instrument that might be found in an orchestra. Some possible instruments could include: bass drums, violins, trombones, cellos, trumpets, flutes, clarinets, cymbals or other instruments. The facilitator should ask the groups to get together and determine what the sound will be that they will collectively make using their voices that could imitate that instrument. Ask the group to prepare to use their vocal "instruments" to do a song such as "Row your boat" or "Twinkle Little Star" for the rest of the group. Once that is complete, the whole group should be asked to "warm up" like an orchestra would (practicing notes, etc.) and then become quiet as a "conductor" reaches the stage. The conductor can be a participant or the facilitator. The group will perform the song as an orchestra might. The conductor can also ask for specific subgroups to raise their volumes or lower them as needed.

Facilitation Questions:

- Why do we do this activity? How might it warm up a group?
- How did the group communicate during the planning of the activity?

PAPER BAGS

Number of People:	Between 8-30
Materials:	Paper bags, a variety of odd objects to place in the bags; paper, writing instruments
Activity Level:	Low
Risk Level:	Low
Time Required:	8-15 minutes

Prior to the activity, the facilitator should place an obscure or random object in each of the paper bags (no more than 10 bags.) Line the bags up on a table and stick them to the base so that participants cannot pick up the bags. Participants should then go around individually and by using sense of touch only, reach into a bag and attempt to identify what is in each of the bags. S/he should then write what s/he thinks it is on a sheet of paper. Once everyone has had a chance to go through the bags, ask people to name what was in each bag. Prizes can be awarded to participants that guess most of the items correctly.

Facilitation Questions:

- What were your initial thoughts about the contents of the bags?
- What were your feelings going into this exercise?

PEOPLE TO PEOPLE

Number of People: Between 12-60

Materials: None (music if desired)

Activity Level: High

Risk Level: Medium

Time Required: 10-20 minutes

Each participant should find a partner for this activity. Once everyone is paired up, one of the partners should form an outer circle while the other person forms an inner circle. A person without a partner (or the facilitator if equal teams) will be calling out the exercise. Once the caller/facilitator is ready (or the music begins,) the inner circle should rotate in one direction and the outer circle should rotate in the opposite direction. At any point in time, the caller should shout out the names of two body parts (keeping it clean is good – remember where body parts may go!) At this point, everyone should move to find his/her partner and touch those two body parts together. It doesn't matter which person is which body part. The partners that are last to contact each other are "out" for the rest of the game. Alternatively, if the caller wishes, s/he can say, "People to People" instead, which causes <u>everyone</u> (including the people that are out) to get to the middle and requires them to find a new partner. The person left without a partner is the new leader, continuing the pairing of the body parts.

Facilitation Questions:
- What was challenging about this activity? What did you enjoy most?
- Which were the most difficult combinations?

POSTURE RELAY

Number of People:	Between 8-15
Materials:	One bean bag (or similar item) per team
Activity Level:	Medium
Risk Level:	Low
Time Required:	5-8 minutes

Break participants into teams if there are more people than will work in a single group. Participants should line up next to one other. The first person in line will take the bean bag, place it on his/her head, run over to and around a specific location, and return back to the rest of the team without having the bag drop off his/her head. That person will give the bean bag to the next person in line, who does the same course, and so on. If the bean bag is touched with one's hands, or if it falls off, then that person must start again. The game ends when the relay is completed.

Facilitation Questions:

- Who had a difficult time with this exercise? Who thought it was relatively easy?
- How did people support each other during this activity? How could that support play a role with the group in the future?

PUZZLE JUMBLE

Number of People:	Between 14-100
Materials:	Various puzzles (children's puzzles or large ones work best) with one piece per person or a series of pictures cut into puzzle pieces.
Activity Level:	Low
Risk Level:	Low
Time Required:	8-15 minutes

Before the activity begins, give each person a puzzle piece or allow him/her to select one at random. The participants will keep their piece to themselves until the facilitator says to begin. At that point, the group members should try to locate the other members of the group with similar pieces to form a complete puzzle. As an alternative to this exercise, you can have a single puzzle with smaller pieces and require people to work together to put it together. Alternatively, you can also remove pieces or put pieces from other puzzles in the mix to challenge the group in other ways. (This is a good activity to break people into smaller groups for future exercises as well)

Facilitation Questions:

- Why do we do this activity?
- Who was taking the lead in your group? How was that selected? What roles did people play?
- What strategies and thoughts do you have about the communication during this activity?

RAID

Number of People:	Between 14-50
Materials:	Markers for play area
Activity Level:	High
Risk Level:	Low
Time Required:	10-20 minutes

The facilitator should define the borders of the game and designate a small area as a "hot spot" in one corner. Two participants will be "exterminators" while the rest are ants. The exterminators will be chasing and attempting to tag the ants. A tagged ant falls on his/her back and puts all four limbs in the air facing upward. Four other untagged ants may pick up their hurt ant friend by the limbs and place him/her on the designated "hot spot" in the corner. The once-dead ant is now brought to life and may continue playing. Note that any time a living ant is helping a dead ant, they cannot be tagged. This only works if all four ants are lifting the dead ant. The "hot spot" is also an area where no ant can be tagged, but ants cannot hide there just to avoid being caught....there is a 15 second period allowed to rest in the hot spot.

Facilitation Questions:

- Why do we do this activity?
- This is a high-energy activity...what does this mean for the energy level of the group right now? How do you feel?

RANDOM POETRY

Number of People:	Between 6-20
Materials Needed:	Cut up sheets of 30-50 random words
Activity Level:	Low
Risk Level:	Low
Time Required:	12-25 minutes

Divide participants into small groups of about 3-6. They will be receiving a collection of words as well as some blank pieces. Their objective is to create a team poem or story using those words. The poem should have some meaning, although not necessarily a serious one. They could compare it to the magnetic poetry kits that exist in stores. Participants should be given six minutes to arrange the words into a poem or story. Groups may write their own words on the blank pieces provided, but the groups must use ALL of the paper sheets given to them. Once complete, the groups will then read their poetry and explain what it might mean. An example of some words can be found on the next page.

Facilitation Questions:

- What strategies did you use during this exercise?
- How did your group reach a decision about the order of the words?
- Why did you choose the "blank" words that you did?
- How does this exercise test your creativity? Why is that important?

Ultimate Icebreaker & Teambuilder Guide © 2007

platypus	like	-ed
squirming	salsa	-ing
cello	moonlight	throw
otter	floating	stand
madly	shimmering	drop
where	and	plethora
strawberries	books	is
ocean	love	_____
dance	guilty	_____
lawn	the	_____
gnome	a	_____
tea	a	_____
gazing	and	_____
dappled	barf	
popsicles	-ing	
many		

RHYTHM & MOTION

Number of People: Between 10-50

Materials: None

Activity Level: Low

Risk Level: Low

Time Required: 12-20 minutes

All of the participants will form into a circle. One group member is selected to leave the room, cover his/her ears and/or close his/her eyes. At this time, the facilitator will select the "Pooba". The Pooba will establish a rhythm of clapping, stomping, snapping, or other noise making. The rest of the group will follow, careful to not give away the identity of the Pooba, especially with eye contact. The Pooba is the only one allowed to initiate changes in the rhythm. The person asked to leave will return to the middle of the circle and try to guess who the Pooba is. The Pooba can choose to alter the rhythm at any point in time, forcing the others to try to match the rhythm, but keeping the identity of the Pooba secret. The person is granted three chances to guess. If the original Pooba is successful in hiding his/her identity, a glorious round of applause will be given and a new player will leave the room. If the Pooba is successfully guessed, a new guesser and Pooba are chosen after a big cheer and applause.

Facilitation Questions:

- If you were in the middle, how did you figure out who the Pooba was?
- What did it feel like to be in the middle?
- How did you track the changes in the rhythm?

Ultimate Icebreaker & Teambuilder Guide © 2007

RHYTHM ICE BREAKER

Number of People:	Between 10-40
Materials:	"Instruments" made of household supplies, cans, wood, cup of paper clips, etc.
Activity Level:	Low
Risk Level:	Low
Time Required:	8-15 minutes

Arrange participants in a "U" shape and ask for some volunteers who would like to play an "instrument" for this activity. Musical talent is not required, but somewhat helpful. Everyone else will be stomping and creating a beat. It is important for everyone to keep the activity and the beat together. Ask people to create the steady beat and then one-by-one, add instruments every 8-10 seconds. Allow the music to continue for a bit and then take away one instrument at a time until only the beat remains. The rhythm may fall apart at some point. Encourage participants to start over or even select someone that can conduct or assist the group in pulling the music together.

Facilitation Questions:

- Why did you choose your instrument and music? What sparked that creativity?
- How did it sound? What would you change if you were to do this activity again?

ROAD TRIP!

Number of People:	Between 6-24
Materials:	Various maps, atlases, travel books, a small model "Hot Wheels" car per group, paper, writing instruments
Activity Level:	Low
Risk Level:	Low
Time Required:	45-60 minutes

Divide participants into subgroups of 3-5 people and explain that each group is going to need to plan a road trip from their current location to some other location. Where they go and how the teams will get there is up to them. Explain that they may use the materials provided as well as access the internet in order to plan their trip. Money isn't an issue (or it may be if the facilitator wishes to challenge the group) and each team must be able to explain the following questions: How did their "car" choice impact their plans? What sights did they choose to see or not see? Who was driving? Did they stop to visit anyone? Was the group focused on reaching the destination or the process of getting there? Each group will then recount their journey to the rest of the participants. Groups should be realistic with their trip planning and must be driving their car at some point in time. Other information could be tourist spots they wish to see, where they will be staying, how long at locations, etc.

Facilitation Questions:

- How did you decide where you were going and what you were doing?
- Did you see any patterns with the choices being made?
- Who was leading the group in the exercise? Did everyone feel like their voice was being heard and acknowledged? How might this influence group dynamics in the future?

SCISSORS

Number of People:	Between 8-28
Materials Needed:	One scissors per group
Activity Level:	Low
Risk Level:	Low
Time Required:	8-15 minutes

This brain teaser activity requires participants to sit in a circle facing the middle. The first person will start by turning to the person on his/her right and say, "I am passing these scissors to you _____" (Fill in either "crossed" or "open.") The phrase s/he uses depends upon whether the receiver's legs are crossed or open. They can do whatever they want with the scissors in terms of how they pass them to the next person (open or closed). The person who is receiving the scissors must say, "I am receiving these scissors _____" (The ending should reflect how the giver had his/her legs positioned – NOT how they passed the scissors.) If the receiver or giver is incorrect in passing, the person who leads the activity and knows the "trick" of the game should interrupt and say, "I'm sorry, that is not correct." The game continues around the circle until everyone has figured out the game. Participants may get frustrated if they cannot figure out the game…be patient and encouraging.

Facilitation Questions:

- How did you figure out this exercise?
- Why do we do an exercise that challenges your perceptions?
- What does this exercise mean for the future of this group? What lessons can be learned?

SCOOTERBALL

Number of People:	Between 6-18 in groups of 3
Materials Needed:	One rubber playground ball (or other ball) per team
Activity Level:	High
Risk Level:	Medium
Time Required:	8-15 minutes

Divide participants up into groups of three and give each group a ball. The objective is for the one person in the middle to pretend to "walk" on the ball for a set distance, with his/her arms around the person on either side for support. In order for the ball to move forward, the person has to walk on the ball as if the ball were a treadmill going backwards. The person in the middle may not kick or move the ball forward in any other manner nor can the people on either side touch the ball under any circumstances. This activity can be done competitively or cooperatively challenge the groups. You may also substitute other balls (footballs, etc.) to increase the challenge of this activity. Be aware of safety during this activity and the people on the sides must be able to significantly support the weight of the middle person so no ankle injuries result. In essence, the side people are holding up the middle person and the middle person should be able to lift his/her legs completely off the ground and be supported by the two side people!

Facilitation Questions:

- How was this activity?
- What was most challenging for you?
- What was it like to rely upon or have others rely upon you for your success?

SELF INTRODUCTION STORY TIME

Number of People:	Between 6-25
Materials:	One story copy and writing instrument per person.
Activity Level:	Low
Risk Level:	Low
Time Required:	15-25 minutes

The objective of this exercise is to help group members learn more about each other. Each individual will be asked to fill in the blanks of their story and then share it with the rest of the group! Remember that the blank story should make sense and include words like "noun" or "adjective" to help the writer fill in the gaps. An example of a story can be found on the next page or you can create your own. This activity can lead to more self-disclosure and higher risk depending upon the questions and statements in the story.

Facilitation Questions:

- Why do we do this activity?
- What did you learn about others in the group through this activity?
- Why did you take the story in the direction you did?

Hello, my name is _____. I am _____ years
                    (Proper Name)   (Number)

old and was a _____ type of kid. I grew up in
                    (Adjective)

_____ and I really felt _____ there because of the
    (Location)   (Adjective)

_____ . I have always dreamed that someday I would be
      (Noun)

able to go to _____because of the _____ and
            (Noun)   (Noun)

_____. Some things I like to do in my spare time include
      (Noun)

_____, which is great because it makes me feel
      (Noun)

_____ . There are many things that I am good at and
      (Adjective)

one of them is _____. I did an interesting thing once when
             (Noun)

I was _____. You'll have to ask me about it sometime.
      (Number)

There is one thing I would change about myself, it is _____. Still, I
                                    (Noun)

am very glad to be here now because I want _____. The one
                                (Nouns)

thing that I hope to be remembered for someday is _____. As far
                                    (Verb)

as my future, I hope to _____ soon and then take some time to
                  (Verb)

_____. Thanks for getting to know me and I hope to
      (Verb)

_____ you soon.
      (Verb)

SENTENCE STEMS

Number of People:	Between 4-50
Materials:	List of sentence stems on pieces of paper or posted for groups to see.
Activity Level:	Low
Risk Level:	Medium
Time Required:	15-30 minutes

Participants should be in small groups of between two and six people. The facilitator will ask participants to answer a sentence for the other members of the group. Each person should draw a piece of paper or choose one from a list that is posted. Some examples could be:

- The way I would describe my family is…
- My fondest memories of high school are…
- The things I value most are…
- My favorite pastimes are…
- My best vacation would be…
- Something I wish I could change about myself is…
- The item I would rescue in case of a fire would be…

Everyone should participate in sharing in this exercise and once complete, the group should move on to the next question. In this activity, each person can answer her/his own one question and the next person can have a different question or everyone can take turns answering each question. Remind participants to keep their answers brief and meaningful.

Facilitation Questions:

- How did it feel to share in this activity?
- Why do we do self-disclosure activities such as this?
- What stands out as something you learned during this exercise?

SEVEN-ELEVEN

Number of People: Between 4-60

Materials: None

Activity Level: Low

Risk Level: Low

Time Required: 6-10 minutes

Ask the participants to sit in a circle on the floor, facing the middle. A volunteer from the circle will start the game by saying, "One." The person to his/her right will count up to the next number loud enough so everyone can hear him/her. The game continues around the circle until the number 7, a multiple of seven (14, 21, 28, 35, etc.), 11, or a multiple of 11 (22, 33, 44, etc.) comes up. The individual who has that number will nod his/her head instead of saying the number aloud. When that person nods his/her head, the game continues in the opposite direction around the circle. If a mistake is made, the game restarts with the person that goofed back at one. The game should be fairly fast-paced and no stalling to count is allowed.

Facilitation Questions:

- Why do we do this activity?
- How was this exercise challenging for you?

Ultimate Icebreaker & Teambuilder Guide © 2007

SHOE FACTORY

Number of People:	Between 8-40
Materials:	Shoes for everyone
Activity Level:	Medium
Risk Level:	Low
Time Required:	6-15 minutes

The facilitator should ask the group to form a circle and stand shoulder to shoulder facing inwards. Everyone is to then remove his/her shoes and put them in the center of the circle, mixing them up. After the group has formed a pile of shoes, everyone in the circle should then go in and grab two different shoes that are not their own from the pile. S/he should try to put them on his/her feet (as best s/he can) and attempt to match the shoes with its shoe partner in the crowd. Once partners are found, people should stand next to the person that is wearing the other shoe. Groups may have to be creative in order to figure out how to do this and the shapes may be out-of-the-ordinary. Encourage participants to figure it out as best they can!

Facilitation Questions:

- Was there a successful solution to this activity?
- Who was wearing particularly nice shoes? Whose shoes didn't fit their new owners?

SHOE SORT

Number of People:	Between 8-30
Materials:	None
Activity Level:	Low
Risk Level:	Low
Time Required:	8-15 minutes

This activity will challenge the senses and methods to communicate. Everyone should keep their eyes closed or use blindfolds for this activity. Explain that the objective is for everyone to line up in order of shoe size from smallest to largest without the use of sight or sound. Ask people to stand and cross their arms in front of their chest and move slowly for safety. Once the group has completed the task, process what happened. Participants should go strictly by the number of shoe size with the same for women and men. If the facilitator would like to increase the difficult a little, explain that it must be lined up by actual foot size.

Facilitation Questions:

- What was challenging about this activity? What did you enjoy most?
- How did the group communicate? Was it successful?
- What would you do differently the next time you participate in this activity?

Ultimate Icebreaker & Teambuilder Guide © 2007

SING DOWN

Number of People:	Between 9-200
Materials:	Paper and pen for each team.
Activity Level:	Low
Risk Level:	Low
Time Required:	15-30 minutes

Participants should be divided up into at least three teams, but not more than six. The facilitator will give the groups a word (i.e. love, dance, boy, etc.) and three minutes to think of as many songs as they can with that word in the lyrics (not just the title). All songs brainstormed by the group must be written down to be valid. Teams may NOT add additional songs to their list once the brainstorming period has ended. Once the time has passed, one team will begin by having the entire group sing a few seconds of a song from their list with that word in it. All team members must sing it. NO SONGS CAN BE REPEATED. If a prior group sings a song on your team's list, you must cross it off and you can never use it again. The next team responds with another song and sings that. The group that has the most songs at the end wins. The process can then be repeated with another word for another game.

Facilitation Questions:

- How did brainstorming work within your group?
- Who definitely should and should not have been singing in your group?

SLAPS

Number of People:	Between 8-24
Materials:	None
Activity Level:	Low
Risk Level:	Low
Time Required:	6-12 minutes

Ask the participants to lie on their stomachs in a circle (close to their neighbors) with their heads facing the middle of the circle. Every participant's arms should extend outwards toward the middle. Each person should also overlap hands with their neighbors - the right arm goes underneath the left arm of the person to their right. The left arm should then be over the right arm of the person on the left. One person will be designated to start by patting/slapping the ground with one of his/her hands. The person whose hand is on the right will do the same and continue counterclockwise. If someone decides to slap the ground twice, the direction reverses. If a hand misses, hesitates for more than two seconds, slaps prematurely or out of order, then that hand is removed from the game. Once a player has removed both of his/her hands, s/he is out of the game. That person can then sit on the sidelines or do things to try and distract those remaining. When there are only two people remaining, the game ends.

Facilitation Questions:
- How did your eyes fool you?
- What was challenging about this activity?

Ultimate Icebreaker & Teambuilder Guide © 2007

SNAKE'S TAIL

Number of People: Between 12-45

Materials: None

Activity Level: High

Risk Level: Low

Time Required: 10-20 minutes

A line of participants is formed with everyone holding hands. One end of the line is the head of the snake and the other becomes the tail of the snake. The object of the game is for the head to try to catch the tail, while the tail is trying to escape from the head. Let participants know not to break the grip (if possible). Another variation is to have multiple snakes and have the heads of groups chase the tails of the other groups. Once that tail is captured, the new longer snake tries to eat the other snakes.

Facilitation Questions:

- Why do we do this activity?
- What was challenging about this activity? What did you enjoy most?

SNAPS

Number of People:	Between 10-35
Materials:	None
Activity Level:	Low
Risk Level:	Low
Time Required:	12-20 minutes

This is another mind reading game that has a secret pattern. The leader will select a category (such as US states) and people will need to guess what that state is using the leader's cryptic questions. First, the leader should ask someone to whisper a state's name to him/her. Once that is heard, the leader will explain to the group that "Snaps is the name of the game." The leader will then spell out the name of the state by giving snaps and sentence statement/question clues.

For example, if the state is "Colorado," then the leader will ask a question or make a statement that starts with the first letter in the name of the state. The "C" in Colorado may be a question like, "Can you guess it?" To continue spelling, the leader will snap fingers the number of times for each vowel – one for "A", two for "E", three for "I", four for "O" and five for "U". So the leader would snap four times for an "O". Perhaps the "L" could be, "Let's hear any guesses," followed by four snaps again, followed by, "Ready yet?" and so on. This is to be done each time until the state is guessed. People will start catching on and be able to guess the names right away, so encourage them to also take the lead on "Snaps." These people should try to keep the solution quiet while others are figuring it out for themselves. Later, the facilitator can choose a new category like fruit or something else that would challenge the group.

Facilitation Questions:
- What was frustrating about this activity?
- How did people figure out the solution to this exercise?

SOCK GAME

Number of People:	Between 8-32
Materials:	None
Activity Level:	High
Risk Level:	Medium
Time Required:	6-10 minutes

Ask participants to remove their shoes, but make sure everyone is wearing socks – no sandals for this game! The object of the game is for participants to remain on their knees at all times and try to de-sock everyone else before they de-sock you. Remember to play on a soft surface so bloody knees are kept to a minimum.

Facilitation Questions:

- How do you feel about this activity?
- What role does silliness play within the group?
- Who was most ticklish?

SOLEMN AND SILENT

Number of People:	Between 8-120
Materials:	None
Activity Level:	Low
Risk Level:	Low
Time Required:	8-12 minutes

Explain to the participants that this will be an exercise in self-control. Everyone should pair up and stand back-to-back. On the count of three, everyone will face their partner, look into his/her eyes and then try to remain solemn and silent. No speaking or sounds allowed! The first person of the pair to smile or laugh has to sit down. People can make faces or use non-verbals, but they must remain locked with their eyes. All who win the round will then pair up with a new partner and then go again, while the losing people wait on the sideline. The contest repeats pairing and competition until one final person remains. If there are an odd number of people, you may form a group of three that all compete against each other at the same time or have an "observer" of the activity. If you get people that are both keeping a straight face for an extended period of time, you can encourage the rest of the group to heckle and disrupt them, while being solemn and silent as well.

Facilitation Questions:

- Why do we do this kind of activity?
- What did your partner do to provoke a reaction?

SPONGE PASS

Number of People:	Between 10-60
Materials:	A bucket of water, one large sponge, and a jar or other empty container per group
Activity Level:	Low
Risk Level:	Medium
Time Required:	10-20 minutes

Ask participants to form a line about a foot apart from each other, all facing the same direction. The facilitator should place the bucket of water at the end of one line and give a sponge to the first participant. The empty jar or other container should be placed at the other end of the line. Be aware that this exercise will get people and the floor wet! Explain that the object of the game is to fill the empty container of water by soaking the sponge in the water and passing it <u>overhead</u> to the next person, and so on down the line until the last person can squeeze the water into the empty container at the end. They can then pass the sponge back over the line. The game continues until the end container is full. Alternatively, you may have the end person run to the front with the squeezed-out sponge and dip it back into the bucket to pass behind again.

Facilitation Questions:

- What was most memorable about this activity?
- What were you feeling during this activity? Fear? Elation?

SPOON FEED ME

Number of People:	Between 3-13
Materials:	A big bowl of ice cream, three spoons per person, napkins, and towels (you may also have ice cream toppings if you wish)
Activity Level:	Low
Risk Level:	Medium
Time Required:	6-12 minutes

The facilitator should scoop out a large bowl of ice cream and then ask everyone to get into a circle, lying down on their backs with their heads at the inner part of the circle and feet spread out on the outside. Participants should be so that their heads are right next to each other. Verify before starting the activity whether anyone has any allergies to ice cream flavors or dairy before you begin! Explain that what is going to happen is that each person is going to take a spoonful of ice cream from the bowl in the middle and attempt to feed it to the person on their left, but s/he must remain laying flat with her/his head on the ground! Once that person has been fed the ice cream, then go to the right and with a fresh spoon, the next person will feed the person there. Rotate people or ask the group to take turns alphabetically. Do this activity a couple of times and let the laughter ensue. Once a few spoonfuls have been fed by everyone, encourage everyone to take a fresh spoon and finish the dish themselves or clean up!

Facilitation Questions:

- How does trust figure in to this exercise?
- How did it feel to be out of control of your own fate during this activity?

S-P-U-D

Number of People:	Between 8-32
Materials:	One Kick-ball or other relatively soft ball (Optional cones to mark the playing field area)
Activity Level:	High
Risk Level:	Low
Time Required:	12-25 minutes

Arrange all of the participants in a line and ask everyone to count off, remembering his/her number. The facilitator will start off as "it" and will throw the ball high in the air and call a number. The person whose number was just called scrambles to retrieve the ball, while everyone else scatters within a designated area. As soon as the person whose number is called retrieves the ball (has it clearly in his/her possession and control), s/he shouts, "Stop!" Everyone must freeze in their places at that point. The person with the ball can take up to three giant steps in any direction and throw the ball at whomever they think they can hit. The person who is hit by the ball is then "it", and receives a letter (S-P-U-D…just like in a basketball game of "horse"). The cycle then starts again. If one person gets all four letters, s/he is eliminated. When someone is frozen, they cannot move their feet from their spots, but can move their bodies, duck, etc. to try to avoid being hit. If the group size is too large for four letters, you can give people two or three letters instead.

Facilitation Questions:

- How do playground games help our group?
- How important is 'play' in our lives? Do we do enough of it? Why?

SQUEEZE

Number of People:	Between 12-30
Materials:	An object people can grab (ball, plastic bottle, etc.)
Activity Level:	Low
Risk Level:	Low
Time Required:	10-20 minutes

Arrange people into two teams and ask them to sit in two parallel lines, front to back with members of their own team. At the front end of the team should be placed the item to be grabbed, equidistant from the both teams. (It is also important to have a judge or second facilitator track a mistake or success.) Each team should join one hand with their neighbor and everyone should close their eyes. The facilitator will sit down, grab the free hands on either side of the leaders of both teams at the back of the line and will squeeze them simultaneously at some random point in time. At that point, that person should squeeze the hand of the next person (whose hand s/he is holding), who will squeeze the next person down and so on. Once the squeeze reaches the person at the front, the first person to grab the object successfully will win that round. The winning team will rotate so that the person who grabbed the item moves to the back of the line and everyone shifts forwards. The winning team overall is the first to successfully get through to their original positions successfully. If a team grabs the item too early, the hand wasn't squeezed by the facilitator or other infraction, the team rotates <u>backwards</u> one person! Note that the facilitator in the back can pause as long as s/he wishes before squeezing or as quickly as they wish. Alternatively, this activity can also be done with a game of chance. The facilitator can flip a coin and whenever the coin comes up heads (flip so both leaders can see), that is the cue for the team to start squeezing.

Facilitation Questions:

- How did competition affect this activity?
- What kind of pressure was placed on the people in front? How did people respond?
- How can this parallel real, everyday situations?

STATUES

Number of People:	Between 6-60
Materials:	None
Activity Level:	Medium
Risk Level:	Low
Time Required:	8-15 minutes

Ask participants to spread out so that there is freedom to move. Explain to everyone that they'll be participating in an activity that will help people relax their minds and bodies. The facilitator will give a title of a statue and everyone will need to physically give their interpretations of the statues and hold that pose for 15 seconds. After those 15 seconds, everyone can relax. This process will continue until everyone has gone through all of the statues. Participants or observers can vote for the best or most creative of each example. Alternatively, for groups that are very familiar with each other, you may give names of participants to try to imitate as statues. The statues to interpret could be (but invent your own if you wish):

- Child at Play
- Anteater with a Full Stomach
- Runner at Starting Line
- Frozen in Fear
- Reflection
- The Dancer
- Cat with Cream
- Happy Dog
- Rubber Band

Facilitation Questions:
- Why did you interpret something the way you did?
- How did your creativity come out during this exercise? Why is that important?

STINGER

Number of People:	Between 15-60
Materials:	None
Activity Level:	Low
Risk Level:	Low
Time Required:	10-20 minutes

Ask the participants to form a circle and close their eyes. The facilitator will circle the group and explain that s/he is going to select someone to be the "stinger" in the game by squeezing an individual's shoulder. Once the facilitator has chosen a stinger, the group can open their eyes and should spend time introducing themselves to people while shaking hands. The stinger is going to try to eliminate everyone else in the game without getting caught. S/he will do this by shaking hands and "injecting poison" with their index finger while shaking hands (poking index finger on the wrist or hand of the other person). A person stung will then "die" five to eight seconds after they have been stung. The more dramatic the death, the better. When one of the living (and not stung) participants thinks that they have discovered who the stinger is, s/he may announce what s/he knows by yelling, "Stinger!" Everyone freezes at that point and waits for someone else to "second" the claim. If there is a second, then the two can make a public accusation. If there is no second, the accuser will fall down from exhaustion, and the game continues. If another person does step forward to second, both count to three and on three, point to who they think the stinger is. If they don't point to the same person at the same time, or both point to the wrong person, then they are both automatically out of the game. If they select the correct person, the stinger is caught and that game is over.

Facilitation Questions:
- How did people figure out who the stinger was in this activity?
- Were people paranoid about this game? Who had heightened senses?

SUMO

Number of People:	Between 11-30
Materials:	None
Activity Level:	High
Risk Level:	Medium
Time Required:	12-20 minutes

This is a game that is known for potential rug burns, but is a lot of fun for a group that knows enough about each other to be comfortable with a lot of physical contact. Ask players to pair up and ask one extra person needs to be in the middle. That middle person is the "sumo master". Players should form a large circle about three feet apart and the pairs should <u>sit</u> with one person directly in front of the other, facing the sumo master. The object of the game is for the person who is the inside of the pair to touch the sumo master before the count of 10. The sumo master will call the names of two people that are sitting in the front pair position. These two people must crawl and scrape to touch the sumo master (who must remain still), but the people sitting behind them are grabbing their partner to prevent that inside person from doing so. Often times, there is some wrestling and struggling as the pairs attempt to get close enough to touch the sumo master. The sumo master can count as slowly or quickly as s/he wishes. If one of the inner people is successful in touching the sumo master, then s/he is promoted to the sumo master position. If no one touches the sumo master by the count of ten, the players, go back to their pairs, but are now <u>behind</u> their partners. (Switch roles) The sumo master can then call another two names. There are variations of the game where the sumo master can call as many or as few names as s/he wishes – one, two, three, ten, etc. In addition, the sumo master can say, "breadbasket" where ALL of the front participants in the circle must try to touch the sumo master. Periodically, the facilitator can request that one of the circles rotates two or three people in one direction to mix up the players. In addition, it is vital to remember that this activity is very physical and to be safe while doing the exercise!

Facilitation Questions:
- Who were the aggressive people during this exercise?
- What surprised you during this activity?
- Was it important for you to win or were you more interested in having fun?
- What does that say about motivations during competitive activities?

T-SHIRT TALES

Number of People: Between 8-30

Materials: T-Shirts that participants bring with them

Activity Level: Low

Risk Level: Low

Time Required: 10-25 minutes

Ask participants before the activity to bring a T-shirt that has some sort of memory or history attached to it. Ask participants to go around and explain what the T-shirt says and why it is important to them. Pay particular attention to why the shirt has meaning, what the context of the shirt was, etc.

Facilitation Questions:

- What did you learn about people here today?
- What memories are the strongest for you? How do you want to create future memorable moments with this group?

TEAM CROSSWORD

Number of People:	Between 8-30
Materials:	3" x 3" cards of paper (one per letter in participant's names), tape, and markers
Activity Level:	Low
Risk Level:	Low
Time Required:	10-18 minutes

There should be a large blank wall or large papered surface to use for this activity. Explain to participants that they should each write the letters of their first name on separate slips of paper, taking up the entire card for each letter. The group must then arrange the letters of their names on the blank wall in the form of a crossword puzzle so that everyone fits. Each name must share at least one letter with another person's name so everyone is interconnected. If the names can be interconnected in more than one space, even better. This puzzle can then be posted in a visible location to show unity and the connections that the group shares.

Facilitation Questions:

- Was this a challenging activity for the group? Was there an easy solution?
- How did the group get to a solution? Was there someone taking the lead or was it a joint effort?
- How does the finished product look to you?

THE CREATURE

Number of People:	Between 4-40 and possible subgroups
Materials:	None
Activity Level:	Medium
Risk Level:	Low
Time Required:	12-18 minutes

Divide people into groups as necessary and explain to participants that they are to create some make-believe creature in this exercise. The creature will need to be mobile and should use the group's creativity and imagination. Each person can play one or more parts of the creature's body (tail, head, leg, mouth, arm, snout, etc.) Participants will then need to demonstrate their creature to the rest of the participants. Give groups of people 5-10 minutes to design their "creature" (anything their imagination can create) and then have each creature move across the room to show its mobility. The facilitator can then ask everyone to explain what each body "part" does, the significance of the creature, where it comes from, etc.

Facilitation Questions:

- How did your group decide upon your creature?
- Imagine the environment where your creature would live…what would that look like?
- How did your group work together to create your creature?

THINK FAST

Number of People:	Between 8-28
Materials Needed:	Some random object
Activity Level:	Low
Risk Level:	Low
Time Required:	10-20 minutes

Participants should stand in a circle facing the middle for this exercise. The facilitator will explain that this game will need to be played very quickly. A volunteer will stand in the middle of the circle and close his/her eyes, keeping them closed throughout his/her <u>entire</u> time in the center. A person standing in the outer circle is given an object. When the center person says, "Start!" the object is to be <u>passed</u> (not tossed) around the circle to the right from one participant to the next. The center person will then call out, "Stop!" at any time. The center person then will quickly say a letter of the alphabet and the person holding the object must quickly say three nouns that begin with that specified letter. If the participant says three nouns within five seconds, the game continues on immediately, passing the object to the right again. If the person cannot think of three nouns in that amount of time or gets one wrong, s/he becomes the person in the center. The facilitator may take the role of "referee" for the nouns to determine whether they are valid or not.

Facilitation Questions:

- How did this game challenge you? How did you respond to the challenge of thinking fast?
- How might fast thinking affect this team (or you as an individual) in the future?

TOILET PAPER GAME

Number of People:	Between 8-30
Materials:	One big roll of toilet paper (possibly two for larger groups)
Activity Level:	Low
Risk Level:	Low
Time Required:	12-25 minutes

Explain to the group that everyone is going camping and to take as much toilet paper as they are going to need for a weekend trip. Once everyone has a good supply, explain to the group that for every square of toilet paper in his/her possession, they will have to share one thing about themselves to the rest of the group. Alternatively, since this amount of paper may take awhile, you can break into pairs to share or ask people to take a smaller amount!

Facilitation Questions:

- Why do we do this activity?
- What did you learn about others during this activity?

TOUCHEE FEELEE

Number of People: Between 10-50

Materials: None

Activity Level: Medium

Risk Level: Medium

Time Required: 10-18 minutes

This activity involves touching other participants, so remind people about what is and is NOT appropriate for this activity! Everyone will stand together in a relatively small area to start. Explain that the facilitator will give some statement and a body part. Everyone will need to prepare to play a game of Twister, requiring everyone playing to touch the body part of someone that fits the statement. For example, the facilitator could say, "Touch the forehead of someone wearing an earring." Everyone must then use some body part (not necessarily the hand) to touch the forehead of someone who this applies to. The facilitator will then read another statement, and while still maintaining contact with the first person, must touch a second person that fits the bill. Once someone cannot touch all of the people required, they are out. Alternatively, for an easier game, the people can just hold one touch at a time instead of stacking touches on top of each other or don't designate body parts. For a lesson in teamwork, require the group to do their best to make sure everyone can touch for each statement.

Facilitation Questions:

- How does touch influence you? Is it important or not?
- What was challenging about this activity?
- How did the group work together for success?

TWO TRUTHS AND A LIE

Number of People:	Between 5-40
Materials:	Paper and writing instruments per person (or do by memory for small groups)
Activity Level:	Low
Risk Level:	Low
Time Required:	8-15 minutes

This is a small group activity, but subgroups can be formed from a larger number of people. The facilitator should ask the group to take about 2-3 minutes to think of and/or write down two things about themselves that are true and one thing that is not – a lie. The truths can be anything that a person has done, something about themselves or about possessions. The lies should be made up but done in the same context as the truths. When complete, each group member will then share all three things about him/herself in random order while the rest of the group has to determine which one of the three is the lie. Participants should think of lies that might be believable in order to try and fool the other participants. An alternative to this activity can be played with up to 30-40 people. The same statements can be collected from participants on note cards, but only 5-6 can be revealed at the start of an activity. For example with a week-long training, five or six of the cards can be revealed at the beginning of each training session and participants can guess as an icebreaker.

Facilitation Questions:

- Which was easier to create, the lies or the truth? Why?
- Which people had intriguing truths? Convincing lies?
- What did you learn about people through this exercise?

WATER BALANCE

Number of People:	Between 8-18
Materials:	Child's sandcastle bucket, water
Activity Level:	Medium
Risk Level:	Medium
Time Required:	10-20 minutes

The biggest challenge for this activity is that participants have a strong likelihood of getting wet at some point during the exercise. Participants should lay down in a circle with everyone's legs extended so that they meet in the middle of the circle. The facilitator will explain to participants that they are to take a bucket of water and pass it from person to person using only their legs/feet. Each person's legs will be extended into the air while s/he is lying on his/her back. The objective is to pass the bucket of water to each person in the circle without spilling it. Obviously the exercise is going to get people wet, so this might work best as an outdoor activity. Failure in this activity will mean a lot of people will get very wet, so having towels on hand would help too! As a conversation about rules, it doesn't say anywhere that the bucket has to be passed completely around the circle if the group is having a challenging time.

Facilitation Questions:

- What was challenging about this activity? What did you enjoy most?
- What were you thinking about as the bucket neared you? How did you respond to the pressure and threat of getting wet?

WATERFALL GAME

Number of People:	Between 8-40
Materials:	Paper, writing instruments
Activity Level:	Low
Risk Level:	High
Time Required:	8-18 minutes

This activity is probably more for an adult audience. Each participant should write his/her favorite color, favorite animal, and favorite body of water on a piece of paper, keeping her/his information to him/herself. Next to each, ask people to write three adjectives that describe that color, animal, and body of water. Once that everyone has completed, explain that the color, animal and body of water are actually metaphors for other things. Explain that the adjectives describing their favorite color represent how they view themselves. Ask people to share their color and adjectives with others or in small groups. Following that, explain that their favorite animal represents how others view them and then ask people to share again. The final one with the body of water could represent how individuals might describe their views about sex. Group members are asked to then share their bodies of water and adjectives. The answers truly don't represent these issues, but are often a humorous analogy for people to have as a warm-up for other activities.

Facilitation Questions:

- Some of these answers are often humorous, what role does humor play in this group?
- Why might it be important to not take ourselves seriously sometimes?

Ultimate Icebreaker & Teambuilder Guide © 2007

WHAT I CARRY

Number of People:	Between 8-40 in subgroups
Materials:	Just what people bring with them
Activity Level:	Low
Risk Level:	Low
Time Required:	15-20 minutes

Participants should be split into small groups of three or four. Give them about 10 minutes total (about 2-3 minutes each) to have each person go through his/her possessions (wallets, purses, bags, keys,) explain the items that they possess (those they wish to share) and what they mean. Rotate around until each person has had a chance to go through his/her items for the group. If participants don't have any items or aren't satisfied with an item, have them describe an item that is in a car or is close by that they could share with the group.

Facilitation Questions:

- Why do people carry things of importance to them?
- What did you learn about people through this exercise?

WHERE WERE YOU?

Number of People:	Between 6-40
Materials:	None
Activity Level:	Low
Risk Level:	Low
Time Required:	15-25 minutes

Ask people to get comfortable in groups of 6-12 and organize themselves into small circles. As the facilitator, pick a year or a date before the meeting. Once everyone is ready, ask participants to take a couple of minutes to think about and share where they were and what they were doing on that date (Summer of 1999 or January 2003, etc.) with the group. Encourage people to ask questions to try and jog memories as needed. This information can be shared with the large group or broken into smaller groups.

Facilitation Questions:

- Who knew exactly what they were doing? Who had a more difficult time?
- Why did you choose the event or memory from that time period? Why was it important or memorable to you?

WOOOOOOOOO

Number of People:	Between 10-50
Materials:	One set of number cards per "hider"
Activity Level:	Low
Risk Level:	Low
Time Required:	15-40 minutes

This is a nighttime activity to be played outside that is a reverse game of hide and seek, where you have more seekers than hiders! There should be four or five volunteers to be "hiders" who will remain in one place while they are hiding. They must go out and hide in the nearby forest. These people should pick a spot that allows their clothing to blend into the dark and shades of gray. Each hider should have a set of about 20 identically numbered pieces of small paper (or one paper for every participant.) They should then take a few minutes and go find a spot of their choosing. Then let the seekers begin their individual searches. The facilitator should set clear boundaries for this exercise so no one goes too far but large enough so that people won't see each other that easily. Be aware of any safety issues in the dark and the terrain. Each hider has the option to make a characteristic sound occasionally to help the searchers, particularly if no one is close. When a seeker finds a hider, the hider soundlessly hands a numbered piece of paper to the discoverer. When a seeker has collected a slip of paper from all the hiders, s/he can retire from the game to watch things (or confuse others by making animal calls of his/her own!). No flashlights are allowed in this game and facilitators should encourage safety and fun with this activity!

Facilitation Questions:

- This activity is a lot of fun, but who was nervous about this exercise?
- What was frustrating about the activity?
- What is most memorable for you?
- What does this exercise do for the group in terms of fun, creativity, or energy?

TEAM BUILDERS

Teambuilders are those activities that have a message or learning that takes place with the experience, and often work best with an established group. These are the best activities for facilitation and follow-up after the completion of the activity, so don't forget that this processing is often the most important part! There might be goals involved in these activities or it might just be a test to a team's group dynamics. These activities are great ways of continuing to challenge a team to know each other better, trust, communicate, and have shared experiences together.

AFFIRMATIVE FOLD-UPS

Number of People:	Between 4-35
Materials:	Blank paper and a writing instrument per person
Activity Level:	Low
Risk Level:	Medium
Time Required:	10-18 minutes

Ask the group to sit comfortably in a circle facing the middle and give everyone a piece of the paper and writing instrument. Explain that each person should write his/her name on the very top of the paper (not too big) and then put that paper face-down in the center of the circle. Once done, each participant should then draw someone else's sheet from the center and look at the name on the top of the paper. S/he should then write one word (or a few words) of praise or compliment about that person on the BOTTOM of the sheet. Once s/he has written that information, fold the paper up, covering that comment. S/he should then to wait until everyone is done and then pass that paper to the left. If someone gets their own, just hold it for a round. The writing and folding should continue (accordion-style) until the name is the only thing showing on the piece of paper. At the end, the facilitator can collect the papers and give them to the owners. This is a great closure activity for an established group or team or to wrap up a section of training. The facilitator may wish to photocopy a starter sheet with pre-made lines so everyone knows where to fold the paper.

Facilitation Questions:

- What is the importance of recognition within this group?
- How does it feel to be recognized by your peers?
- What methods of recognition and praise should we be doing that we currently do not?
- What are informal methods of providing encouragement and positive feedback that can be done on a daily basis?
- What surprised you about your own fold-up?

AMAZING TEAMCOAT

Number of People:	Between 5-36
Materials:	Coat, pieces of material and assorted fabric for each participant, sewing needles, spools of thread.
Activity Level:	Low
Risk Level:	Low
Time Required:	30-60 minutes

This activity allows the group of participants to take an old coat and sew pieces of fabric physically on to the coat. This teambuilder then has something tangible that can be given out at meetings, be an honorary award, or designate the team in some public way. The facilitator can designate the coat will rotate to people as a reward every week, keep it visible for everyone to see or use it as a symbol for success and achievement for the team. As an addition to the activity, you may arrange for fabric markers, paint, or other ways of decorating the material to individualize what goes on to the coat.

Facilitation Questions:

- What is the symbolism that this coat represents?
- Why did you choose the fabric that you did? What meaning might it have for you?
- What occasions should this group use this coat? How should the group determine who gets it and for what period of time?

ARTIST, CLAY, MODEL

Number of People:	Between 6-80 in subgroups of 3
Materials:	None (Blindfolds if you wish)
Activity Level:	Low
Risk Level:	Medium
Time Required:	8-20 minutes

Participants should be divided into groups of three. Each person should choose to be the artist, a model, or some clay. The artist should close his/her eyes and the person who is the model should then "strike a pose." The artist will then take the person that is the clay and try to mold that person into a replica of the artist without actually seeing that pose. This may be done via sound or touch, as the facilitator designates. Once complete, roles can be switched.

Facilitation Questions:

- How did it feel to be doing this activity?
- What were your impressions of being the model? The Artist? The Clay?

AUTOBIOGRAPHY

Number of People:	Between 5-30
Materials:	Writing instrument and paper for each person (or use the example that follows)
Activity Level:	Low
Risk Level:	Low
Time Required:	15-40 minutes

Give each participant paper and materials to write with. The facilitator should start the exercise and explain the following scenario to the group: "I am wandering through the library when I notice a book that carries your name on it. It is your autobiography! Being a curious person I am, I turn to page 94 and begin reading." Explain that the exercise is now to write page 94 of the autobiography, with whatever period in time or event that they would choose. There is no "right way" to write the page and any style would work well. After everyone has written his/her page, participants will come back to the group to read what that page says for each of them. A template to use is included on the next page.

Facilitation Questions:

- What prompted you to choose the particular event or moment that you did as page 94?
- What were your thoughts while listening to people share their stories?
- Who would like to share "the rest of the story" that couldn't be finished on page 94?

Using the space below, please write page 94 of your autobiography.

_____

_____

_____

_____

_____

_____

_____

_____

_____

_____

_____

_____

_____

BLIND GOLF

Number of People:	Between 6-50 in pairs
Materials:	Golf course sheets, colored pencils (one per person), blindfolds (optional)
Activity Level:	Low
Risk Level:	Low
Time Required:	10-20 minutes

This exercise is good for communication and following directions. Use the golf course sheets on the following pages or create your own. In pairs, the object is to have the drawer close his or her eyes and attempt to draw a single, connected line from the tee box to the green and ultimately the hole. The partner will be the person that verbally directs the drawer's direction and where s/he moves the pencil! The lines need not be straight and will likely be all over the page. The person that can see cannot guide the hand of the other player – no touching allowed (unless you'd like to leave this rule out to challenge a group to think "outside the box.") When a player goes off the paper or in the "water", there is a 2-shot penalty. If the player goes in the "sand," they add one shot to his/her score. As a facilitator, take a practice run on each hole and set a realistic, but challenging amount of time to complete each hole. If the player completes it in under that time, s/he counts it as one shot (plus penalties). If s/he is 0-5 seconds longer than the set time, s/he completes it in two shots (plus any penalties!), 6-10 seconds is three shots, 11-15 is four shots and any longer is five shots (plus penalties). You may wish to create your own golf holes, use markers and butcher paper for large versions of this game, or have other teams design the holes themselves as a competition. After a period of time, switch roles and encourage the teams to communicate!

Facilitation Questions:

- How did you communicate with your partner? What was effective and what could be improved?
- What did you do more effectively as the golf holes went further along? Did your strategies change? Did you communication methods improve?
- What can this exercise show us about communication within this group?

Ultimate Icebreaker & Teambuilder Guide © 2007

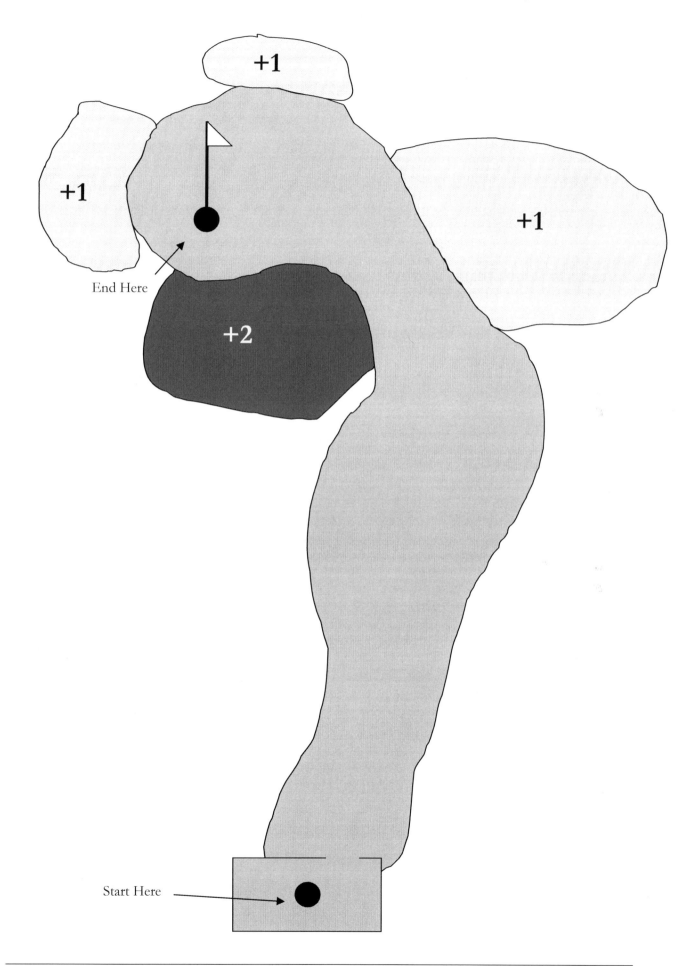

+1

+1

+1

+2

End Here

Start Here

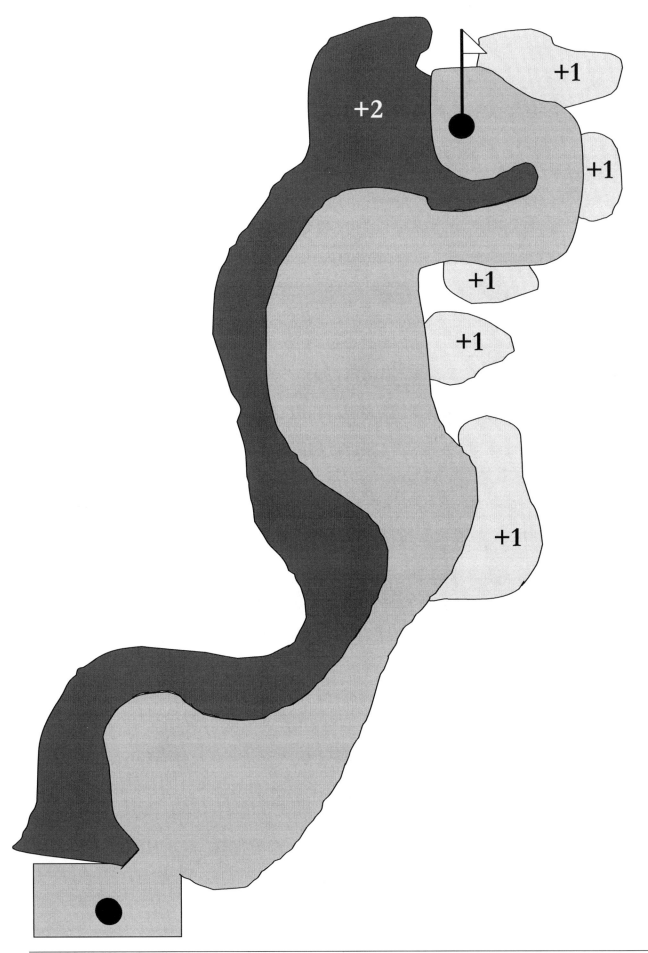

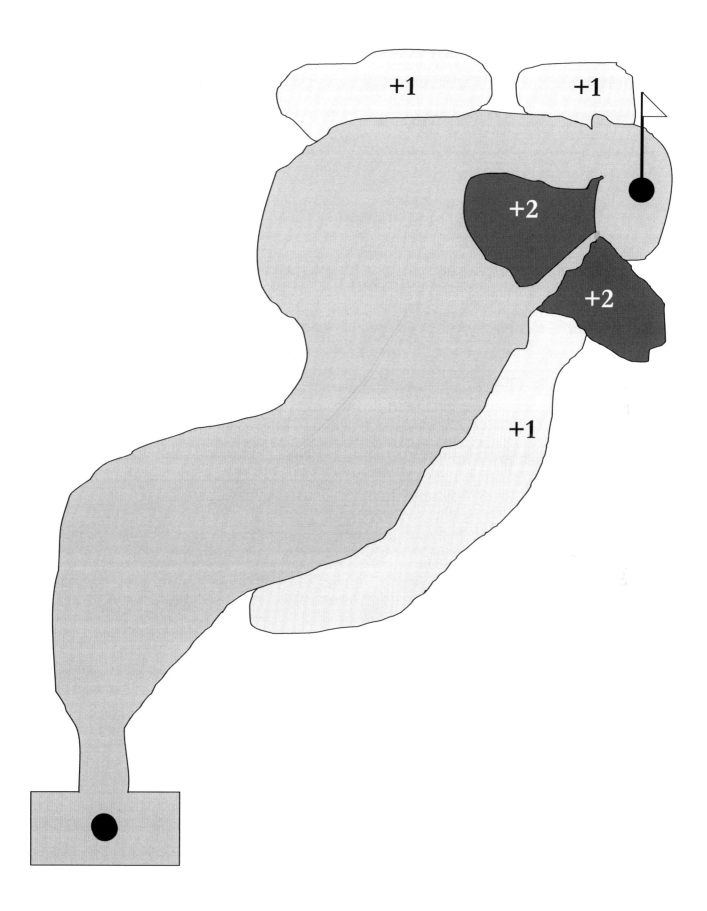

BUILD MY HOUSE

Number of People:	Between 5-40
Materials:	One sheet of paper per participant with a photocopied stick figure of a house on it, writing instruments
Activity Level:	Low
Risk Level:	Medium
Time Required:	20-30 minutes

Ask participants to prepare to write on their paper and follow the instructions as you read them out loud. This activity is a way for people to use a house metaphor to understand more about each other. Encourage participants to take the activity seriously, realize they get out of any activity what they put into it.

- In the foundation of the house, write a concept or idea that you govern your life by.
- Along the walls, write the methods which you support and strengthen this idea or concept.
- In the roof, write the things you use to keep harm out of your life.
- In the window, write something which you are proud of and want others to see.
- In the door, write an important part of you that you borrowed from someone else and the name of the person you got it from.
- In the chimney, write how do you "release" stress and the unwanted attributes in your life.
- For the front yard, write how you relax.
- For the background, write the place you go to be at harmony with yourself.

Ask people to share their answers as they feel comfortable in large groups or smaller subgroups. Recognize that all people have similar facets to our personalities and that sharing can help a team understand each other better.

Facilitation Questions:

- Which parts of the house were easiest and which were most difficult to complete?
- What similarities did you find between people's houses? Any recurring themes?
- Why don't we have conversations about such things unless forced to do so in some activity? What does that say about people in general? Is that a good or bad thing?

Ultimate Icebreaker & Teambuilder Guide © 2007

CAPTURE THE FLAG

Number of People:	Between 16-50 in 2+ teams of at least 8 people
Materials:	One flag per team (Optional: cones to market boundaries or if really dark, use glow sticks instead of flags)
Activity Level:	High
Risk Level:	Low
Time Required:	30-75 minutes

The designated playing area is divided into equal areas for each time. Each back section has a rectangle that is known as the jail. The group is then divided into teams. Each team should secretly decide where to place their flag, as long as it is somewhere in their territory and within reach. The object of the game is for a team to get another team's flag and return it back to its territory. Once the game has started, anyone who steps into an opponent's area is eligible to be tagged and taken to jail. A player must get through the enemy's lines without getting tagged. People in jail may be rescued by teammates who get through the enemy lines without being tagged, and are able to touch the prisoner's hand. The prisoners can line themselves up by holding hands and stretching towards the center line as long as one person is still holding on to the jail area. If people are linked, then all are rescued at the same time. If rescued, both the prisoner and rescuer must walk with their hands up to their own side. They cannot be tagged at this time. If a player has the flag and gets tagged, the flag can either go back to where it was, or be dropped where the person got tagged, the facilitator's choice. That player then goes to jail. Teams may only have one person within 30 feet of protecting the flag (unless an opponent is within that space.) The flag must be in full view and not placed out of reach, nor attached to any participant. Once a team's flag is placed, ready to be captured, the team may not touch their own flag. Remind players the spirit of "fair play," encourage fun, but not being overly competitive. Other rules can be decided by the group as needed. Encourage teams to use strategy to accomplish their objective.

Facilitation Questions:
- What strategies did you use during this exercise?
- What roles did people play?
- What moments were memorable for the teams?

CHAIN BACK RUB

Number of People: Between 4-150

Materials: None

Activity Level: Low

Risk Level: Medium

Time Required: 8-10 minutes

The nature of this activity is probably better for a group that knows each other fairly well. Participants should form a circle, standing shoulder-to-shoulder, and then make a turn to their right. The leader will then instruct participants that they should reach forward and give the person in front of them a well-deserved backrub. After 2-4 minutes, ask everyone to turn around the other direction and "pay back" that person with a final backrub. This activity can be done to foster relaxation, question people's comfort levels, same gender touching and stigmas with that, etc.

Facilitation Questions:

- What does touch mean to you? Is it welcome or an invasion of your space? Why are both answers OK?
- How do you feel after this activity?

CHART A LIFE

Number of People: Between 4-30

Materials: Paper for each person (Easel or butcher paper and markers for large visuals) and writing instrument.

Activity Level: Low

Risk Level: Medium

Time Required: 12-30 minutes

Each participant will draw a chart similar to, or use copies of what is shown on the next page. On one side, the chart indicates the level of feeling (the highs and lows) in that person's life. The horizontal axis represents time and should indicate key points in life such as Birth, Childhood, Teenage Years, High School, College, Grad. School, First Job, and continue on into the future. Each group member is going to chart his or her life with the past, present and anticipate the future according to the level of feeling, both positive and negative, associated with that moment. Members will then share their charts with other members of the group as comfort levels allow.

Facilitation Questions:

- How did it feel to share your life with the rest of the group?
- Why did you include the aspects of your future that you did?
- Which memories are the most powerful from your chart? What made them so?

FEELING

Negative   Neutral   Positive

TIME

CLIPBOARDS

Number of People:	Between 5-30
Materials:	One clipboard per participant; magazine cutouts; stickers; markers; paper; other craft materials; and several pairs of scissors. Lamination paper to seal the designs is optional, but good for the exercise.
Activity Level:	Low
Risk Level:	Low
Time Required:	45-60 minutes

There are two versions of this activity, depending upon how well the group knows each other. 1.) Ask each participant to take a clipboard and decorate it in a way that best represents aspects of his/her personality or who s/he is. Clip pictures or phrases from magazines, add color, stickers, glitter or other materials available to create a distinct item. Once complete, give every participant some lamination paper (clear contact paper) to cover the clipboard, so that it will last a longer period of time. When everyone is done, people should explain what their clipboard means to them and what goes into the clipboard. 2.) The second way to do the activity is to draw names at random and ask that person to decorate a clipboard for the name that s/he drew! It should be kept as secret as possible so that no one knows who is decorating whose clipboard. Set aside an area where plenty of materials can be found for people to use. A good amount of time should be given to facilitate this activity. The group should come back together at a later point, unveil the clipboards, and present them to who they belong to!

Facilitation Questions:

- Why did you decorate the clipboard as you did? What meaning did it hold?
- Are there any themes or patterns with your clipboard?
- How personal is this? Did you feel yourself getting "into" or "involved" in this project. Was it important to make it legitimate?

DEBATE

Number of People:	Between 6-16
Materials:	None
Activity Level:	Low
Risk Level:	Low
Time Required:	30-60 minutes

.This activity should be for a well-established group. Explain to participants that they may very well be arguing for a side of the issue that they don't believe in. Divide participants up into two different groups and explain that they will be given an issue relevant to current events, the team, or society. Each group will need to take a side on the issue (or assign them) and prepare to dialogue about that issue. Give each team time to prepare their thoughts and to speak for a designated length of time about that issue. The other team should have a chance to state their own side following that. As a facilitator, you may wish to have a time for rebuttal following their opening statements. By understanding both sides of that issue though, it can serve to strengthen resolve and clarify positions in the future. Facilitate this by talking about ethics and values and how they can conflict.

Facilitation Questions:

- What was it like to take a stand on an issue? Did you always agree with the stand you were taking?
- How does disagreement or conflict benefit this team?
- How does this activity affect your communication skills or your confidence level?
- Was it hard to not get personal? Was it important to win? Why or why not?

DESIGN YOUR PERFECT

Number of People:	Between 6-40
Materials:	A bottle of glue per group, large amounts of newsprint or poster board, tape
Activity Level:	Low
Risk Level:	Low
Time Required:	30-45 minutes

The facilitator should explain to participants that they are going to create the perfect _____ (something.) This could be the perfect team, staff member, volunteer, project, or anyone/anything that the group needs to focus on for the future. The participants should collect items that could go into this creation. Things that are disposable and not of value are best. After a set period of time gathering items, bring participants back to the main area and provide them with the materials to physically construct their design. Everyone participating in the group should then explain what they have made. The "perfect item" can be hung in a visible area to demonstrate their teamwork and vision. Alternatively, for an added challenge, you may also explain to the groups if you wish that no talking is allowed during the exercise.

Facilitation Questions:

- Why did you choose the items that you did? What do they represent?
- Were there things you would add, but could not? What were they and why?
- What symbolism does this hold? What ideals does it represent?
- Is this an ideal that people can live up to? How might you personally try to reach this ideal?
- What commitment are you willing to make to reach this perfection?

DOT BRAINSTORMING

Number of People: Between 3-60

Materials Needed: Large sheets of paper, markers, and sticker dots

Activity Level: Low

Risk Level: Low

Time Required: 6-20 minutes

The facilitator should have a prepared topic or idea that is going to need some sort of brainstorming by the group. Explain to the group that they will be doing the brainstorming and then evaluating their suggestions. As the group brainstorms, write the ideas on the paper, leaving about 6″ of room on the side of the list. Once the brainstorming is complete, hand out sticky dots to each person and explain that the participants can list their favorite ideas by putting their sticky dots next to the ideas they like. S/he may put more than one dot next to any idea that s/he is particularly fond of. Use the results to continue a discussion about what choices the group has made and continue the process of talking about specific issues related to that brainstorming.

Facilitation Questions:

- How did the dot brainstorming affect the dynamics of the activity? Was it helpful?
- Do you feel that your voice was effectively heard through this activity?

EACH ONE, TEACH ONE

Number of People:	Between 3-25
Materials:	None
Activity Level:	Low
Risk Level:	Low
Time Required:	15-40 minutes

Ask participants to think of some activity or skill that they possess. The activity can be something as simple as learning how to tie a shoe, tell a joke well, or even make some odd bodily noise. The participants will then be asked to explain and teach it to the rest of the people in the group. The facilitator may wish to provide some lead time prior to the actual activity to give participants a chance to think of and prepare ahead of time. Each participant should be able to go through the process of step-by-step instruction to show others how to complete the task. This exercise works well when taking a complicated task and reducing it down to manageable steps as well as teaching skills at instructing others in a group. The facilitator for this activity may wish to assign a time limit for each presentation of about 3-4 minutes, otherwise people have the tendency to run long. Also, arrange to have every rotate through the activity as time allows.

Facilitation Questions:

- Why do we do this activity?
- What was important when conveying instructions for this activity?
- How did it feel to be in a position to teach others something? What will you remember about this activity to help you in the future?
- How might you do things differently in the future?

EGG BREAK

Number of People:	Between 9-80
Materials:	One egg, 40-50 straws, 3 feet of masking tape per group as well as markers, poster board, towels, and a prize for winning group(s).
Activity Level:	Low
Risk Level:	Low
Time Required:	30-45 minutes

This exercise can challenge different people in groups to take leadership roles and also have some established leaders learn to step aside! Divide participants into subgroups as appropriate and provide each group with a raw egg, straws, and masking tape. Explain to the groups that using only the materials provided, they are to create a product that will protect the egg from breaking when dropped from a designated height (20 feet or so). Eggs must remain in the same condition they received them but the straws and other materials can be altered as needed using only what was provided. Find a suitable location and make arrangements to actually drop the egg casing, tally the results, and process what went well and didn't go well for each group. Groups that have their egg product survive can have a prize and if more than one is successful, you can award multiple prizes or have a second test to determine ultimate winners. In addition, each group can also be asked to create a name for the egg protection device and how they would choose to market it to the world. Each group would then present the proposal for marketing this invention. Focus facilitation on creativity, group decision-making and roles within the group.

Facilitation Questions:

- Talk about your team's strategies and ideas. How did your group reach a decision on the design?
- How were decisions made in this group? Were all voices heard? What could be improved in this process?
- What kind of creativity did you use? How was the quality control and creation of the actual project?
- Who took the lead with this activity? Was it someone that you would expect? What expertise did people bring to this project?
- What would you do differently if you were to do this activity again?

FEAR FACTOR

Number of People:	Between 6-30
Materials:	Variety of materials (see below)
Activity Level:	Medium
Risk Level:	High
Time Required:	30-60 minutes

This activity is based upon the popular television show, "Fear Factor." There are no death-defying stunts, but merely activities to encourage a discussion about risk taking, competition and teamwork. Below are some examples of stunts that you may ask your teams to participate in.

- Nasty Blender – go to the store and get a collection of items that would create a disgusting or difficult concoction to eat or drink. Blend it together with ice for a smoothie. Good suggestions for products include: sardines, chocolate, broccoli, Tabasco, Cheese-Its, Clam Juice, Canned Beets, etc.
- Public Embarrassment – participants will go into public locations and sing a song at the top of their lungs for anyone who is around. Good songs include "Doe, a deer…" from *The Sound of Music*, Spice Girls, I'm a Little Teapot, etc. You can a dance into things for a little more flavor.
- Balloon Building – participants need to create a "bed" made of inflated balloons that one of the participants will need to lay down upon. The balloons must be able to support the person completely off the ground for a total of 10 seconds. Balloons should be provided to participants (no more than 30 or so.) The group with the fewest balloons supporting someone will win.

You can issue points for competitions, create your own unique (but safe) challenges, and create a title of "Fear Factor Champion" for the team that completes the stunts successfully.

Facilitation Questions:
- What did you think of this activity? Was it worth it?
- How does risk-taking play a role in your life? How does it influence this group?
- What would you do differently looking back at this activity?

FINGER PAINT COLLAGE

Number of People:	Between 5-25
Materials:	Newsprint or butcher paper, finger paint, masking tape, clean-up materials
Activity Level:	Low
Risk Level:	Low
Time Required:	25-45 minutes

Explain to participants that they will be creating a group mural using the materials provided. The object of the activity is to express themselves and what they feel about the group (or some other topic area) through their artwork. Remember that there is limited space (taping several pieces of newsprint or butcher paper together may be necessary depending upon the size of the group.) Everyone will take a turn painting. Allow participants to paint whatever they would like on the mural. Once it is complete, ask the group what to do with the design. You may include the option of displaying this in some prominent location where all can see. Alternatively, you may hold a discussion prior to painting with the group to discuss the overall concept or theme for the design.

Facilitation Questions:

- What images is part of this design? What do they represent?
- How is this both an individual and a group effort? What does that mean for this team?
- How did decisions get made about what went into the mural? Was that effective?

FIVE THINGS I WANT TO LEARN

Number of People: Between 15-60

Materials Needed: Paper and writing instruments

Activity Level: Low

Risk Level: Low

Time Required: 10-20 minutes

Ask participants to take a few minutes to write down five things in life that they want to learn. After they have completed that, below the list they should write down five things that they are able to teach to the rest of the group. These skills can be professional or personal; tangible or not, depending upon individual preferences. Once complete the facilitator should ask participants to wander the room and meet people while discussing their lists to determine any matches. Alternatively, people can sit in a circle and state the things that they wish to learn or can teach. Ask people to identify if they also wish to learn or can teach that task for them. This activity works well with larger groups since people are more likely to have matches. Encourage communication within the group in case people don't list something that they wish to teach and learn. There very well may be things that people forgot they had as talents or things they've really wanted to learn how to do!

Facilitation Questions:

- What did you learn through this activity?
- What surprised you about this exercise?
- Who is going to actually go out and learn these five things? What is preventing people from doing so? How can this team help make it happen for you?
- What does this exercise have to say about the range of skills for people in this group?

FLASH CARD REVELATIONS

Number of People:	Between 12-40
Materials:	One set of index cards per person with everyone's names printed on them (or have participants write the names on their own cards)
Activity Level:	Low
Risk Level:	High (potentially)
Time Required:	20-40 minutes

Ask participants to sit in a circle facing the middle. Explain that the facilitator will be reading a series of questions. Each person will need to reveal the name of a person that best fits that category on the card. This is a more public version of the activity "Touchstones." Fit the questions asked to the level of risk appropriate for the group as well as a range so that it would likely apply to a variety of people in the group and not just the same people. This activity works best for an established group where people know each other well. The facilitator should ask that this be a quiet activity for full impact. Questions can include:

- Who do you believe most enjoys their life?
- Who makes you feel welcomed?
- Who is good with giving praise and recognition?
- Who holds opinions different than your own?

You can also use humorous questions (but not inappropriate) to lighten the mood on some of the occasions as well. Process the activity afterwards so that people understand the activity and how it felt for people. Participants can share the rationale behind the cards they use or they can sit silently and observe. Ask plenty of questions so that multiple answers for each person can be assured.

Facilitation Questions:
- How do you feel after this exercise?
- How did it feel to be recognized by people?
- What do you wish you could have asked or said to people during this activity? Did the silence make this more or less challenging?
- How important is affirmation and praise for the success of the group?

GROUP RÉSUMÉ

Number of People:	Between 4-20
Materials Needed:	Poster paper and markers for each group
Activity Level:	Low
Risk Level:	Low
Time Required:	20-40 minutes

Explain to participants that they are going to create a group résumé composed of the skills and abilities that the group collectively possesses. They will need to determine what skills, education and experience they possess and compile all of that in a résumé format. If it is easier for the group, the facilitator can determine some job or position that the group is "applying" for. The résumé should include information on such areas as: educational background, total years of experience, positions held, professional skills, hobbies, talents, awards, accomplishments, publications, conferences or trainings that they've attended, etc. Once complete, each group should post their résumé and allow people to go around the room to view them. A volunteer should volunteer to share the group's résumé during processing time.

Facilitation Questions:

- What were your thoughts and observations about this activity?
- What surprised you?
- What does this activity have to say about the composition of the people doing this exercise?
- What are some resources in this group that you can tap into that you didn't know where there?

IMPORTANT ITEM

Number of People: Between 6-32

Materials: Each person should bring his/her own item

Activity Level: Low

Risk Level: High

Time Required: 20-90 minutes (+)

Each person should be given advance notice to come to the activity with something that is special, memorable or means a lot to him/her. The activity will ask each person to share with the group what that item is and why it is important. Go around the room and ask everyone to share, keeping respect for people's objects and such. The facilitator and group may wish to set up groundrules for the activity and discussion afterwards, particularly about confidentiality and sharing. Depending upon the trust level and environment, this exercise could lead to some intense sharing, so facilitators should be aware of that possibility and the need for follow up.

Facilitation Questions:
- Why did you see during this exercise? What did you feel?
- What did it feel like to share?
- How was it to listen to other people talk about their objects?
- What was the level of respect during this activity?
- How does this level of respect and care continue beyond this exercise?

 Ultimate Icebreaker & Teambuilder Guide © 2007

INFORMATION FUN SHEET

Number of People: Between 8-35

Materials: Sheets of paper and writing instruments

Activity Level: Low

Risk Level: Medium

Time Required: 30-60 minutes

The facilitator may designate questions for participants prior to the beginning of the activity. Ask the group to answer a series of questions about themselves in an honest fashion. Ask people to write answers on separate sheets of paper. These questions should be able to define a person and involve at least a moderate amount of self-disclosure. For example, you may ask people to answer questions such as, "One thing that no one knows about me is…," "The song that represents me the best is…," or "The proudest moment in my life would be…." Tell participants to not put their names on the question sheets. When everyone has answered, the facilitator can ask the questions out loud so that participants can answer them or even guess who they believe each answer belongs to. The group members can then clarify and explain more things about themselves. Remember that sharing answers in a group setting will also require additional amounts of time. Alternatively, you may also ask people to type answers for a later session or hang the responses on a wall for people to answer by a set time.

Facilitation Questions:

- Why do we do this activity?
- How does this activity help build relationships within the group? Why is that even important?

LAST WILL & TESTAMENT

Number of People: Between 8-35

Materials: Paper and writing instruments

Activity Level: Low

Risk Level: High

Time Required: 15-30 minutes

In this exercise, the facilitator will ask individuals to create their "last will and testament" for the group and write it on some paper. Explain that s/he can include real material possessions or aspects of his/her personality that s/he values and would like to share. Write what each item is and who it should go to. Items can go to people who are either within the group or in outside lives as a whole. After people have completed writing answers down, volunteers can share this information with the group. Ask everyone to share in turn. This activity can work well for group closure. The wills can be posted in visible locations for team members or others to see.

Facilitation Questions:

- What were the memorable moments about this activity?
- Why is closure important for a group? What does this mean for us?
- How do you deal with change? Is that positive all the time?
- Why did you bequeath what you did to someone? Is there a story behind it?

LEVITATION

Number of People:	Between 8-100
Materials:	None
Activity Level:	Medium
Risk Level:	Medium
Time Required:	8-20 minutes

This is a trust activity for the participants and safety and trust should be topics of discussion prior to, and following the event. One person will lie on his/her back on the ground with his/her eyes closed (if comfortable). The rest of the group will place their hands underneath the person lying down. One person will be designated as the captain and place him/herself by the person's head. The person lying down should concentrate on being as rigid and stiff as a board. Once everyone is ready and the person lying down has said that s/he is ready, the captain will softly count to three and the group will lift the person up to their waist level. The captain will wait a couple of seconds to verify safety and then count to three again and everyone will lift to shoulder height. Another count to three and then the group will lift the person to a level overhead. Finally, the captain will count to three and the group will gently rock the person forward and then backward down to the ground. The group should remember to take this activity seriously, not to talk, and keep the person's head higher than the feet at all times.

Facilitation Questions:

- How did it feel to be the one lifted? How did it feel to be a person doing the lifting?
- Discuss for me what the trust level was like during this exercise.
- What did you see during this activity?
- How did silence affect the exercise?

LISTENING SKILLS DRAWINGS

Number of People:	Between 6-150 in pairs
Materials:	A piece of paper and writing instrument per person as well as two diagrams for each pair (examples on the next page)
Activity Level:	Low
Risk Level:	Low
Time Required:	15-30 minutes

Everyone must find a partner for this activity. Ask partners to sit back-to-back and decide who will be the first drawer and who will be the first talker. Give the talker a copy of the first diagram. (Note: put each diagram on separate pieces of paper so that no one can see future diagrams.) There are multiple rounds for this activity. Alternate between each partner drawing and listening. Allow 2-3 minutes per round or longer if time permits. Participants should then compare drawings to see how close s/he is to the original.

Diagram #1: The talker will provide only verbal instructions while the drawer must draw the shape they hear described. In this round, the drawer is not allowed to speak, look at the person giving instructions or ask any questions. This is "one-way communication."

Diagram #2: The second round will have partners switch roles and attempt to improve upon the last round's results. In the second round, the talker gets a different diagram and the drawer is allowed to ask yes/no questions.

Diagram #3: Switch back to original roles and now the drawer can ask any questions s/he wishes. Compare results again and talk about the benefits of two-way communication versus one-way with respect to the drawing skill, time it took to complete, etc.

Diagram #4: Roles switch for a final time, but partners are allowed to look and face each other. They can all communicate freely during this diagram.

Facilitation Questions:
- What were the differences between the communication styles? How did they compare with the results of the drawings?
- How can you tie this exercise in to differing learning styles?
- What lessons can you take from this exercise for future efforts where communication is a key?

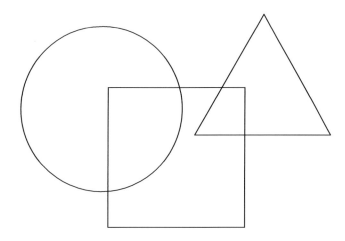

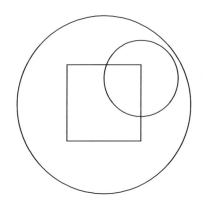

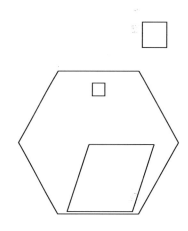

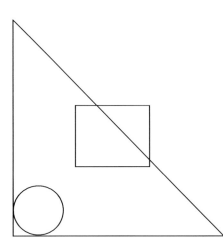

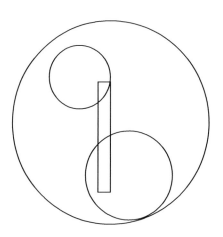

MASKS I WEAR

Number of People: Between 7-40

Materials: Scissors, pieces of poster board, yarn, markers and other decorative materials

Activity Level: Low

Risk Level: High

Time Required: 30-45 minutes

Each participant should receive a piece of poster board and have access to the other supplies. Each person must cut out a face-like shape, about the same size as his/her head. Ask people to also cut out eyes to see through and a mouth they would like. Each person is going to create a mask and then decorate the face. On one side, the mask should represent what other people see/know/believe about him/her (the outside.) The inside should be decorated to represent what s/he feels about him/herself (things going on inside, what people don't necessarily know or see, etc.) Everything can be done with designs, drawings, symbols or words. The participants will then share their masks with the group or small groups as they feel comfortable.

Facilitation Questions:

- What are the images on your mask and what do they represent?
- What is the symbolism of a mask?
- How much of a difference is there between the inside and outside of the mask? Why is that?

MASKS OF ME

Number of People:	Between 6-40
Materials:	Paper Maché rolls (3″ wide or so) cut into strips (about 100 strips per person – about 75 strips should be about ¾″ wide and 25 should be about ¼ inch wide), one bowl of warm water per person, facial tissues, scissors, soft music, towels. Second part will require paper plates, bottles of acrylic paint, paintbrushes and water in bowls.
Activity Level:	Low
Risk Level:	High
Time Required:	Two sessions of 60 (+) minutes

This activity involves significant set-up time and preparation, but can be very impactful to a group. It also fosters a high level of trust and cooperation among participants. Participants should know each other and have some basic level of trust before pairing up for this activity. If there are an odd number of participants, then the facilitator should participate as a partner. Participants will be making paper maché masks of each other during the exercise – over the face if people feel comfortable, but on the hands if people do not. The facilitator should challenge people to attempt to do a face mask as they feel comfortable.

One of the pairs should lay on his/her back and take a tissue to place on his/her face, tearing a hole out for his/her nose only. Place this on top of his/her face. The partner will begin by wetting the paper maché and applying the moist strips on top of the Kleenex on the face in layers to make a form mask of the person's face. The person lying down should try very hard to keep the same relaxed facial features the entire time. Use gentle pressure and cover the person's eyes and mouth, but leave an opening at the nostrils for the person to use to breathe! Try to form the mask to the contours of the partner's face as closely as possible. Use the little narrow strips for detail work around the nose and eyes. Each person will use approximately 100 strips (but it could be more) and the mask should be at least a couple of layers deep for stability. Smooth the strips with water to create as smooth of a texture as possible, keeping the features of the person intact. The mask should go up above the forehead to the hairline, to the sides by the edges of the ears and down <u>below</u> the chin about an inch or so. Once the creation of the mask is complete, allow it to dry for a few minutes on the person's face until the paper maché has hardened. The person should then remove the mask by asking the person with the mask to crinkle his/her nose and blow out through his/her mouth.

Gently remove the mask from the person and set it aside to completely dry. Once dry, remove the tissue paper that has stuck to the inside of the mask to allow it to completely dry overnight. Repeat the process with the partners in reverse roles. If someone is claustrophobic or unable to do a face mask, complete the same process with the hand, forming contours around fingers, etc. Remind participants to continually soothe the people receiving the masks and ask them if they are ok, how they are doing, etc. This encouragement can be vital since people are unable to see what is going on around them. This activity deals with trust and failure to keep that trust during vulnerable activities can have an effect on the team.

The second part of the activity takes place after the masks are completely dry. With scissors, participants should carefully trim the edges of the mask to create a smooth line. Following that, everyone should paint the exterior to represent themselves or with some artistic design that they like. Allow the paint to dry and then arrange a time in the future for everyone to share their masks as a group.

Facilitation Questions:
- How did this feel to be receiving the mask? What were your thoughts about trust during this activity?
- How did it feel to be putting the mask on someone else?
- How important was communication and feedback during this exercise?
- When you were painting your masks, what did your mask represent for you?
- What might you do with your mask? What can it mean for you?

OBSERVATION

Number of People:	Between 5-100
Materials:	Strangely dressed "visitor," list of clothing worn and items carried by that visitor, paper & writing instruments for participants.
Activity Level:	Low
Risk Level:	Low
Time Required:	15-25 minutes

Before the session, the facilitator should arrange for a person to enter the room, ask the group a question such as, "Excuse me, I am looking for the restroom," stay for a few seconds and then leave. The "visitor" should be dressed strangely, wearing odd articles of clothing and jewelry, etc. After the visitor leaves, explain to the participants that this exercise deals with observation. Individually ask participants to write down everything they observed about the person. When they are done, ask them to compile the list in small groups of 3-4 people. Discuss the changes from individual and group observation. Include all aspects about the visitor including clothing and jewelry, objects carried, what was asked, etc. Discuss changes in observation when one person is making the determination versus group determinations.

Facilitation Questions:

- Why is observation important to us as leaders or in a group?
- What were details that some people got while others completely missed?
- Were you surprised by the number of things you could or could not remember?
- How does this exercise relate to situations in the "real world?"

PEANUT BUTTER AND JELLY

Number of People:	Between 10-40
Materials:	Paper and writing instrument per person; loaf of bread; jar of peanut butter; jar of jelly; butter knife; spoon; paper plates; napkins; clean up materials
Activity Level:	Low
Risk Level:	Low
Time Required:	20-35 minutes

There should be 2-4 people who will be the actors/facilitators of this activity and the rest of the participants will be observing. Ask participants to write down on their paper exactly how to make a peanut butter and jelly sandwich. Once they have done writing and you have collected all of the answers, scan them for an example of a sandwich that is detailed and uses very clear instructions (or have one ready that you wrote if none of them meets this standard). Also select one or two examples (anonymously) of instructions that are vague and unclear. Tell the group that the facilitators will now make the peanut butter and jelly sandwiches according to the instructions that they wrote. The facilitators should then read the instructions verbatim from the paper and make a sandwich according to those guidelines. Actors should use a lot of freedom to interpret instructions as they wish. For example, if the instructions say to "spread the peanut butter," the facilitators may elect to spread the peanut butter on the table, the plate, the other facilitators, etc. Once complete, the instructions for the detailed/accurate paper should be followed. This example should provide clear ideas about the importance of detail when doing tasks in the group!

Facilitation Questions:

- What are your reactions to this activity?
- What messages are being conveyed through this exercise?
- How many of you have been in situations where instructions were not as clear as you would like? How did you feel about that?
- This exercise is also about teamwork and understanding, how do you see those messages with this activity?

PENNY FOR YOUR THOUGHTS

Number of People:	Between 10-30
Materials:	One bag of pennies per person, each holding an equal number of pennies as members of the group.
Activity Level:	Low
Risk Level:	Medium
Time Required:	15-25 minutes

All participants should be given a bag with the pennies to start the activity. Explain that everyone is to mill around the room with each other and trade a "penny for a thought." Participants will give a penny to another person and that person will give the first person a compliment. The roles are then reversed and the second person receives a compliment in exchange for a penny. The activity continues until all participants have shared with every other member of the group and have a new bag of "pennies" from the other members.

Facilitation Questions:

- How important was this feedback for you (both giving and receiving)?
- What did you think and feel about this exercise?
- How do people prefer their recognition, publicly or privately? What does this mean for the future?

PERPETUAL TAG

Number of People:	Between 10-35
Materials:	None
Activity Level:	Low
Risk Level:	Low
Time Required:	Up to weeks…

This activity is good for an established and long-term group or organization. It is an on-going tag game that can be initiated during a long session or over the course of several days or weeks. The facilitator should privately designate one person as "it" and tell the group that one of them has been told that s/he is "it." The object of the game is to not be "it." The "it" may tag another person in any way they like (i.e. touch, telephone, IM, fax, e-mail, mail, through a friend, internet, telegram, text message, etc.) as long as the person being tagged can realize that they are now it. The game can last for as long as you wish and can lead to funny stories. The group need not know who "it" is so that the surprise factor is increased and on-going. There are no rules and no limit to the number of times the "it" can change in any given time period, but there are no "touch-backs" where the "it" goes right back to the previous person. Alternatively, the exercise could be done where the method of delivering a tag cannot be duplicated while the game goes on – posting a giant centralized poster board for all people to see the methods that the tag has been completed.

Facilitation Questions:
- What were some of the creative ways that people were tagged?
- What efforts did you go through to tag someone or avoid being tagged?

PERSONAL QUOTATION

Number of People:	Between 6-30
Materials:	Collection of quote books, quotation references or internet resources
Activity Level:	Low
Risk Level:	Medium
Time Required:	8-20 minutes

Prior to the activity, ask participants to go through a list of quotations (or alternatively, have them search the internet or library resources) for a quote they can identify with that represent themselves. It can be their personal philosophies on work and/or life, or their hopes and ambitions for the future. Participants will then share their quotes and meaning in the group or subgroups, depending upon total participants in the activity.

Facilitation Questions:

- Why did you choose a particular quote to represent you? What does it mean for you?
- What were some of the sources for the quotes? Are the sources as motivating as the quotes themselves?
- What would you like to do to live up to the messages given in your quotations?

PERSPECTIVES

Number of People:	Between 6-18
Materials:	Index cards, paper, writing instruments
Activity Level:	Low
Risk Level:	Medium
Time Required:	30-60 minutes

The purpose of this activity is for participants to realize the potentially wide range of experiences and positions on issues that can occur in an environment or group. It helps people understand that while one topic could be life changing for one group it may have only a marginal impact for others. Before participants begin, create a series of cards (or use some examples from higher education on the following page) that list some examples of different individuals that could be associated with your group. Then prepare a list of topic cards that relate to issues or concerns in the group, the community or the world at large. Distribute the cards to participants and prepare them to assume that role. Draw a topic card at random and explain that everyone will need to jump into that role for the next 5-8 minutes before a new card and topic is drawn. This activity should be designed to provoke discussion and help demonstrate the point of diverse thoughts and attitudes towards a variety of issues that people may not have thought of. For the purpose of this activity, ask participants to think of a specific person when playing their role if questioned about stereotypes.

Facilitation Questions:

- How did it feel to jump into someone else's shoes?
- Did you find yourself stereotyping the person on your card? Why or why not?
- What does this exercise show about the diversity of people around us and the people that we work with?

Single mother with two small children	Senior white lacrosse player
International student from Cuba	Gay student
Student actress from a small town	African-American student
Computer science student from China	Non-Traditional student coming back to school after 25 years
Ex-military student	Liberal, nature-loving student and child of hippie parents

PIECE OF THE PUZZLE

Number of People:	Between 8-40
Materials:	Pre-cut pieces of poster paper in puzzle shapes – one piece per participant, markers, and other decoration materials. Each piece should be about 12 inches in size (poster board works well to cut), magazines, glue, markers, etc.
Activity Level:	Low
Risk Level:	Medium
Time Required:	30-45 minutes

Each person should be given a blank puzzle piece and asked to decorate the piece of the puzzle in some way that represents him/herself. Make sure that everyone is decorating on the same side of the puzzle piece by writing something on the back of each piece! This activity works well if the participants can use magazines to cut up quotes and pictures and make a collage! Once everyone is done gluing and creating their piece, each and should share what the piece represents to her/him. Once everyone has shared, then the pieces should all be assembled together in some location that is visible for the entire group. The impact for the team and the final product can be very dramatic and lead to a great discussion!

Facilitation Questions:

- What are the images and pieces of your puzzle piece and what do they mean for you?
- What does the entire puzzle mean for this group?
- How do the pieces hold themselves together? How will this group keep itself together to keep a unified image for the future?

POETRY GROUP

Number of People:	Between 5-35
Materials:	Paper and writing instruments
Activity Level:	Low
Risk Level:	Medium
Time Required:	20-45 minutes

This exercise can all be done at once or split into two separate sessions. Explain to participants that everyone has some sort of creativity inside that can be tapped. There are many different styles of poetry from free verse to haiku to sonnets to other forms. There are no "right" or "wrong" poems, but participants will be asked to write a poem that discusses how they view themselves, their hopes and dreams, their history or future aspirations, or any other topic that they wish to focus on. Emphasize that no one is here to judge the poetry, but the group will be asked to read their poems (or portions thereof) to the rest of the group. The facilitator can set the environment of the exercise with couches, lower lighting and provide coffee or cocoa to the group to provide a coffee house atmosphere as well. Encourage humor, variety and ask that everyone be sensitive to the creative works since time and effort went into each. You may wish to set a specific amount of time for each poem so everyone can present.

Facilitation Questions:

- How did it feel to do this activity? What was most challenging?
- Poetry can be an intensely private thing…what does this sharing mean for the group?
- How important is freedom of expression for the group and the ability to take risks?

PSYCHIATRIST

Number of People:	Between 10-30
Materials:	None
Activity Level:	Low
Risk Level:	Low
Time Required:	30-60 minutes

This is a secret game and activity, but one that requires participants to know each other pretty well and be comfortable enough with each other to joke about idiosyncrasies. Arrange everyone in a circle and ask for a "brave" volunteer. In this game, everyone but the volunteer will know the secret to the game. The volunteer will need to guess it what that secret is. The premise of the activity is that the volunteer is the psychiatrist and everyone else in the room has the same problem that only the psychiatrist can help him/her with. When the volunteer is out of the room and can't see or hear, explain to the other participants that everyone here has the same problem. The problem is that they are all going to act and behave like the person to their left. This should include phrases, mannerisms, and other behaviors. Explain that it should be subtle at first and more obvious as time goes on.

Once everyone is ready, the psychiatrist will be allowed to come back in the room. S/he is told that s/he can only ask yes/no questions to individual people to try and determine what their problem is. The respondent must answer as if they were the person on her/his left, which could lead to some funny moments. If the respondent gives an answer that the person on his/her left feels is incorrect, the person on the left may say "Psychiatrist" and everyone must get up and change seats. Everyone will now have to act like their newest neighbor on his/her left. The game continues until more obvious clues allow the volunteer to figure out the pattern. In addition to playing as if the person on the left, other maladies could include: all act like someone specific that is famous, all act like the facilitator, all can't tell the truth, women tell the truth and men lie, answer like their parents, slowly is turning into a barnyard animal, etc.

Facilitation Questions:
- What was memorable about this activity?
- How did it feel to be the person in the middle?
- What quirks or idiosyncrasies did you use to describe your neighbor?

QUILTING

Number of People:	Between 10-35
Materials:	Quilt panels for the entire group (1' x 1' or larger – think of the end size and adjust), material, thread, needles
Activity Level:	Low
Risk Level:	Low
Time Required:	Over 2 hours

This activity requires someone with knowledge of quilting, a significant amount of time, and the materials used in the activity. Explain to the group that everyone will be each constructing a quilt using the combined panels of each person on the team. You may decide to have team members create their own panels, find fabric that represents themselves, or some other way of individualizing each quilt panel (puffy paint, etc.) As an activity, participants can be asked to quilt the panels together after receiving instruction or the activity can be to decorate and design the quilts to be assembled later, depending upon the time and interest level of the group. Note that this activity is extensive and may take an extended period of time, up to one hour per person for each quilt square and three or more hours for the entire quilt itself so prepare accordingly.

Alternatively, you could construct one quilt for the entire team. Each person is responsible for creating his/her own panel that would then be sewn into one quilt. It could be used as a reward for high-performing team members or displayed as a show of team unity.

Facilitation Questions:

- Why did you choose your specific panel and what does it mean?
- How did it feel to put the quilt together?
- What will this quilt mean and how will the group use it for the future?

RISKY

Number of People:	Between 6-24
Materials:	High, medium, low-risk cards; pair of dice
Activity Level:	Low
Risk Level:	Medium
Time Required:	20-40 minutes

Before beginning the activity, the facilitator should create a series of questions that people in the group will be asking and answering during the activity. Create about an equal number of low, medium and high-risk questions and separate them into different stacks. Participants will roll the dice to determine which type of card to select from. You may set the results of the dice to be: a 2-6 is a Medium card, 7-9 is a Low card and a 10-12 is a High card. S/he will read the card and then answer the question for the group. Continue and rotate around the group until most of the cards and questions have been answered. Example questions could include:

- "What is your scariest moment?"
- "What is your biggest fear and why?"
- "Where is the best place you've ever been romantic"
- "What is your favorite ice cream flavor?"
- "What is a secret that no one knows about?"
- "What was your best vacation?"
- "Who was your best friend growing up?"

Facilitation Questions:

- What did you think of this activity?
- What did you learn about the others that were participating?
- Did you find yourself wanting higher risk questions or lower risk questions? Why is that?

SELF I SEE, SELF U SEE

Number of People: Between 6-40

Materials: One blank piece of paper and pen per person (use paper size appropriate to number of people)

Activity Level: Low

Risk Level: High

Time Required: 30-75 minutes

The facilitator should prepare enough sheets of paper and markers for everyone that participates. Larger groups may require poster board or large sheets of newsprint. Each person will take a minute to write on one side at the top of the paper his/her name. On the other side, write twenty characteristics about him/herself that s/he feels represents who s/he truly is. Once complete, the paper will be passed around (or if large paper and groups, hang the paper on walls throughout the room with tape) and everyone will write comments on the name side of the paper with positive affirmations about what they see! The papers will rotate around until everyone has had a chance to sign them and then the paper is returned to the owner. Groups can process what this activity felt like and make statements about what they appreciate from members of the group, including what people believe they see and do not see. This is often a great closure activity for a group to use to reflect together.

Facilitation Questions:

- What were the contrasts between who you thought you were and what other people thought of you?
- How do you feel after reading what people said?
- Why might this be an important activity for this group?

SILENT COOKIE BAKING

Number of People:	Between 4-12
Materials:	Cookie making ingredients, cookie recipes, oven
Activity Level:	Low
Risk Level:	Low
Time Required:	40-60 minutes

The participants in this exercise will be asked to bake a batch (or two) of cookies, but they will be unable to talk throughout the entire exercise. Groups will be responsible for everything from opening and securing ingredients to getting the cookies off of the pan! Let the participants set their own roles and determine how everyone will work together. There are a lot of variations for this activity as well. For example, you may mix in participants that are unable to see during the exercise or even (if safety permits) some/all participants are unable to see <u>or</u> hear for a bigger challenge. In addition, team members can have arms tied to one another as well. Process the activity following the baking and allow people to eat their creations!

Facilitation Questions:

- What were the challenges during this activity?
- How did everyone work to achieve the goals?
- How did communication work within this exercise? What could be improved upon for the future?
- How do this activity's tasks tie into the real world?

SPIRITUAL FOCUS

Number of People:	Between 5-32
Materials:	Paper and writing instruments
Activity Level:	Low
Risk Level:	High
Time Required:	20-45 minutes

In this activity, the facilitator will ask participants to create a "spirituality development timeline." This topic can be sensitive for many members of the group, so setting groundrules about sharing, discussion and appreciation for differences is a wise idea. During this activity, include areas such as major events, times of awareness, and definitions starting from the time of birth until present day. You can also ask participants to extend the timeline out beyond the present and to forecast a possible future. Ideas and specifics about spiritual development should be defined by the participants themselves. After everyone has finished, participants can share particular moments or events that were meaningful or ask participants to form small groups to share the timelines and the major events. This activity can bring a discussion of spirituality and religion to the group as a whole. (Spirituality is defined as broader than strictly religion, but participants should feel free to define the exercise as they wish to meet their needs.)

Facilitation Questions:

- What does your spirituality mean for you? How does it feel to share a piece of it?
- What did you feel during this exercise? How do you feel about the people in the group?

STRAW TOWER

Number of People:	Between 8-40 in subgroups of 6-10 people
Materials:	Plastic straws – at least 500 per group, measuring tape
Activity Level:	Low
Risk Level:	Low
Time Required:	20-35 minutes

Divide participants into subgroups and explain that the challenge of this activity is going to be to create a freestanding tower of the greatest height. Teams will not be able to brace the tower, use anything other than straws and will have approximately 15 minutes to complete their task. The tallest freestanding tower will be declared the winner. Once completed, allow teams to examine each other's towers and process the activity and the communication that took place. Similar activities can be done using tinker toys or asking teams to create a bridge from one chair to another that is free standing and will support the most weight! Another option is to change the activity so that one person in each sub-group is secretly a "bad apple." This person would have the responsibility to try to dominate the activity by ignoring other's ideas and presenting some bad ideas of his/her own. That could then be processed about how building the structures went and suggestions for effective communication and teamwork. There are many variations that this activity can bring, but the processing about roles in the group, how that may change from existing roles and implications team dynamics will be key.

Facilitation Questions:

- Why do we do this activity?
- Who took the lead in the groups? What did you think of the ideas used to determine a course of action?
- How was communication facilitated in the groups and what was, and was not effective about that?
- If you were to do this activity again differently, what might you do next time?
- How do lessons in the straw tower relate to this group working together in the future?

TAKE A STAND

Number of People: Between 8-75

Materials: Strongly Agree/Disagree signs

Activity Level: Low

Risk Level: High

Time Required: 25-45 minutes

Post the signs on opposite sides of the space of the room, high enough for people to see. One side of the room represents "Strongly Agree" and the other side of the room represents "Strongly Disagree." There are some groundrules and expectations that you should set as a facilitator to make this activity work more effectively. Remind participants that this activity is not about judging, but is meant to spur awareness in the group. In addition, there will be no arguing about specific issues or commenting negatively about someone who holds a different view than you. Remind people about professional and personal distinctions during discourse. You may find sample questions on the next page.

Explain to the group that you will be offering statements and after the statement is read, they should stand at the place in the room that shows what their belief is. Think of the space between the signs as a continuum. This is a quiet activity and people should not speak during the activity except when called upon during the follow-up sharing. Read the first statement and ask people to move to the spot in the room that best represents their opinion. If people have questions or need interpretation about a question asked, tell them to interpret the question however they see fit. Explain to people that it is OK to move if they feel that their answer shifts during this exercise. People in the middle are either ambivalent about the issue or undecided. Ask anyone that wishes to respond why they are standing there, or who would like to speak about this issue. As a facilitator, you must be comfortable with making sure all voices are heard, and no one person dominates any discussion. It is advisable to limit the comments to perhaps 5-8 statements for each question and get a good balance from both sides (and the middle) on every issue. People may not actually straddle the middle line so that people are forced to choose one side or the other for this activity as well.

An alternative to this activity would be to tailor questions specifically to the group and an upcoming project, training, or task that they will be involved with. For example, "I am feeling nervous about the upcoming training" or "When I get stressed, I tend to not ask for help." Generating these questions can lead to a dialogue about areas of importance to the group.

Facilitation Questions:

- Do we all have the same values?
- What felt awkward during this exercise?
- When were you unsure?
- Was there conflict between some of the right answers?
- What does this mean for working together?
- What assumptions did you make about others prior to this exercise?

Take a Stand Questions

1.   I think the drinking age should be lowered to 18.
2.   Pre-marital sex is OK.
3.   My right to a healthy environment supersedes another person's right to smoke.
4.   It is OK to euthanize a pet if it is old or in pain.
5.   It is OK to euthanize a human if s/he is old or in pain.
6.   Student government should fund a white student organization if asked through proper channels.
7.   Leaders should be held to higher moral standards than others.
8.   It is alright to lie to someone if you believe that it will benefit them.
9.   A Seminole (Native American nation) is an appropriate mascot for a university athletic team.
10. I believe that as a person it is appropriate to single out ethnic groups that sponsor terrorism as part of the "public good."
11. I believe that it is OK to suspend some civil liberties for the sake of the war on terrorism.
12. The premise for the war on Iraq was justified and "right".
13. I believe that religion has a place within our public school system.
14. I believe that the Pledge of Allegiance should include the phrase, "Under God."
15. I believe that people living in the United States should have to speak English.
16. I believe that GLBT people should not be employed in certain jobs in society.
17. I believe that GLBT people should not be allowed to adopt children.
18. I believe in a woman's right to choose.
19. I believe human cloning should be allowed.
20. Marijuana should be legalized.
21. I trust the US Government.
22. Religion doesn't play enough of a role in society today.
23. There is too much of a focus on issues of race in US society today.
24. I believe that cameras should be more prevalent to record possible illegal activity in society.
25. I believe that prostitution should be legalized.
26. Spying on US Citizens without a warrant is OK with me. I have nothing to hide.

TEAM ACRONYM

Number of People: Between 4-30

Materials: Paper and markers

Activity Level: Low

Risk Level: Low

Time Required: 10-20 minutes

Ask participants to think of the name of a group that they work with (or the group that brings them together now.) For example, if the group that is working together is the Orientation Team on campus, ask each person to write down some word for each letter in the team's name that describes the team. For example, the Orientation "PLUS" Team might be: Purposeful, Likable, Uninhibited, and Sensitive. Participants should get into small groups to share their words. From there, those subgroups should select words that they like the best. Finally, the entire group can determine which words best fit the team as a whole. You can then post those words visibly and revisit them on a regular basis to make sure that the team is living up to the ideals that they created in those words.

Facilitation Questions:

- Why did the group choose the words it did?
- What is the symbolism of this exercise for the group?
- Where does the group move with this activity? How might it be useful?

TEAM JEWELRY

Number of People:	Between 6-30
Materials:	Femo clay, beads, string/hemp/leather, etc.
Activity Level:	Low
Risk Level:	Low
Time Required:	45-90 minutes

The facilitator should arrange to have enough clay and a variety of colors to give team members a chance to express themselves through this activity. Explain that the members of the team are going to design and create jewelry (bracelet, necklace) or other item that will each contain a piece that was created by, or represents each member of the team. If you will be using Femo clay, each participant will need to create one bead per person (30 people on the team means creating 30 identical beads). For beads, make sure they all have holes of sufficient size in them for stringing and that they are baked according to the clay instructions. Allow them to cool and then have each person explain their beads to the group while stringing them together. Encourage them to wear and utilize their team's creation. Talk about the activity in terms of team unity and the whole is made up of more than the sum of the individual parts.

Facilitation Questions:

- Who enjoyed this activity? Who thought it was difficult? Why is that?
- What were the beads and what did they represent?
- What is the symbolism of this activity and what does it mean for this group?

TELEPHONE

Number of People: Between 10-30

Materials: None

Activity Level: Low

Risk Level: Low

Time Required: 5-15 minutes

Participants should sit in a circle for this activity. The facilitator should create a 2-3 sentence message that s/he will whisper to one of the people in the circle. The message will not be repeated, but it must be said clearly. That person must then pass on as much of the message s/he can and repeat it to the next person. That person will relay to the next and so on until it reaches the end. At that point, the last person should say aloud what the message was that s/he heard. For the exercise to be purposeful, participants should make a <u>sincere</u> attempt to relay the message as heard. Alternatively, the facilitator could also start another message in the opposite direction at the same time until the messages cross each other, creating a problem with "mixed messages".

Facilitation Questions:

- Communication is the root of this exercise…what went wrong with communication here?
- What could you have done to eliminate those problems?
- What effect does rumor and gossip have on a team? What is the group's opinion of it right now? Are there changes that you wish to make now about gossip/rumors that would benefit the team?

TOUCHSTONES

Number of People:	Between 10-60
Materials:	List of questions on next page
Activity Level:	Low
Risk Level:	High
Time Required:	30-60 minutes

This activity is often best for closure in a group. On the next page, you will find a list of potential questions to ask for this activity. Instruct participants to sit down in a circle facing the <u>outside</u> of the circle. The facilitator will stay in the middle of the circle during the entire activity and read off the statements. The facilitator should explain to the group that everyone in the room has touched the lives of people here in some way. Participants will be called to the middle of the circle and prompted to recognize other members of the group by touching the shoulders of people that fit the specific criteria read by the facilitator. As a facilitator, this activity works if there are about 7-10 separate groups doing the touching or about 3-6 people at one time. Ask participants to count off into subgroups. It is vitally important that all participants remain silent with eyes closed during the activity. People in the middle can touch as many people as they would like, but try to limit it in the interest of time. After the facilitator reads about 5-7 statements from the list, ask the touchers to sit down. The facilitator should call a new group of people to come into the center. The facilitator will then read another set of statements. The pattern continues until everyone has had a chance to be in the middle. The facilitator should make a point to notice which people are or are not being touched as often and make a point to touch them so that everyone feels "mattered" in the group. It can be disheartening if you are only touched once for 25 different categories! At the end of the activity, ask people to turn around and process the experience. Feel free to create lists more appropriate to your group. Remember to be genuine, emotional and funny – the best questions are a mixture of all three.

Facilitation Questions:

- How do you feel after this activity?
- What were some memorable moments about this exercise?
- What do you wish you could have said or done differently?

1. who fascinates you
2. who would sacrifice for you
3. who you'd like to spend more time with
4. who is a champion for diversity
5. who has (or would) influence you to work on being a better person
6. who has integrity
7. who you hope you don't lose touch with in the future
8. who is (or will be) a great friend
9. who knows how to get things done
10. who you admire
11. who you feel a connection with
12. who is a pleasant surprise to you
13. who you want to get to know better
14. who you feel is a quiet leader
15. who you think is a good listener
16. who really enjoys the role/job they play/do
17. who is quiet
18. who looks out for others in the group
19. who you would go to when you need a lift
20. who has helped you out when you were stressed out
21. who you would want to take a road trip with
22. who you'd like to see speak out more often
23. who you could cry with
24. who loves competition
25. who you think is a future leader
26. who you think is creative
27. who is well-rounded
28. who has even more to offer
29. who you feel is very important to you
30. who works hard behind-the-scenes
31. whose opinion you highly value
32. who you would seek out for advice
33. whose humor you enjoy
34. who you think always has a great attitude
35. you enjoy working with
36. who you feel you could share a secret with
37. who has helped you when you really needed it
38. who has inner strength
39. who is interesting to you
40. who has a positive influence on you
41. who puts in a lot of effort with what they do
42. who works well with diverse individuals
43. who has done something to make you smile
44. who you have shared a good experience with
45. who is very motivational
46. who you would like to share more with
47. who you would like to be more like
48. who makes you feel good about yourself
49. who inspires you
50. who lives an authentic life
51. who is humble
52. who is a mentor but may not know it
53. who is giving
54. who is beautiful inside and out
55. who is great with animals
56. who reminds you of a child sometimes
57. who you want to thank but have not
58. who you have especially enjoyed getting to know
59. who is always in a great mood
60. who would be the best roommate ever
61. who makes you laugh or lift your spirits
62. who can make your heart skip a beat
63. who can tell jokes really well
64. who is brilliant

The examples below are more humorous, but can set the tone for the activity!

1. who you would trade clothes with
2. who would make a good road kill collector.
3. who should become a vegetarian
4. who looks like hell first thing in the morning
5. who has beautiful ears
6. who is sweet enough to dip in chocolate
7. who would look good driving an old pickup truck and wearing boots
8. who is goofy enough to be a Disney character
9. who would do well if they happened to be in prison
10. who can turn any plant into a dead mess
11. who would be a nightmare roommate, but you love anyway
12. who is often flatulent or gassy
13. who has a funny/silly or really weird laugh
14. who reminds you of your grandmother when they drive
15. who needs to "light a match"
16. who you want to pinch their cheeks because they are just soooo adorable
17. who secretly has a dirty mind
18. who would make a good hippie
19. who was one of those kids always in the dirt and eating bugs
20. who is a "spicy vixen"
21. who you want to give a "wedgie"
22. who you could see being in a bad 80's rock band

TV COMMERCIAL

Number of People:	Between 5-60
Materials:	None
Activity Level:	Low
Risk Level:	Low
Time Required:	20-40 minutes

The facilitator should divide participants into groups of no more than six people. Explain that each team will need to develop a 30-second TV commercial that advertises their group (or alternatively some product) to the rest of the world. It should also contain a slogan and visuals that would be effective. Once developed, the team will need to act out the commercial for the rest of the participants (in front of a video camera if you have one.) Give a set period of time for participants to design their commercial. Discuss some of the various methods of successful commercials (creativity, well-known personalities or actors, humor, comparison to competition, sex appeal, etc.) Process this activity and ask why it was important for the team to work together and how these commercials could even be used in real life.

Facilitation Questions:

- Why did we do this activity?
- How was creativity used during this exercise? Why did you choose the method of "selling" that you did?
- What key parts of the group did you address with your commercial? Why did you choose those?

VALUE CARD SORT

Number of People:	Between 6-40
Materials:	Sheet with 40-50 values listed (See the following pages for examples)
Activity Level:	Low
Risk Level:	Medium
Time Required:	20-40 minutes

Gather all of the participants together and ask them to find a spot that they can spread out in for the activity. There are two versions of this activity. The first version will ask participants to take their value cards, look at the values listed and of these values, select the 10 that are most important to her/him. After they have done so, ask them to narrow that list down to 6, then 4, then 2 and finally the one value that is most important them. Once everyone has their values, ask participants to share what value they had selected as being the most important and why. Process the exercise and note the differences in values in the room, the process of narrowing the choices down and what this might mean for working as a team.

The second version of this exercise asks participants to take the list of values and separate them into three stacks. There should be a stack for values that are of high importance, a stack of moderate importance and one of no/little value. Arrange the values so that people could see the list of values in front of you. When everyone is ready, rotate around the room and examine everyone's value priorities to understand more about people in the group.

Facilitation Questions:

- Why are values important to people?
- What did it feel like to have to remove values from your list? How did it feel to have only one value? Were you satisfied with that?
- What were the differences and similarities with the one value chosen by everyone? What does this mean for working in the group as a whole?
- Were you surprised by what you saw? Why or why not?

Leadership & Influence	**Being Liked & Appreciated by Others**
Satisfying Relationship With a Partner/Spouse	**Freedom**
Deep Feelings & Empathy	**Openness & Honesty**
Justice & Fairness	**Self Understanding**
Cooperation & Teamwork	**Pursuit of Truth & Understanding**
A Sense of Order	**Personal Achievement**

Lifelong Learning	**Personal Independence**
Great Sense of Humor	**Health & Fitness**
Friendship	**Creativity**
Intelligence	**Family Life**
Class & Poise	**Having Financial Resources**
Deep Spiritual Beliefs	**Treating others as you would want to be treated**

Service to Others	**Laid Back Attitude**
Physical Relationships	**Capacity to Give & Receive Love**
Humility	**Adventure**
Living Congruent to Values & Beliefs	**Job Satisfaction & Success**
Betterment of the World	**Beauty**
Communication	**Power & Authority**

Life of Leisure	Fiscal Responsibility
Diversity & Social Justice	Flexibility
Self-Challenge	Being Genuine
Ambition	Courage
Optimism	Patience & Perseverance
Trust	Hope

WEB WE WEAVE

Number of People:	Between 8-35
Materials:	Big ball of string or yarn
Activity Level:	Low
Risk Level:	Low
Time Required:	15-30 minutes

Ask participants to stand in a large circle a couple of feet apart from each other. The facilitator will begin the activity by asking a question that everyone in the group is going to answer such as, "What is one thing that you are looking forward to with this team?" The facilitator will answer the question and then toss the yarn ball across the circle to another person while keeping a hold of the end, creating a string across the group. That person then answers the question, holds the corner of the yarn and tosses the yarn ball to someone else. Everyone should keep hold of their part of yarn until a web is formed as the yarn ball crosses the circle multiple times. This continues until everyone has answered the question and the yarn ball returns to the facilitator. The facilitator can ask as many questions as appropriate to create a good network of yarn, depending upon the size of the group. The facilitator can then ask two or three people to release their string and notice how the web sags and appears weak and6 vulnerable. Draw comparisons between the need of the group to "keep their strings up" and share expectations with the group.

Facilitation Questions:

- How did it feel to share during this activity?
- What does this exercise show about teamwork? What is the metaphor?
- What happens when the string is dropped? What happens when everyone keeps their string tight? What metaphor can this tie in to with the group in the "real world?"
- What will you commit to so that the team does not fall apart in the future?

REFERENCES

The author would like to acknowledge the many different resources available on the topic of icebreakers and teambuilding activities. Many of these activities have been recycled so that the original source is unknown. If you know of the original source material for any of the activities in this guide, please contact the author who will properly reference it in future printings.

Forbess-Greene, S., *The Encyclopedia of Icebreakers*, © 1983, John Wiley and Sons, Inc. Reprinted with permission of John Wiley & Sons, Inc.

Newstrom and Scannell, *Still More Games Trainers Play*, © 1991, The McGraw-Hill Companies. Material reproduced and adapted with permission of the McGraw-Hill Companies.

Rohnke, Karl, *The Bottomless Bag Again!?*, © 1994, Reprinted and adapted with permission of author.

CATEGORY INDEX

Activity Name	Category	Min. # of Part.	Max # of Part.	Materials?	Activity Level	Risk Level	Minutes Required	Page
A to Z	Ice Breaker	6	200	No	Low	Low	5 – 10	46
Amoeba Tag	Ice Breaker	14	125	No	High	Low	10 – 20	47
Arc Ball	Ice Breaker	14	60	Yes	Medium	Low	8 – 20	48
Assassin	Ice Breaker	10	80	Yes	Low	Low	Weeks…	49
Back to Back	Ice Breaker	8	300	No	High	Low	5 – 15	50
Balloon Blow Out	Ice Breaker	5	80	Yes	Low	Low	4 – 10	51
Balloon Tag	Ice Breaker	8	50	Yes	Medium	Low	4 – 10	52
Banana Relay	Ice Breaker	10	60	Yes	Medium	Medium	8 – 18	53
Barnyard	Ice Breaker	8	30	Yes	Low	Low	8 – 20	54
Barnyard Animals	Ice Breaker	15	300	No	Low	Medium	6 – 15	55
Basket	Ice Breaker	6	60	Yes	Low	Low	10 – 25	56
Birdie on a Perch	Ice Breaker	15	80	No	High	Medium	6 – 15	57
Birthday Line	Ice Breaker	12	200	No	Low	Low	1 – 5	58
Bite the Bag	Ice Breaker	6	60	Yes	Medium	Medium	5 – 15	59
Black Magic	Ice Breaker	10	40	No	Low	Low	12 – 40	60
Blind Identify	Ice Breaker	10	30	Yes	Low	Medium	8 – 15	61
Blindfold Line-Up	Ice Breaker	7	40	Yes	Medium	Medium	5 – 10	62
Body English	Ice Breaker	6	70	No	Medium	Low	5 – 10	63
Brain Benders	Ice Breaker	8	80	Yes	Low	Low	10 – 20	64
Buzz	Ice Breaker	10	40	No	Low	Low	8 – 15	66
Calls of the Night	Ice Breaker	6	24	Yes	Low	Low	12 – 20	67
Catch Me If You Can	Ice Breaker	6	200	No	Low	Low	4 – 10	68
Chalkboard Sentences	Ice Breaker	12	48	Yes	Low	Low	10 – 18	69
Charlie's Angels	Ice Breaker	12	45	No	Low	Low	15 – 25	70
Chocalotaschnizzel	Ice Breaker	8	30	Yes	Medium	Low	12 – 20	72
Chubby Bunny	Ice Breaker	4	30	Yes	Low	Medium	6 – 15	73
Clam Free	Ice Breaker	16	60	Yes	High	Low	12 – 20	74
Clapping Clues	Ice Breaker	6	60	No	Low	Low	10 – 20	75
Clothespin Tag	Ice Breaker	8	50	Yes	Medium	Low	5 – 12	76
Color, Car, Character	Ice Breaker	10	40	No	Low	Low	12 – 30	77
Comic Strip Chaos	Ice Breaker	20	100	Yes	Low	Low	4 – 8	78
Confusion Bingo	Ice Breaker	10	100	Yes	Medium	Medium	8 – 15	79
Count Off	Ice Breaker	8	25	No	Low	Low	5 – 8	81
Dead Fish	Ice Breaker	8	50	No	Low	Low	4 – 10	82
Detective	Ice Breaker	12	50	No	Low	Low	8 – 15	83
Dizzy Bat	Ice Breaker	8	60	Yes	High	Medium	6 – 15	84
Do You Love Your Neighbor?	Ice Breaker	14	80	No	Medium	Low	10 – 20	85
Drip, Drip, Drop	Ice Breaker	15	40	Yes	High	High	10 – 20	86
Ducky Wucky	Ice Breaker	10	40	Yes	Low	Medium	8 – 15	87
Elbow Tag	Ice Breaker	14	36	No	High	Medium	12 – 20	88
Elves, Giants and Chickens	Ice Breaker	15	250	No	Medium	Low	8 – 12	89
Evolution	Ice Breaker	16	50	No	Low	Low	10 – 20	90

Activity Name	Category	Min. # of Part.	Max # of Part.	Materials?	Activity Level	Risk Level	Minutes Required	Page
Famous Pairs	Ice Breaker	16	80	Yes	Low	Low	12 – 20	91
Five Things	Ice Breaker	6	75	Yes	Low	Low	20 – 30	103
Flour Game	Ice Breaker	6	24	Yes	Low	Medium	15 – 30	104
Follow the Leader	Ice Breaker	10	50	No	High	Low	10 – 18	105
Freeze Tag	Ice Breaker	15	150	No	High	Medium	10 – 18	106
Group Story	Ice Breaker	4	40	No	Low	Low	6 – 12	107
Guard the Bone	Ice Breaker	8	30	Yes	Medium	Low	6 – 15	108
Ha!	Ice Breaker	10	30	No	Medium	Medium	8 – 12	109
Height Line	Ice Breaker	10	60	No	Low	Low	4 – 8	110
Hog Call	Ice Breaker	20	200	No	Low	Medium	4 – 8	111
How You Doin'?	Ice Breaker	15	70	No	Low	Medium	8 – 12	112
Hula Hoop Relay	Ice Breaker	9	50	Yes	Medium	Low	8 – 15	113
Hum That Tune	Ice Breaker	15	300	No	Low	Low	4 – 8	114
Human Knot	Ice Breaker	6	40	No	High	Medium	12 – 25	115
Human Taco (or Burger)	Ice Breaker	20	300	Yes	Low	Low	8 – 20	116
Human Twister	Ice Breaker	6	40	Yes	Low	Medium	8 – 15	118
I Love You Baby, But I Just Can't Smile	Ice Breaker	10	45	No	Low	Low	6 – 12	119
Ice Cubes	Ice Breaker	6	60	Yes	Medium	Medium	8 – 20	120
I'm Thinking of Someone	Ice Breaker	10	45	No	Low	Low	10 – 20	121
Imaginary Dough	Ice Breaker	6	50	No	Low	Low	10 – 25	122
Keep It Up	Ice Breaker	6	20	Yes	Medium	Low	6 – 15	123
Killer	Ice Breaker	16	50	No	Low	Low	10 – 20	124
Lap Sit	Ice Breaker	6	300	No	Medium	Medium	6 – 10	125
Life Saver Relay	Ice Breaker	12	50	Yes	Low	Medium	5 – 10	126
Line Relay	Ice Breaker	10	60	No	High	Low	6 – 12	127
List Stories	Ice Breaker	6	36	Yes	Low	Low	10 – 20	128
Lollipop	Ice Breaker	4	30	Yes	Low	Low	15 – 40	129
M&M Game	Ice Breaker	4	30	Yes	Low	Low	15 – 40	130
M&M Swap	Ice Breaker	5	50	Yes	Medium	Low	8 – 15	131
Machine Game	Ice Breaker	10	120	No	Medium	Low	10 – 20	132
Mafia	Ice Breaker	8	25	Yes	Low	Low	20 +	133
Make a Date	Ice Breaker	8	50	Yes	Low	Low	12 – 20	136
Man Overboard	Ice Breaker	12	125	No	Medium	Medium	20 – 30	137
Mirror, Mirror	Ice Breaker	8	30	Yes	Low	Low	6 – 15	139
Mrs. Mumbles	Ice Breaker	8	40	No	Low	Low	10 – 18	140
Musical Interpretation	Ice Breaker	10	200	Yes	Medium	Low	5 – 10	141
My Favorite Place	Ice Breaker	5	30	Yes	Low	Low	15 – 25	142
Number Groups	Ice Breaker	15	300	No	Low	Low	3 – 8	143
Ooo, Aaaah, Ooooh!	Ice Breaker	9	32	No	Low	Low	8 – 15	144
Orange Pass	Ice Breaker	7	50	Yes	Medium	Medium	6 – 12	145
Orchestra	Ice Breaker	10	200	No	Low	Low	6 – 10	146
Paper Bags	Ice Breaker	8	30	Yes	Low	Low	8 – 15	147
People to People	Ice Breaker	12	60	No	High	Medium	10 – 20	148

Activity Name	Category	Min. # of Part.	Max # of Part.	Materials?	Activity Level	Risk Level	Minutes Required	Page
Posture Relay	Ice Breaker	8	15	Yes	Medium	Low	5 – 8	149
Puzzle Jumble	Ice Breaker	14	100	Yes	Low	Low	8 – 15	150
Raid	Ice Breaker	14	50	Yes	High	Low	10 – 20	151
Random Poetry	Ice Breaker	6	20	Yes	Low	Low	12 – 25	152
Rhythm & Motion	Ice Breaker	10	50	No	Low	Low	12 – 20	154
Rhythm Ice Breaker	Ice Breaker	10	40	Yes	Low	Low	8 – 15	155
Road Trip!	Ice Breaker	6	24	Yes	Low	Low	45-60	156
Scissors	Ice Breaker	8	28	Yes	Low	Low	8 – 15	157
Scooterball	Ice Breaker	6	18	Yes	High	Medium	8 – 15	158
Self Introduction Story Time	Ice Breaker	6	25	Yes	Low	Low	15 – 25	159
Sentence Stems	Ice Breaker	4	50	Yes	Low	Medium	10 – 20	161
Seven-Eleven	Ice Breaker	4	60	No	Low	Low	6 – 10	162
Shoe Factory	Ice Breaker	8	40	No	Medium	Low	6 – 15	163
Shoe Sort	Ice Breaker	8	30	No	Low	Low	8 – 15	164
Sing Down	Ice Breaker	9	200	Yes	Low	Low	15 – 30	165
Slaps	Ice Breaker	8	24	No	Low	Low	6 – 12	166
Snake's Tail	Ice Breaker	12	45	No	High	Low	10 – 20	167
Snaps	Ice Breaker	10	35	No	Low	Low	12 – 20	168
Sock Game	Ice Breaker	8	32	No	High	Medium	6 – 10	169
Solemn and Silent	Ice Breaker	8	120	No	Low	Low	8 – 12	170
Sponge Pass	Ice Breaker	10	60	Yes	Low	Medium	10 – 20	171
Spoon Feed Me	Ice Breaker	3	13	Yes	Low	Medium	6 – 12	172
S-P-U-D	Ice Breaker	8	32	Yes	High	Low	12 – 25	173
Squeeze	Ice Breaker	12	30	Yes	Low	Low	10 – 20	174
Statues	Ice Breaker	6	60	No	Medium	Low	8 – 15	175
Stinger	Ice Breaker	15	60	No	Low	Low	10 – 20	176
Sumo	Ice Breaker	11	30	No	High	Medium	12 – 20	177
T-Shirt Tales	Ice Breaker	8	35	Yes	Low	Low	10 – 25	178
Team Crossword	Ice Breaker	8	30	Yes	Low	Low	10 – 18	179
The Creature	Ice Breaker	4	40	No	Medium	Low	12 – 18	180
Think Fast	Ice Breaker	8	28	Yes	Low	Low	10 – 20	181
Toilet Paper Game	Ice Breaker	8	30	Yes	Low	Low	12 – 25	182
Touchee Feelee	Ice Breaker	10	50	No	Medium	Medium	10 – 18	183
Two Truths and a Lie	Ice Breaker	5	40	No	Low	Low	8 – 15	184
Water Balance	Ice Breaker	8	18	Yes	Medium	Medium	10 – 20	185
Waterfall Game	Ice Breaker	8	40	Yes	Low	Medium	8 – 18	186
What I Carry	Ice Breaker	8	40	No	Low	Low	15 – 20	187
Where Were You?	Ice Breaker	6	40	No	Low	Low	15 – 25	188
Woooooooooo	Ice Breaker	10	50	Yes	Low	Low	15 - 40	189
Adjective Name Game	Name Game	8	30	No	Low	Low	8 – 20	12
Blanket Name Game	Name Game	10	30	Yes	Low	Low	6 – 15	13
Butt Spelling	Name Game	10	50	No	Low	Medium	8 – 15	14
Concentration	Name Game	10	30	No	Low	Low	6 – 20	15

Activity Name	Category	Min. # of Part.	Max # of Part.	Materials?	Activity Level	Risk Level	Minutes Required	Page
Funny Face	Name Game	6	40	No	Low	Low	4 – 8	16
Group Juggle	Name Game	10	35	Yes	Low	Low	10 – 25	17
Here I Am	Name Game	10	25	Yes	Low	Low	5 – 10	18
Human Bingo	Name Game	10	150	Yes	Low	Low	6 – 15	19
I'm a Gigolo	Name Game	10	35	No	Low	Low	5 – 12	21
Introduction Interview	Name Game	8	30	No	Low	Low	8 – 25	22
Motion Name Game	Name Game	8	30	No	Medium	Low	6 – 30	23
My Three Objects	Name Game	4	40	Yes	Low	Low	8 – 30	24
Shabuya Roll Call	Name Game	8	24	No	Low	Low	8 – 20	25
Shoe Game	Name Game	8	40	No	Low	Low	10 – 25	26
Snort	Name Game	10	35	No	Low	Low	10 – 25	27
Whomp'Em	Name Game	10	30	Yes	Medium	Low	6 - 12	28
All Aboard	Ropes	7	18	Yes	Medium	Medium	15 – 30	31
Blind Squares	Ropes	8	30	Yes	Medium	Medium	15 – 30	32
Build Your Own Game	Ropes	12	100	Yes	High	Low	40 – 60	33
Log Jam	Ropes	10	26	Yes	High	Medium	20 – 30	34
Log Roll	Ropes	10	50	No	High	Medium	5 – 10	35
Mars Probe	Ropes	5	24	Yes	Low	Medium	12 – 30	36
Plane Wreck	Ropes	6	40	Yes	Medium	High	15 – 40	37
Rope Wall	Ropes	8	32	Yes	High	High	12 – 25	38
Three Person Trust Fall	Ropes	3	100	No	High	High	4 – 10	39
Traffic Jam	Ropes	10	60	Yes	Low	Low	12 – 25	40
Trust Walk	Ropes	6	60	Yes	Medium	High	25 – 40	41
Two Person Trust Fall	Ropes	6	150	No	High	High	3 – 8	43
Willow in the Wind	Ropes	7	120	No	High	High	10 – 20	44
Affirmative Fold-Ups	Teambuilder	4	35	Yes	Low	Medium	10 – 18	191
Amazing Teamcoat	Teambuilder	5	36	Yes	Low	Low	30 – 60	192
Artist, Clay, Model	Teambuilder	6	80	No	Low	Medium	8 – 20	193
Autobiography	Teambuilder	5	30	Yes	Low	Low	15 – 40	194
Blind Golf	Teambuilder	6	50	Yes	Low	Low	10 – 20	196
Build My House	Teambuilder	5	40	Yes	Low	Medium	20 – 30	200
Capture the Flag	Teambuilder	16	50	Yes	High	Low	30 – 75	201
Chain Back Rub	Teambuilder	4	150	No	Low	Medium	8 – 10	202
Chart a Life	Teambuilder	4	30	Yes	Low	Medium	12 – 30	203
Clipboards	Teambuilder	5	30	Yes	Low	Low	45 – 60	205
Debate	Teambuilder	6	16	No	Low	Low	30 – 60	206
Design Your Perfect	Teambuilder	6	40	Yes	Low	Low	30 - 45	207
Dot Brainstorming	Teambuilder	3	60	Yes	Low	Low	6 – 20	208
Each One, Teach One	Teambuilder	3	25	No	Low	Low	15 – 40	209
Egg Break	Teambuilder	9	80	Yes	Low	Low	30 – 45	210
Fear Factor	Teambuilder	6	30	Yes	Medium	High	30 – 60	211
Finger Paint Collage	Teambuilder	5	25	Yes	Low	Low	25 – 45	212
Five Things I Want to Learn	Teambuilder	15	60	Yes	Low	Low	10 – 20	213

Activity Name	Category	Min. # of Part.	Max # of Part.	Materials?	Activity Level	Risk Level	Minutes Required	Page
Flash Card Revelations	Teambuilder	12	40	Yes	Low	High	20 – 40	214
Group Résumé	Teambuilder	4	20	Yes	Low	Low	20 – 40	215
Important Item	Teambuilder	6	32	Yes	Low	High	20 – 90 +	216
Information Fun Sheet	Teambuilder	8	35	Yes	Low	Medium	30 - 60	217
Last Will & Testament	Teambuilder	8	35	Yes	Low	High	15 – 30	218
Levitation	Teambuilder	8	100	No	Medium	Medium	8 – 20	219
Listening Skills Drawings	Teambuilder	6	150	Yes	Low	Low	15 – 30	220
Masks I Wear	Teambuilder	7	40	Yes	Low	High	30 – 45	222
Masks Of Me	Teambuilder	6	40	Yes	Low	High	60 +	223
Observation	Teambuilder	5	100	Yes	Low	Low	15 – 25	225
Peanut Butter & Jelly	Teambuilder	10	40	Yes	Low	Low	20 - 35	226
Penny for Your Thoughts	Teambuilder	10	30	Yes	Low	Medium	15 – 25	227
Perpetual Tag	Teambuilder	10	35	No	Low	Low	Weeks…	228
Personal Quotation	Teambuilder	6	30	Yes	Low	Medium	8 – 20	229
Perspectives	Teambuilder	6	18	Yes	Low	Medium	30 – 60	230
Piece of the Puzzle	Teambuilder	8	40	Yes	Low	Medium	30 – 45	232
Poetry Group	Teambuilder	5	35	Yes	Low	Medium	20 – 45	233
Psychiatrist	Teambuilder	10	30	No	Low	Low	30 – 60	234
Quilting	Teambuilder	10	35	Yes	Low	Low	120 +	235
Risky	Teambuilder	6	24	Yes	Low	Medium	20 – 40	236
Self I See, Self U See	Teambuilder	6	40	Yes	Low	High	30 – 75	237
Silent Cookie Baking	Teambuilder	4	12	Yes	Low	Low	40 - 60	238
Spiritual Focus	Teambuilder	5	32	Yes	Low	High	20 – 45	239
Straw Tower	Teambuilder	8	40	Yes	Low	Low	20 – 35	240
Take a Stand	Teambuilder	8	75	Yes	Low	High	25 – 45	241
Team Acronym	Teambuilder	4	30	Yes	Low	Low	10 – 20	243
Team Jewelry	Teambuilder	6	30	Yes	Low	Low	45 – 90	244
Telephone	Teambuilder	10	30	No	Low	Low	5 – 15	245
Touchstones	Teambuilder	10	60	Yes	Low	High	30 – 60	246
TV Commercial	Teambuilder	5	60	No	Low	Low	20 – 40	248
Value Card Sort	Teambuilder	6	40	Yes	Low	Medium	20 – 40	249
Web We Weave	Teambuilder	8	35	Yes	Low	Low	15 - 30	254

ALPHABETICAL LISTING

Activity Name	Category	Min. # of Part.	Max # of Part.	Materials?	Activity Level	Risk Level	Minutes Required	Page
A to Z	Ice Breaker	6	200	No	Low	Low	5 – 10	46
Adjective Name Game	Name Game	8	30	No	Low	Low	8 – 20	12
Affirmative Fold-Ups	Teambuilder	4	35	Yes	Low	Medium	10 – 18	191
All Aboard	Ropes	7	18	Yes	Medium	Medium	15 – 30	31
Amazing Teamcoat	Teambuilder	5	36	Yes	Low	Low	30 – 60	192
Amoeba Tag	Ice Breaker	14	125	No	High	Low	10 – 20	47
Arc Ball	Ice Breaker	14	60	Yes	Medium	Low	8 – 20	48
Artist, Clay, Model	Teambuilder	6	80	No	Low	Medium	8 – 20	193
Assassin	Ice Breaker	10	80	Yes	Low	Low	Weeks...	49
Autobiography	Teambuilder	5	30	Yes	Low	Low	15 – 40	194
Back to Back	Ice Breaker	8	300	No	High	Low	5 – 15	50
Balloon Blow Out	Ice Breaker	5	80	Yes	Low	Low	4 – 10	51
Balloon Tag	Ice Breaker	8	50	Yes	Medium	Low	4 – 10	52
Banana Relay	Ice Breaker	10	60	Yes	Medium	Medium	8 – 18	53
Barnyard	Ice Breaker	8	30	Yes	Low	Low	8 – 20	54
Barnyard Animals	Ice Breaker	15	300	No	Low	Medium	6 – 15	55
Basket	Ice Breaker	6	60	Yes	Low	Low	10 – 25	56
Birdie on a Perch	Ice Breaker	15	80	No	High	Medium	6 – 15	57
Birthday Line	Ice Breaker	12	200	No	Low	Low	1 – 5	58
Bite the Bag	Ice Breaker	6	60	Yes	Medium	Medium	5 – 15	59
Black Magic	Ice Breaker	10	40	No	Low	Low	12 – 40	60
Blanket Name Game	Name Game	10	30	Yes	Low	Low	6 – 15	13
Blind Golf	Teambuilder	6	50	Yes	Low	Low	10 – 20	196
Blind Identify	Ice Breaker	10	30	Yes	Low	Medium	8 – 15	61
Blind Squares	Ropes	8	30	Yes	Medium	Medium	15 – 30	32
Blindfold Line-Up	Ice Breaker	7	40	Yes	Medium	Medium	5 – 10	62
Body English	Ice Breaker	6	70	No	Medium	Low	5 – 10	63
Brain Benders	Ice Breaker	8	80	Yes	Low	Low	10 – 20	64
Build My House	Teambuilder	5	40	Yes	Low	Medium	20 – 30	200
Build Your Own Game	Ropes	12	100	Yes	High	Low	40 – 60	33
Butt Spelling	Name Game	10	50	No	Low	Medium	8 – 15	14
Buzz	Ice Breaker	10	40	No	Low	Low	8 – 15	66
Calls of the Night	Ice Breaker	6	24	Yes	Low	Low	12 – 20	67
Capture the Flag	Teambuilder	16	50	Yes	High	Low	30 – 75	201
Catch Me If You Can	Ice Breaker	6	200	No	Low	Low	4 – 10	68
Chain Back Rub	Teambuilder	4	150	No	Low	Medium	8 – 10	202
Chalkboard Sentences	Ice Breaker	12	48	Yes	Low	Low	10 – 18	69
Charlie's Angels	Ice Breaker	12	45	No	Low	Low	15 – 25	70
Chart a Life	Teambuilder	4	30	Yes	Low	Medium	12 – 30	203
Chocalotaschnizzel	Ice Breaker	8	30	Yes	Medium	Low	12 – 20	72
Chubby Bunny	Ice Breaker	4	30	Yes	Low	Medium	6 – 15	73
Clam Free	Ice Breaker	16	60	Yes	High	Low	12 – 20	74

Activity Name	Category	Min. # of Part.	Max # of Part.	Materials?	Activity Level	Risk Level	Minutes Required	Page
Clapping Clues	Ice Breaker	6	60	No	Low	Low	10 – 20	75
Clipboards	Teambuilder	5	30	Yes	Low	Low	45 – 60	205
Clothespin Tag	Ice Breaker	8	50	Yes	Medium	Low	5 – 12	76
Color, Car, Character	Ice Breaker	10	40	No	Low	Low	12 – 30	77
Comic Strip Chaos	Ice Breaker	20	100	Yes	Low	Low	4 – 8	78
Concentration	Name Game	10	30	No	Low	Low	6 – 20	15
Confusion Bingo	Ice Breaker	10	100	Yes	Medium	Medium	8 – 15	79
Count Off	Ice Breaker	8	25	No	Low	Low	5 – 8	81
Dead Fish	Ice Breaker	8	50	No	Low	Low	4 – 10	82
Debate	Teambuilder	6	16	No	Low	Low	30 – 60	206
Design Your Perfect	Teambuilder	6	40	Yes	Low	Low	30 - 45	207
Detective	Ice Breaker	12	50	No	Low	Low	8 – 15	83
Dizzy Bat	Ice Breaker	8	60	Yes	High	Medium	6 – 15	84
Do You Love Your Neighbor?	Ice Breaker	14	80	No	Medium	Low	10 – 20	85
Dot Brainstorming	Teambuilder	3	60	Yes	Low	Low	6 – 20	208
Drip, Drip, Drop	Ice Breaker	15	40	Yes	High	High	10 – 20	86
Ducky Wucky	Ice Breaker	10	40	Yes	Low	Medium	8 – 15	87
Each One, Teach One	Teambuilder	3	25	No	Low	Low	15 – 40	209
Egg Break	Teambuilder	9	80	Yes	Low	Low	30 – 45	210
Elbow Tag	Ice Breaker	14	36	No	High	Medium	12 – 20	88
Elves, Giants and Chickens	Ice Breaker	15	250	No	Medium	Low	8 – 12	89
Evolution	Ice Breaker	16	50	No	Low	Low	10 – 20	90
Famous Pairs	Ice Breaker	16	80	Yes	Low	Low	12 – 20	91
Fear Factor	Teambuilder	6	30	Yes	Medium	High	30 – 60	211
Finger Paint Collage	Teambuilder	5	25	Yes	Low	Low	25 – 45	212
Five Things	Ice Breaker	6	75	Yes	Low	Low	20 – 30	103
Five Things I Want to Learn	Teambuilder	15	60	Yes	Low	Low	10 – 20	213
Flash Card Revelations	Teambuilder	12	40	Yes	Low	High	20 – 40	214
Flour Game	Ice Breaker	6	24	Yes	Low	Medium	15 – 30	104
Follow the Leader	Ice Breaker	10	50	No	High	Low	10 – 18	105
Freeze Tag	Ice Breaker	15	150	No	High	Medium	10 – 18	106
Funny Face	Name Game	6	40	No	Low	Low	4 – 8	16
Group Juggle	Name Game	10	35	Yes	Low	Low	10 – 25	17
Group Résumé	Teambuilder	4	20	Yes	Low	Low	20 – 40	215
Group Story	Ice Breaker	4	40	No	Low	Low	6 – 12	107
Guard the Bone	Ice Breaker	8	30	Yes	Medium	Low	6 – 15	108
Ha!	Ice Breaker	10	30	No	Medium	Medium	8 – 12	109
Height Line	Ice Breaker	10	60	No	Low	Low	4 – 8	110
Here I Am	Name Game	10	25	Yes	Low	Low	5 – 10	18
Hog Call	Ice Breaker	20	200	No	Low	Medium	4 – 8	111
How You Doin'?	Ice Breaker	15	70	No	Low	Medium	8 – 12	112
Hula Hoop Relay	Ice Breaker	9	50	Yes	Medium	Low	8 – 15	113
Hum That Tune	Ice Breaker	15	300	No	Low	Low	4 – 8	114

Activity Name	Category	Min. # of Part.	Max # of Part.	Materials?	Activity Level	Risk Level	Minutes Required	Page
Human Bingo	Name Game	10	150	Yes	Low	Low	6 – 15	19
Human Knot	Ice Breaker	6	40	No	High	Medium	12 – 25	115
Human Taco (or Burger)	Ice Breaker	20	300	Yes	Low	Low	8 – 20	116
Human Twister	Ice Breaker	6	40	Yes	Low	Medium	8 – 15	118
I Love You Baby, But I Just Can't Smile	Ice Breaker	10	45	No	Low	Low	6 – 12	119
Ice Cubes	Ice Breaker	6	60	Yes	Medium	Medium	8 – 20	120
I'm a Gigolo	Name Game	10	35	No	Low	Low	5 – 12	21
I'm Thinking of Someone	Ice Breaker	10	45	No	Low	Low	10 – 20	121
Imaginary Dough	Ice Breaker	6	50	No	Low	Low	10 – 25	122
Important Item	Teambuilder	6	32	Yes	Low	High	20 – 90 +	216
Information Fun Sheet	Teambuilder	8	35	Yes	Low	Medium	30 - 60	217
Introduction Interview	Name Game	8	30	No	Low	Low	8 – 25	22
Keep It Up	Ice Breaker	6	20	Yes	Medium	Low	6 – 15	123
Killer	Ice Breaker	16	50	No	Low	Low	10 – 20	124
Lap Sit	Ice Breaker	6	300	No	Medium	Medium	6 – 10	125
Last Will & Testament	Teambuilder	8	35	Yes	Low	High	15 – 30	218
Levitation	Teambuilder	8	100	No	Medium	Medium	8 – 20	219
Life Saver Relay	Ice Breaker	12	50	Yes	Low	Medium	5 – 10	126
Line Relay	Ice Breaker	10	60	No	High	Low	6 – 12	127
List Stories	Ice Breaker	6	36	Yes	Low	Low	10 – 20	128
Listening Skills Drawings	Teambuilder	6	150	Yes	Low	Low	15 – 30	220
Log Jam	Ropes	10	26	Yes	High	Medium	20 – 30	34
Log Roll	Ropes	10	50	No	High	Medium	5 – 10	35
Lollipop	Ice Breaker	4	30	Yes	Low	Low	15 – 40	129
M&M Game	Ice Breaker	4	30	Yes	Low	Low	15 – 40	130
M&M Swap	Ice Breaker	5	50	Yes	Medium	Low	8 – 15	131
Machine Game	Ice Breaker	10	120	No	Medium	Low	10 – 20	132
Mafia	Ice Breaker	8	25	Yes	Low	Low	20 +	133
Make a Date	Ice Breaker	8	50	Yes	Low	Low	12 – 20	136
Man Overboard	Ice Breaker	12	125	No	Medium	Medium	20 – 30	137
Mars Probe	Ropes	5	24	Yes	Low	Medium	12 – 30	36
Masks I Wear	Teambuilder	7	40	Yes	Low	High	30 – 45	222
Masks Of Me	Teambuilder	6	40	Yes	Low	High	60 +	223
Mirror, Mirror	Ice Breaker	8	30	Yes	Low	Low	6 – 15	139
Motion Name Game	Name Game	8	30	No	Medium	Low	6 – 30	23
Mrs. Mumbles	Ice Breaker	8	40	No	Low	Low	10 – 18	140
Musical Interpretation	Ice Breaker	10	200	Yes	Medium	Low	5 – 10	141
My Favorite Place	Ice Breaker	5	30	Yes	Low	Low	15 – 25	142
My Three Objects	Name Game	4	40	Yes	Low	Low	8 – 30	24
Number Groups	Ice Breaker	15	300	No	Low	Low	3 – 8	143
Observation	Teambuilder	5	100	Yes	Low	Low	15 – 25	225
Ooo, Aaaah, Oooh!	Ice Breaker	9	32	No	Low	Low	8 – 15	144
Orange Pass	Ice Breaker	7	50	Yes	Medium	Medium	6 – 12	145

Activity Name	Category	Min. # of Part.	Max # of Part.	Materials?	Activity Level	Risk Level	Minutes Required	Page
Orchestra	Ice Breaker	10	200	No	Low	Low	6 – 10	146
Paper Bags	Ice Breaker	8	30	Yes	Low	Low	8 – 15	147
Peanut Butter & Jelly	Teambuilder	10	40	Yes	Low	Low	20 - 35	226
Penny for Your Thoughts	Teambuilder	10	30	Yes	Low	Medium	15 – 25	227
People to People	Ice Breaker	12	60	No	High	Medium	10 – 20	148
Perpetual Tag	Teambuilder	10	35	No	Low	Low	Weeks…	228
Personal Quotation	Teambuilder	6	30	Yes	Low	Medium	8 – 20	229
Perspectives	Teambuilder	6	18	Yes	Low	Medium	30 – 60	230
Piece of the Puzzle	Teambuilder	8	40	Yes	Low	Medium	30 – 45	232
Plane Wreck	Ropes	6	40	Yes	Medium	High	15 – 40	37
Poetry Group	Teambuilder	5	35	Yes	Low	Medium	20 – 45	233
Posture Relay	Ice Breaker	8	15	Yes	Medium	Low	5 – 8	149
Psychiatrist	Teambuilder	10	30	No	Low	Low	30 – 60	234
Puzzle Jumble	Ice Breaker	14	100	Yes	Low	Low	8 – 15	150
Quilting	Teambuilder	10	35	Yes	Low	Low	120 +	235
Raid	Ice Breaker	14	50	Yes	High	Low	10 – 20	151
Random Poetry	Ice Breaker	6	20	Yes	Low	Low	12 – 25	152
Rhythm & Motion	Ice Breaker	10	50	No	Low	Low	12 – 20	154
Rhythm Ice Breaker	Ice Breaker	10	40	Yes	Low	Low	8 – 15	155
Risky	Teambuilder	6	24	Yes	Low	Medium	20 – 40	236
Road Trip!	Ice Breaker	6	24	Yes	Low	Low	45-60	156
Rope Wall	Ropes	8	32	Yes	High	High	12 – 25	38
Scissors	Ice Breaker	8	28	Yes	Low	Low	8 – 15	157
Scooterball	Ice Breaker	6	18	Yes	High	Medium	8 – 15	158
Self I See, Self U See	Teambuilder	6	40	Yes	Low	High	30 – 75	237
Self Introduction Story Time	Ice Breaker	6	25	Yes	Low	Low	15 – 25	159
Sentence Stems	Ice Breaker	4	50	Yes	Low	Medium	10 – 20	161
Seven-Eleven	Ice Breaker	4	60	No	Low	Low	6 – 10	162
Shabuya Roll Call	Name Game	8	24	No	Low	Low	8 – 20	25
Shoe Factory	Ice Breaker	8	40	No	Medium	Low	6 – 15	163
Shoe Game	Name Game	8	40	No	Low	Low	10 – 25	26
Shoe Sort	Ice Breaker	8	30	No	Low	Low	8 – 15	164
Silent Cookie Baking	Teambuilder	4	12	Yes	Low	Low	40 - 60	238
Sing Down	Ice Breaker	9	200	Yes	Low	Low	15 – 30	165
Slaps	Ice Breaker	8	24	No	Low	Low	6 – 12	166
Snake's Tail	Ice Breaker	12	45	No	High	Low	10 – 20	167
Snaps	Ice Breaker	10	35	No	Low	Low	12 – 20	168
Snort	Name Game	10	35	No	Low	Low	10 – 25	27
Sock Game	Ice Breaker	8	32	No	High	Medium	6 – 10	169
Solemn and Silent	Ice Breaker	8	120	No	Low	Low	8 – 12	170
Spiritual Focus	Teambuilder	5	32	Yes	Low	High	20 – 45	239
Sponge Pass	Ice Breaker	10	60	Yes	Low	Medium	10 – 20	171
Spoon Feed Me	Ice Breaker	3	13	Yes	Low	Medium	6 – 12	172

Activity Name	Category	Min. # of Part.	Max # of Part.	Materials?	Activity Level	Risk Level	Minutes Required	Page
S-P-U-D	Ice Breaker	8	32	Yes	High	Low	12 – 25	173
Squeeze	Ice Breaker	12	30	Yes	Low	Low	10 – 20	174
Statues	Ice Breaker	6	60	No	Medium	Low	8 – 15	175
Stinger	Ice Breaker	15	60	No	Low	Low	10 – 20	176
Straw Tower	Teambuilder	8	40	Yes	Low	Low	20 – 35	240
Sumo	Ice Breaker	11	30	No	High	Medium	12 – 20	177
Take a Stand	Teambuilder	8	75	Yes	Low	High	25 – 45	241
Team Acronym	Teambuilder	4	30	Yes	Low	Low	10 – 20	243
Team Crossword	Ice Breaker	8	30	Yes	Low	Low	10 – 18	179
Team Jewelry	Teambuilder	6	30	Yes	Low	Low	45 – 90	244
Telephone	Teambuilder	10	30	No	Low	Low	5 – 15	245
The Creature	Ice Breaker	4	40	No	Medium	Low	12 – 18	180
Think Fast	Ice Breaker	8	28	Yes	Low	Low	10 – 20	181
Three Person Trust Fall	Ropes	3	100	No	High	High	4 – 10	39
Toilet Paper Game	Ice Breaker	8	30	Yes	Low	Low	12 – 25	182
Touchee Feelee	Ice Breaker	10	50	No	Medium	Medium	10 – 18	183
Touchstones	Teambuilder	10	60	Yes	Low	High	30 – 60	246
Traffic Jam	Ropes	10	60	Yes	Low	Low	12 – 25	40
Trust Walk	Ropes	6	60	Yes	Medium	High	25 – 40	41
T-Shirt Tales	Ice Breaker	8	35	Yes	Low	Low	10 – 25	178
TV Commercial	Teambuilder	5	60	No	Low	Low	20 – 40	248
Two Person Trust Fall	Ropes	6	150	No	High	High	3 – 8	43
Two Truths and a Lie	Ice Breaker	5	40	No	Low	Low	8 – 15	184
Value Card Sort	Teambuilder	6	40	Yes	Low	Medium	20 – 40	249
Water Balance	Ice Breaker	8	18	Yes	Medium	Medium	10 – 20	185
Waterfall Game	Ice Breaker	8	40	Yes	Low	Medium	8 – 18	186
Web We Weave	Teambuilder	8	35	Yes	Low	Low	15 - 30	254
What I Carry	Ice Breaker	8	40	No	Low	Low	15 – 20	187
Where Were You?	Ice Breaker	6	40	No	Low	Low	15 – 25	188
Whomp'Em	Name Game	10	30	Yes	Medium	Low	6 - 12	28
Willow in the Wind	Ropes	7	120	No	High	High	10 – 20	44
Woooooooooo	Ice Breaker	10	50	Yes	Low	Low	15 - 40	189

PARTICIPANT NUMBERS

Activity Name	Category	Min. # of Part.	Max # of Part.	Materials?	Activity Level	Risk Level	Minutes Required	Page
Spoon Feed Me	Ice Breaker	3	13	Yes	Low	Medium	6 – 12	172
Each One, Teach One	Teambuilder	3	25	No	Low	Low	15 – 40	209
Dot Brainstorming	Teambuilder	3	60	Yes	Low	Low	6 – 20	208
Three Person Trust Fall	Ropes	3	100	No	High	High	4 – 10	39
Silent Cookie Baking	Teambuilder	4	12	Yes	Low	Low	40 - 60	238
Group Résumé	Teambuilder	4	20	Yes	Low	Low	20 – 40	215
Chart a Life	Teambuilder	4	30	Yes	Low	Medium	12 – 30	203
Chubby Bunny	Ice Breaker	4	30	Yes	Low	Medium	6 – 15	73
Lollipop	Ice Breaker	4	30	Yes	Low	Low	15 – 40	129
M&M Game	Ice Breaker	4	30	Yes	Low	Low	15 – 40	130
Team Acronym	Teambuilder	4	30	Yes	Low	Low	10 – 20	243
Affirmative Fold-Ups	Teambuilder	4	35	Yes	Low	Medium	10 – 18	191
Group Story	Ice Breaker	4	40	No	Low	Low	6 – 12	107
My Three Objects	Name Game	4	40	Yes	Low	Low	8 – 30	24
The Creature	Ice Breaker	4	40	No	Medium	Low	12 – 18	180
Sentence Stems	Ice Breaker	4	50	Yes	Low	Medium	10 – 20	161
Seven-Eleven	Ice Breaker	4	60	No	Low	Low	6 – 10	162
Chain Back Rub	Teambuilder	4	150	No	Low	Medium	8 – 10	202
Mars Probe	Ropes	5	24	Yes	Low	Medium	12 – 30	36
Finger Paint Collage	Teambuilder	5	25	Yes	Low	Low	25 – 45	212
Autobiography	Teambuilder	5	30	Yes	Low	Low	15 – 40	194
Clipboards	Teambuilder	5	30	Yes	Low	Low	45 – 60	205
My Favorite Place	Ice Breaker	5	30	Yes	Low	Low	15 – 25	142
Spiritual Focus	Teambuilder	5	32	Yes	Low	High	20 – 45	239
Poetry Group	Teambuilder	5	35	Yes	Low	Medium	20 – 45	233
Amazing Teamcoat	Teambuilder	5	36	Yes	Low	Low	30 – 60	192
Build My House	Teambuilder	5	40	Yes	Low	Medium	20 – 30	200
Two Truths and a Lie	Ice Breaker	5	40	No	Low	Low	8 – 15	184
M&M Swap	Ice Breaker	5	50	Yes	Medium	Low	8 – 15	131
TV Commercial	Teambuilder	5	60	No	Low	Low	20 – 40	248
Balloon Blow Out	Ice Breaker	5	80	Yes	Low	Low	4 – 10	51
Observation	Teambuilder	5	100	Yes	Low	Low	15 – 25	225
Debate	Teambuilder	6	16	No	Low	Low	30 – 60	206
Perspectives	Teambuilder	6	18	Yes	Low	Medium	30 – 60	230
Scooterball	Ice Breaker	6	18	Yes	High	Medium	8 – 15	158
Keep It Up	Ice Breaker	6	20	Yes	Medium	Low	6 – 15	123
Random Poetry	Ice Breaker	6	20	Yes	Low	Low	12 – 25	152
Calls of the Night	Ice Breaker	6	24	Yes	Low	Low	12 – 20	67
Flour Game	Ice Breaker	6	24	Yes	Low	Medium	15 – 30	104
Risky	Teambuilder	6	24	Yes	Low	Medium	20 – 40	236
Road Trip!	Ice Breaker	6	24	Yes	Low	Low	45-60	156
Self Introduction Story Time	Ice Breaker	6	25	Yes	Low	Low	15 – 25	159

Activity Name	Category	Min. # of Part.	Max # of Part.	Materials?	Activity Level	Risk Level	Minutes Required	Page
Fear Factor	Teambuilder	6	30	Yes	Medium	High	30 – 60	211
Personal Quotation	Teambuilder	6	30	Yes	Low	Medium	8 – 20	229
Team Jewelry	Teambuilder	6	30	Yes	Low	Low	45 – 90	244
Important Item	Teambuilder	6	32	Yes	Low	High	20 – 90 +	216
List Stories	Ice Breaker	6	36	Yes	Low	Low	10 – 20	128
Design Your Perfect	Teambuilder	6	40	Yes	Low	Low	30 - 45	207
Funny Face	Name Game	6	40	No	Low	Low	4 – 8	16
Human Knot	Ice Breaker	6	40	No	High	Medium	12 – 25	115
Human Twister	Ice Breaker	6	40	Yes	Low	Medium	8 – 15	118
Masks Of Me	Teambuilder	6	40	Yes	Low	High	60 +	223
Plane Wreck	Ropes	6	40	Yes	Medium	High	15 – 40	37
Self I See, Self U See	Teambuilder	6	40	Yes	Low	High	30 – 75	237
Value Card Sort	Teambuilder	6	40	Yes	Low	Medium	20 – 40	249
Where Were You?	Ice Breaker	6	40	No	Low	Low	15 – 25	188
Blind Golf	Teambuilder	6	50	Yes	Low	Low	10 – 20	196
Imaginary Dough	Ice Breaker	6	50	No	Low	Low	10 – 25	122
Basket	Ice Breaker	6	60	Yes	Low	Low	10 – 25	56
Bite the Bag	Ice Breaker	6	60	Yes	Medium	Medium	5 – 15	59
Clapping Clues	Ice Breaker	6	60	No	Low	Low	10 – 20	75
Ice Cubes	Ice Breaker	6	60	Yes	Medium	Medium	8 – 20	120
Statues	Ice Breaker	6	60	No	Medium	Low	8 – 15	175
Trust Walk	Ropes	6	60	Yes	Medium	High	25 – 40	41
Body English	Ice Breaker	6	70	No	Medium	Low	5 – 10	63
Five Things	Ice Breaker	6	75	Yes	Low	Low	20 – 30	103
Artist, Clay, Model	Teambuilder	6	80	No	Low	Medium	8 – 20	193
Listening Skills Drawings	Teambuilder	6	150	Yes	Low	Low	15 – 30	220
Two Person Trust Fall	Ropes	6	150	No	High	High	3 – 8	43
A to Z	Ice Breaker	6	200	No	Low	Low	5 – 10	46
Catch Me If You Can	Ice Breaker	6	200	No	Low	Low	4 – 10	68
Lap Sit	Ice Breaker	6	300	No	Medium	Medium	6 – 10	125
All Aboard	Ropes	7	18	Yes	Medium	Medium	15 – 30	31
Blindfold Line-Up	Ice Breaker	7	40	Yes	Medium	Medium	5 – 10	62
Masks I Wear	Teambuilder	7	40	Yes	Low	High	30 – 45	222
Orange Pass	Ice Breaker	7	50	Yes	Medium	Medium	6 – 12	145
Willow in the Wind	Ropes	7	120	No	High	High	10 – 20	44
Posture Relay	Ice Breaker	8	15	Yes	Medium	Low	5 – 8	149
Water Balance	Ice Breaker	8	18	Yes	Medium	Medium	10 – 20	185
Shabuya Roll Call	Name Game	8	24	No	Low	Low	8 – 20	25
Slaps	Ice Breaker	8	24	No	Low	Low	6 – 12	166
Count Off	Ice Breaker	8	25	No	Low	Low	5 – 8	81
Mafia	Ice Breaker	8	25	Yes	Low	Low	20 +	133
Scissors	Ice Breaker	8	28	Yes	Low	Low	8 – 15	157
Think Fast	Ice Breaker	8	28	Yes	Low	Low	10 – 20	181

Activity Name	Category	Min. # of Part.	Max # of Part.	Materials?	Activity Level	Risk Level	Minutes Required	Page
Adjective Name Game	Name Game	8	30	No	Low	Low	8 – 20	12
Barnyard	Ice Breaker	8	30	Yes	Low	Low	8 – 20	54
Blind Squares	Ropes	8	30	Yes	Medium	Medium	15 – 30	32
Chocalotaschnizzel	Ice Breaker	8	30	Yes	Medium	Low	12 – 20	72
Guard the Bone	Ice Breaker	8	30	Yes	Medium	Low	6 – 15	108
Introduction Interview	Name Game	8	30	No	Low	Low	8 – 25	22
Mirror, Mirror	Ice Breaker	8	30	Yes	Low	Low	6 – 15	139
Motion Name Game	Name Game	8	30	No	Medium	Low	6 – 30	23
Paper Bags	Ice Breaker	8	30	Yes	Low	Low	8 – 15	147
Shoe Sort	Ice Breaker	8	30	No	Low	Low	8 – 15	164
Team Crossword	Ice Breaker	8	30	Yes	Low	Low	10 – 18	179
Toilet Paper Game	Ice Breaker	8	30	Yes	Low	Low	12 – 25	182
Rope Wall	Ropes	8	32	Yes	High	High	12 – 25	38
Sock Game	Ice Breaker	8	32	No	High	Medium	6 – 10	169
S-P-U-D	Ice Breaker	8	32	Yes	High	Low	12 – 25	173
Information Fun Sheet	Teambuilder	8	35	Yes	Low	Medium	30 - 60	217
Last Will & Testament	Teambuilder	8	35	Yes	Low	High	15 – 30	218
T-Shirt Tales	Ice Breaker	8	35	Yes	Low	Low	10 – 25	178
Web We Weave	Teambuilder	8	35	Yes	Low	Low	15 - 30	254
Mrs. Mumbles	Ice Breaker	8	40	No	Low	Low	10 – 18	140
Piece of the Puzzle	Teambuilder	8	40	Yes	Low	Medium	30 – 45	232
Shoe Factory	Ice Breaker	8	40	No	Medium	Low	6 – 15	163
Shoe Game	Name Game	8	40	No	Low	Low	10 – 25	26
Straw Tower	Teambuilder	8	40	Yes	Low	Low	20 – 35	240
Waterfall Game	Ice Breaker	8	40	Yes	Low	Medium	8 – 18	186
What I Carry	Ice Breaker	8	40	No	Low	Low	15 – 20	187
Balloon Tag	Ice Breaker	8	50	Yes	Medium	Low	4 – 10	52
Clothespin Tag	Ice Breaker	8	50	Yes	Medium	Low	5 – 12	76
Dead Fish	Ice Breaker	8	50	No	Low	Low	4 – 10	82
Make a Date	Ice Breaker	8	50	Yes	Low	Low	12 – 20	136
Dizzy Bat	Ice Breaker	8	60	Yes	High	Medium	6 – 15	84
Take a Stand	Teambuilder	8	75	Yes	Low	High	25 – 45	241
Brain Benders	Ice Breaker	8	80	Yes	Low	Low	10 – 20	64
Levitation	Teambuilder	8	100	No	Medium	Medium	8 – 20	219
Solemn and Silent	Ice Breaker	8	120	No	Low	Low	8 – 12	170
Back to Back	Ice Breaker	8	300	No	High	Low	5 – 15	50
Ooo, Aaaah, Oooh!	Ice Breaker	9	32	No	Low	Low	8 – 15	144
Hula Hoop Relay	Ice Breaker	9	50	Yes	Medium	Low	8 – 15	113
Egg Break	Teambuilder	9	80	Yes	Low	Low	30 – 45	210
Sing Down	Ice Breaker	9	200	Yes	Low	Low	15 – 30	165
Here I Am	Name Game	10	25	Yes	Low	Low	5 – 10	18
Log Jam	Ropes	10	26	Yes	High	Medium	20 – 30	34
Blanket Name Game	Name Game	10	30	Yes	Low	Low	6 – 15	13

Activity Name	Category	Min. # of Part.	Max # of Part.	Materials?	Activity Level	Risk Level	Minutes Required	Page
Blind Identify	Ice Breaker	10	30	Yes	Low	Medium	8 – 15	61
Concentration	Name Game	10	30	No	Low	Low	6 – 20	15
Ha!	Ice Breaker	10	30	No	Medium	Medium	8 – 12	109
Penny for Your Thoughts	Teambuilder	10	30	Yes	Low	Medium	15 – 25	227
Psychiatrist	Teambuilder	10	30	No	Low	Low	30 – 60	234
Telephone	Teambuilder	10	30	No	Low	Low	5 – 15	245
Whomp'Em	Name Game	10	30	Yes	Medium	Low	6 - 12	28
Group Juggle	Name Game	10	35	Yes	Low	Low	10 – 25	17
I'm a Gigolo	Name Game	10	35	No	Low	Low	5 – 12	21
Perpetual Tag	Teambuilder	10	35	No	Low	Low	Weeks…	228
Quilting	Teambuilder	10	35	Yes	Low	Low	120 +	235
Snaps	Ice Breaker	10	35	No	Low	Low	12 – 20	168
Snort	Name Game	10	35	No	Low	Low	10 – 25	27
Black Magic	Ice Breaker	10	40	No	Low	Low	12 – 40	60
Buzz	Ice Breaker	10	40	No	Low	Low	8 – 15	66
Color, Car, Character	Ice Breaker	10	40	No	Low	Low	12 – 30	77
Ducky Wucky	Ice Breaker	10	40	Yes	Low	Medium	8 – 15	87
Peanut Butter & Jelly	Teambuilder	10	40	Yes	Low	Low	20 - 35	226
Rhythm Ice Breaker	Ice Breaker	10	40	Yes	Low	Low	8 – 15	155
I Love You Baby, But I Just Can't Smile	Ice Breaker	10	45	No	Low	Low	6 – 12	119
I'm Thinking of Someone	Ice Breaker	10	45	No	Low	Low	10 – 20	121
Butt Spelling	Name Game	10	50	No	Low	Medium	8 – 15	14
Follow the Leader	Ice Breaker	10	50	No	High	Low	10 – 18	105
Log Roll	Ropes	10	50	No	High	Medium	5 – 10	35
Rhythm & Motion	Ice Breaker	10	50	No	Low	Low	12 – 20	154
Touchee Feelee	Ice Breaker	10	50	No	Medium	Medium	10 – 18	183
Wooooooooo	Ice Breaker	10	50	Yes	Low	Low	15 - 40	189
Banana Relay	Ice Breaker	10	60	Yes	Medium	Medium	8 – 18	53
Height Line	Ice Breaker	10	60	No	Low	Low	4 – 8	110
Line Relay	Ice Breaker	10	60	No	High	Low	6 – 12	127
Sponge Pass	Ice Breaker	10	60	Yes	Low	Medium	10 – 20	171
Touchstones	Teambuilder	10	60	Yes	Low	High	30 – 60	246
Traffic Jam	Ropes	10	60	Yes	Low	Low	12 – 25	40
Assassin	Ice Breaker	10	80	Yes	Low	Low	Weeks…	49
Confusion Bingo	Ice Breaker	10	100	Yes	Medium	Medium	8 – 15	79
Machine Game	Ice Breaker	10	120	No	Medium	Low	10 – 20	132
Human Bingo	Name Game	10	150	Yes	Low	Low	6 – 15	19
Musical Interpretation	Ice Breaker	10	200	Yes	Medium	Low	5 – 10	141
Orchestra	Ice Breaker	10	200	No	Low	Low	6 – 10	146
Sumo	Ice Breaker	11	30	No	High	Medium	12 – 20	177
Squeeze	Ice Breaker	12	30	Yes	Low	Low	10 – 20	174
Flash Card Revelations	Teambuilder	12	40	Yes	Low	High	20 – 40	214
Charlie's Angels	Ice Breaker	12	45	No	Low	Low	15 – 25	70

Activity Name	Category	Min. # of Part.	Max # of Part.	Materials?	Activity Level	Risk Level	Minutes Required	Page
Snake's Tail	Ice Breaker	12	45	No	High	Low	10 – 20	167
Chalkboard Sentences	Ice Breaker	12	48	Yes	Low	Low	10 – 18	69
Detective	Ice Breaker	12	50	No	Low	Low	8 – 15	83
Life Saver Relay	Ice Breaker	12	50	Yes	Low	Medium	5 – 10	126
People to People	Ice Breaker	12	60	No	High	Medium	10 – 20	148
Build Your Own Game	Ropes	12	100	Yes	High	Low	40 – 60	33
Man Overboard	Ice Breaker	12	125	No	Medium	Medium	20 – 30	137
Birthday Line	Ice Breaker	12	200	No	Low	Low	1 – 5	58
Elbow Tag	Ice Breaker	14	36	No	High	Medium	12 – 20	88
Raid	Ice Breaker	14	50	Yes	High	Low	10 – 20	151
Arc Ball	Ice Breaker	14	60	Yes	Medium	Low	8 – 20	48
Do You Love Your Neighbor?	Ice Breaker	14	80	No	Medium	Low	10 – 20	85
Puzzle Jumble	Ice Breaker	14	100	Yes	Low	Low	8 – 15	150
Amoeba Tag	Ice Breaker	14	125	No	High	Low	10 – 20	47
Drip, Drip, Drop	Ice Breaker	15	40	Yes	High	High	10 – 20	86
Five Things I Want to Learn	Teambuilder	15	60	Yes	Low	Low	10 – 20	213
Stinger	Ice Breaker	15	60	No	Low	Low	10 – 20	176
How You Doin'?	Ice Breaker	15	70	No	Low	Medium	8 – 12	112
Birdie on a Perch	Ice Breaker	15	80	No	High	Medium	6 – 15	57
Freeze Tag	Ice Breaker	15	150	No	High	Medium	10 – 18	106
Elves, Giants and Chickens	Ice Breaker	15	250	No	Medium	Low	8 – 12	89
Barnyard Animals	Ice Breaker	15	300	No	Low	Medium	6 – 15	55
Hum That Tune	Ice Breaker	15	300	No	Low	Low	4 – 8	114
Number Groups	Ice Breaker	15	300	No	Low	Low	3 – 8	143
Capture the Flag	Teambuilder	16	50	Yes	High	Low	30 – 75	201
Evolution	Ice Breaker	16	50	No	Low	Low	10 – 20	90
Killer	Ice Breaker	16	50	No	Low	Low	10 – 20	124
Clam Free	Ice Breaker	16	60	Yes	High	Low	12 – 20	74
Famous Pairs	Ice Breaker	16	80	Yes	Low	Low	12 – 20	91
Comic Strip Chaos	Ice Breaker	20	100	Yes	Low	Low	4 – 8	78
Hog Call	Ice Breaker	20	200	No	Low	Medium	4 – 8	111
Human Taco (or Burger)	Ice Breaker	20	300	Yes	Low	Low	8 – 20	116

MATERIALS

Activity Name	Category	Min. # of Part.	Max # of Part.	Materials?	Activity Level	Risk Level	Minutes Required	Page
A to Z	Ice Breaker	6	200	No	Low	Low	5 – 10	46
Amoeba Tag	Ice Breaker	14	125	No	High	Low	10 – 20	47
Back to Back	Ice Breaker	8	300	No	High	Low	5 – 15	50
Barnyard Animals	Ice Breaker	15	300	No	Low	Medium	6 – 15	55
Birdie on a Perch	Ice Breaker	15	80	No	High	Medium	6 – 15	57
Birthday Line	Ice Breaker	12	200	No	Low	Low	1 – 5	58
Black Magic	Ice Breaker	10	40	No	Low	Low	12 – 40	60
Body English	Ice Breaker	6	70	No	Medium	Low	5 – 10	63
Buzz	Ice Breaker	10	40	No	Low	Low	8 – 15	66
Catch Me If You Can	Ice Breaker	6	200	No	Low	Low	4 – 10	68
Charlie's Angels	Ice Breaker	12	45	No	Low	Low	15 – 25	70
Clapping Clues	Ice Breaker	6	60	No	Low	Low	10 – 20	75
Color, Car, Character	Ice Breaker	10	40	No	Low	Low	12 – 30	77
Count Off	Ice Breaker	8	25	No	Low	Low	5 – 8	81
Dead Fish	Ice Breaker	8	50	No	Low	Low	4 – 10	82
Detective	Ice Breaker	12	50	No	Low	Low	8 – 15	83
Do You Love Your Neighbor?	Ice Breaker	14	80	No	Medium	Low	10 – 20	85
Elbow Tag	Ice Breaker	14	36	No	High	Medium	12 – 20	88
Elves, Giants and Chickens	Ice Breaker	15	250	No	Medium	Low	8 – 12	89
Evolution	Ice Breaker	16	50	No	Low	Low	10 – 20	90
Follow the Leader	Ice Breaker	10	50	No	High	Low	10 – 18	105
Freeze Tag	Ice Breaker	15	150	No	High	Medium	10 – 18	106
Group Story	Ice Breaker	4	40	No	Low	Low	6 – 12	107
Ha!	Ice Breaker	10	30	No	Medium	Medium	8 – 12	109
Height Line	Ice Breaker	10	60	No	Low	Low	4 – 8	110
Hog Call	Ice Breaker	20	200	No	Low	Medium	4 – 8	111
How You Doin'?	Ice Breaker	15	70	No	Low	Medium	8 – 12	112
Hum That Tune	Ice Breaker	15	300	No	Low	Low	4 – 8	114
Human Knot	Ice Breaker	6	40	No	High	Medium	12 – 25	115
I Love You Baby, But I Just Can't Smile	Ice Breaker	10	45	No	Low	Low	6 – 12	119
I'm Thinking of Someone	Ice Breaker	10	45	No	Low	Low	10 – 20	121
Imaginary Dough	Ice Breaker	6	50	No	Low	Low	10 – 25	122
Killer	Ice Breaker	16	50	No	Low	Low	10 – 20	124
Lap Sit	Ice Breaker	6	300	No	Medium	Medium	6 – 10	125
Line Relay	Ice Breaker	10	60	No	High	Low	6 – 12	127
Machine Game	Ice Breaker	10	120	No	Medium	Low	10 – 20	132
Man Overboard	Ice Breaker	12	125	No	Medium	Medium	20 – 30	137
Mrs. Mumbles	Ice Breaker	8	40	No	Low	Low	10 – 18	140
Number Groups	Ice Breaker	15	300	No	Low	Low	3 – 8	143
Ooo, Aaaah, Oooh!	Ice Breaker	9	32	No	Low	Low	8 – 15	144
Orchestra	Ice Breaker	10	200	No	Low	Low	6 – 10	146

Activity Name	Category	Min. # of Part.	Max # of Part.	Materials?	Activity Level	Risk Level	Minutes Required	Page
People to People	Ice Breaker	12	60	No	High	Medium	10 – 20	148
Rhythm & Motion	Ice Breaker	10	50	No	Low	Low	12 – 20	154
Seven-Eleven	Ice Breaker	4	60	No	Low	Low	6 – 10	162
Shoe Factory	Ice Breaker	8	40	No	Medium	Low	6 – 15	163
Shoe Sort	Ice Breaker	8	30	No	Low	Low	8 – 15	164
Slaps	Ice Breaker	8	24	No	Low	Low	6 – 12	166
Snake's Tail	Ice Breaker	12	45	No	High	Low	10 – 20	167
Snaps	Ice Breaker	10	35	No	Low	Low	12 – 20	168
Sock Game	Ice Breaker	8	32	No	High	Medium	6 – 10	169
Solemn and Silent	Ice Breaker	8	120	No	Low	Low	8 – 12	170
Statues	Ice Breaker	6	60	No	Medium	Low	8 – 15	175
Stinger	Ice Breaker	15	60	No	Low	Low	10 – 20	176
Sumo	Ice Breaker	11	30	No	High	Medium	12 – 20	177
The Creature	Ice Breaker	4	40	No	Medium	Low	12 – 18	180
Touchee Feelee	Ice Breaker	10	50	No	Medium	Medium	10 – 18	183
Two Truths and a Lie	Ice Breaker	5	40	No	Low	Low	8 – 15	184
What I Carry	Ice Breaker	8	40	No	Low	Low	15 – 20	187
Where Were You?	Ice Breaker	6	40	No	Low	Low	15 – 25	188
Adjective Name Game	Name Game	8	30	No	Low	Low	8 – 20	12
Butt Spelling	Name Game	10	50	No	Low	Medium	8 – 15	14
Concentration	Name Game	10	30	No	Low	Low	6 – 20	15
Funny Face	Name Game	6	40	No	Low	Low	4 – 8	16
I'm a Gigolo	Name Game	10	35	No	Low	Low	5 – 12	21
Introduction Interview	Name Game	8	30	No	Low	Low	8 – 25	22
Motion Name Game	Name Game	8	30	No	Medium	Low	6 – 30	23
Shabuya Roll Call	Name Game	8	24	No	Low	Low	8 – 20	25
Shoe Game	Name Game	8	40	No	Low	Low	10 – 25	26
Snort	Name Game	10	35	No	Low	Low	10 – 25	27
Log Roll	Ropes	10	50	No	High	Medium	5 – 10	35
Three Person Trust Fall	Ropes	3	100	No	High	High	4 – 10	39
Two Person Trust Fall	Ropes	6	150	No	High	High	3 – 8	43
Willow in the Wind	Ropes	7	120	No	High	High	10 – 20	44
Artist, Clay, Model	Teambuilder	6	80	No	Low	Medium	8 – 20	193
Chain Back Rub	Teambuilder	4	150	No	Low	Medium	8 – 10	202
Debate	Teambuilder	6	16	No	Low	Low	30 – 60	206
Each One, Teach One	Teambuilder	3	25	No	Low	Low	15 – 40	209
Levitation	Teambuilder	8	100	No	Medium	Medium	8 – 20	219
Perpetual Tag	Teambuilder	10	35	No	Low	Low	Weeks…	228
Psychiatrist	Teambuilder	10	30	No	Low	Low	30 – 60	234
Telephone	Teambuilder	10	30	No	Low	Low	5 – 15	245
TV Commercial	Teambuilder	5	60	No	Low	Low	20 – 40	248
Arc Ball	Ice Breaker	14	60	Yes	Medium	Low	8 – 20	48
Assassin	Ice Breaker	10	80	Yes	Low	Low	Weeks…	49

Activity Name	Category	Min. # of Part.	Max # of Part.	Materials?	Activity Level	Risk Level	Minutes Required	Page
Balloon Blow Out	Ice Breaker	5	80	Yes	Low	Low	4 – 10	51
Balloon Tag	Ice Breaker	8	50	Yes	Medium	Low	4 – 10	52
Banana Relay	Ice Breaker	10	60	Yes	Medium	Medium	8 – 18	53
Barnyard	Ice Breaker	8	30	Yes	Low	Low	8 – 20	54
Basket	Ice Breaker	6	60	Yes	Low	Low	10 – 25	56
Bite the Bag	Ice Breaker	6	60	Yes	Medium	Medium	5 – 15	59
Blind Identify	Ice Breaker	10	30	Yes	Low	Medium	8 – 15	61
Blindfold Line-Up	Ice Breaker	7	40	Yes	Medium	Medium	5 – 10	62
Brain Benders	Ice Breaker	8	80	Yes	Low	Low	10 – 20	64
Calls of the Night	Ice Breaker	6	24	Yes	Low	Low	12 – 20	67
Chalkboard Sentences	Ice Breaker	12	48	Yes	Low	Low	10 – 18	69
Chocalotaschnizzel	Ice Breaker	8	30	Yes	Medium	Low	12 – 20	72
Chubby Bunny	Ice Breaker	4	30	Yes	Low	Medium	6 – 15	73
Clam Free	Ice Breaker	16	60	Yes	High	Low	12 – 20	74
Clothespin Tag	Ice Breaker	8	50	Yes	Medium	Low	5 – 12	76
Comic Strip Chaos	Ice Breaker	20	100	Yes	Low	Low	4 – 8	78
Confusion Bingo	Ice Breaker	10	100	Yes	Medium	Medium	8 – 15	79
Dizzy Bat	Ice Breaker	8	60	Yes	High	Medium	6 – 15	84
Drip, Drip, Drop	Ice Breaker	15	40	Yes	High	High	10 – 20	86
Ducky Wucky	Ice Breaker	10	40	Yes	Low	Medium	8 – 15	87
Famous Pairs	Ice Breaker	16	80	Yes	Low	Low	12 – 20	91
Five Things	Ice Breaker	6	75	Yes	Low	Low	20 – 30	103
Flour Game	Ice Breaker	6	24	Yes	Low	Medium	15 – 30	104
Guard the Bone	Ice Breaker	8	30	Yes	Medium	Low	6 – 15	108
Hula Hoop Relay	Ice Breaker	9	50	Yes	Medium	Low	8 – 15	113
Human Taco (or Burger)	Ice Breaker	20	300	Yes	Low	Low	8 – 20	116
Human Twister	Ice Breaker	6	40	Yes	Low	Medium	8 – 15	118
Ice Cubes	Ice Breaker	6	60	Yes	Medium	Medium	8 – 20	120
Keep It Up	Ice Breaker	6	20	Yes	Medium	Low	6 – 15	123
Life Saver Relay	Ice Breaker	12	50	Yes	Low	Medium	5 – 10	126
List Stories	Ice Breaker	6	36	Yes	Low	Low	10 – 20	128
Lollipop	Ice Breaker	4	30	Yes	Low	Low	15 – 40	129
M&M Game	Ice Breaker	4	30	Yes	Low	Low	15 – 40	130
M&M Swap	Ice Breaker	5	50	Yes	Medium	Low	8 – 15	131
Mafia	Ice Breaker	8	25	Yes	Low	Low	20 +	133
Make a Date	Ice Breaker	8	50	Yes	Low	Low	12 – 20	136
Mirror, Mirror	Ice Breaker	8	30	Yes	Low	Low	6 – 15	139
Musical Interpretation	Ice Breaker	10	200	Yes	Medium	Low	5 – 10	141
My Favorite Place	Ice Breaker	5	30	Yes	Low	Low	15 – 25	142
Orange Pass	Ice Breaker	7	50	Yes	Medium	Medium	6 – 12	145
Paper Bags	Ice Breaker	8	30	Yes	Low	Low	8 – 15	147
Posture Relay	Ice Breaker	8	15	Yes	Medium	Low	5 – 8	149
Puzzle Jumble	Ice Breaker	14	100	Yes	Low	Low	8 – 15	150

Activity Name	Category	Min. # of Part.	Max # of Part.	Materials?	Activity Level	Risk Level	Minutes Required	Page
Raid	Ice Breaker	14	50	Yes	High	Low	10 – 20	151
Random Poetry	Ice Breaker	6	20	Yes	Low	Low	12 – 25	152
Rhythm Ice Breaker	Ice Breaker	10	40	Yes	Low	Low	8 – 15	155
Road Trip!	Ice Breaker	6	24	Yes	Low	Low	45-60	156
Scissors	Ice Breaker	8	28	Yes	Low	Low	8 – 15	157
Scooterball	Ice Breaker	6	18	Yes	High	Medium	8 – 15	158
Self Introduction Story Time	Ice Breaker	6	25	Yes	Low	Low	15 – 25	159
Sentence Stems	Ice Breaker	4	50	Yes	Low	Medium	10 – 20	161
Sing Down	Ice Breaker	9	200	Yes	Low	Low	15 – 30	165
Sponge Pass	Ice Breaker	10	60	Yes	Low	Medium	10 – 20	171
Spoon Feed Me	Ice Breaker	3	13	Yes	Low	Medium	6 – 12	172
S-P-U-D	Ice Breaker	8	32	Yes	High	Low	12 – 25	173
Squeeze	Ice Breaker	12	30	Yes	Low	Low	10 – 20	174
Team Crossword	Ice Breaker	8	30	Yes	Low	Low	10 – 18	179
Think Fast	Ice Breaker	8	28	Yes	Low	Low	10 – 20	181
Toilet Paper Game	Ice Breaker	8	30	Yes	Low	Low	12 – 25	182
T-Shirt Tales	Ice Breaker	8	35	Yes	Low	Low	10 – 25	178
Water Balance	Ice Breaker	8	18	Yes	Medium	Medium	10 – 20	185
Waterfall Game	Ice Breaker	8	40	Yes	Low	Medium	8 – 18	186
Wooooooooo	Ice Breaker	10	50	Yes	Low	Low	15 - 40	189
Blanket Name Game	Name Game	10	30	Yes	Low	Low	6 – 15	13
Group Juggle	Name Game	10	35	Yes	Low	Low	10 – 25	17
Here I Am	Name Game	10	25	Yes	Low	Low	5 – 10	18
Human Bingo	Name Game	10	150	Yes	Low	Low	6 – 15	19
My Three Objects	Name Game	4	40	Yes	Low	Low	8 – 30	24
Whomp'Em	Name Game	10	30	Yes	Medium	Low	6 - 12	28
All Aboard	Ropes	7	18	Yes	Medium	Medium	15 – 30	31
Blind Squares	Ropes	8	30	Yes	Medium	Medium	15 – 30	32
Build Your Own Game	Ropes	12	100	Yes	High	Low	40 – 60	33
Log Jam	Ropes	10	26	Yes	High	Medium	20 – 30	34
Mars Probe	Ropes	5	24	Yes	Low	Medium	12 – 30	36
Plane Wreck	Ropes	6	40	Yes	Medium	High	15 – 40	37
Rope Wall	Ropes	8	32	Yes	High	High	12 – 25	38
Traffic Jam	Ropes	10	60	Yes	Low	Low	12 – 25	40
Trust Walk	Ropes	6	60	Yes	Medium	High	25 – 40	41
Affirmative Fold-Ups	Teambuilder	4	35	Yes	Low	Medium	10 – 18	191
Amazing Teamcoat	Teambuilder	5	36	Yes	Low	Low	30 – 60	192
Autobiography	Teambuilder	5	30	Yes	Low	Low	15 – 40	194
Blind Golf	Teambuilder	6	50	Yes	Low	Low	10 – 20	196
Build My House	Teambuilder	5	40	Yes	Low	Medium	20 – 30	200
Capture the Flag	Teambuilder	16	50	Yes	High	Low	30 – 75	201
Chart a Life	Teambuilder	4	30	Yes	Low	Medium	12 – 30	203
Clipboards	Teambuilder	5	30	Yes	Low	Low	45 – 60	205

Activity Name	Category	Min. # of Part.	Max # of Part.	Materials?	Activity Level	Risk Level	Minutes Required	Page
Design Your Perfect	Teambuilder	6	40	Yes	Low	Low	30 - 45	207
Dot Brainstorming	Teambuilder	3	60	Yes	Low	Low	6 – 20	208
Egg Break	Teambuilder	9	80	Yes	Low	Low	30 – 45	210
Fear Factor	Teambuilder	6	30	Yes	Medium	High	30 – 60	211
Finger Paint Collage	Teambuilder	5	25	Yes	Low	Low	25 – 45	212
Five Things I Want to Learn	Teambuilder	15	60	Yes	Low	Low	10 – 20	213
Flash Card Revelations	Teambuilder	12	40	Yes	Low	High	20 – 40	214
Group Résumé	Teambuilder	4	20	Yes	Low	Low	20 – 40	215
Important Item	Teambuilder	6	32	Yes	Low	High	20 – 90 +	216
Information Fun Sheet	Teambuilder	8	35	Yes	Low	Medium	30 - 60	217
Last Will & Testament	Teambuilder	8	35	Yes	Low	High	15 – 30	218
Listening Skills Drawings	Teambuilder	6	150	Yes	Low	Low	15 – 30	220
Masks I Wear	Teambuilder	7	40	Yes	Low	High	30 – 45	222
Masks Of Me	Teambuilder	6	40	Yes	Low	High	60 +	223
Observation	Teambuilder	5	100	Yes	Low	Low	15 – 25	225
Peanut Butter & Jelly	Teambuilder	10	40	Yes	Low	Low	20 - 35	226
Penny for Your Thoughts	Teambuilder	10	30	Yes	Low	Medium	15 – 25	227
Personal Quotation	Teambuilder	6	30	Yes	Low	Medium	8 – 20	229
Perspectives	Teambuilder	6	18	Yes	Low	Medium	30 – 60	230
Piece of the Puzzle	Teambuilder	8	40	Yes	Low	Medium	30 – 45	232
Poetry Group	Teambuilder	5	35	Yes	Low	Medium	20 – 45	233
Quilting	Teambuilder	10	35	Yes	Low	Low	120 +	235
Risky	Teambuilder	6	24	Yes	Low	Medium	20 – 40	236
Self I See, Self U See	Teambuilder	6	40	Yes	Low	High	30 – 75	237
Silent Cookie Baking	Teambuilder	4	12	Yes	Low	Low	40 - 60	238
Spiritual Focus	Teambuilder	5	32	Yes	Low	High	20 – 45	239
Straw Tower	Teambuilder	8	40	Yes	Low	Low	20 – 35	240
Take a Stand	Teambuilder	8	75	Yes	Low	High	25 – 45	241
Team Acronym	Teambuilder	4	30	Yes	Low	Low	10 – 20	243
Team Jewelry	Teambuilder	6	30	Yes	Low	Low	45 – 90	244
Touchstones	Teambuilder	10	60	Yes	Low	High	30 – 60	246
Value Card Sort	Teambuilder	6	40	Yes	Low	Medium	20 – 40	249
Web We Weave	Teambuilder	8	35	Yes	Low	Low	15 - 30	254

RISK LEVEL

Activity Name	Category	Min. # of Part.	Max # of Part.	Materials?	Activity Level	Risk Level	Minutes Required	Page
A to Z	Ice Breaker	6	200	No	Low	Low	5 – 10	46
Amoeba Tag	Ice Breaker	14	125	No	High	Low	10 – 20	47
Arc Ball	Ice Breaker	14	60	Yes	Medium	Low	8 – 20	48
Assassin	Ice Breaker	10	80	Yes	Low	Low	Weeks…	49
Back to Back	Ice Breaker	8	300	No	High	Low	5 – 15	50
Balloon Blow Out	Ice Breaker	5	80	Yes	Low	Low	4 – 10	51
Balloon Tag	Ice Breaker	8	50	Yes	Medium	Low	4 – 10	52
Barnyard	Ice Breaker	8	30	Yes	Low	Low	8 – 20	54
Basket	Ice Breaker	6	60	Yes	Low	Low	10 – 25	56
Birthday Line	Ice Breaker	12	200	No	Low	Low	1 – 5	58
Black Magic	Ice Breaker	10	40	No	Low	Low	12 – 40	60
Body English	Ice Breaker	6	70	No	Medium	Low	5 – 10	63
Brain Benders	Ice Breaker	8	80	Yes	Low	Low	10 – 20	64
Buzz	Ice Breaker	10	40	No	Low	Low	8 – 15	66
Calls of the Night	Ice Breaker	6	24	Yes	Low	Low	12 – 20	67
Catch Me If You Can	Ice Breaker	6	200	No	Low	Low	4 – 10	68
Chalkboard Sentences	Ice Breaker	12	48	Yes	Low	Low	10 – 18	69
Charlie's Angels	Ice Breaker	12	45	No	Low	Low	15 – 25	70
Chocalotaschnizzel	Ice Breaker	8	30	Yes	Medium	Low	12 – 20	72
Clam Free	Ice Breaker	16	60	Yes	High	Low	12 – 20	74
Clapping Clues	Ice Breaker	6	60	No	Low	Low	10 – 20	75
Clothespin Tag	Ice Breaker	8	50	Yes	Medium	Low	5 – 12	76
Color, Car, Character	Ice Breaker	10	40	No	Low	Low	12 – 30	77
Comic Strip Chaos	Ice Breaker	20	100	Yes	Low	Low	4 – 8	78
Count Off	Ice Breaker	8	25	No	Low	Low	5 – 8	81
Dead Fish	Ice Breaker	8	50	No	Low	Low	4 – 10	82
Detective	Ice Breaker	12	50	No	Low	Low	8 – 15	83
Do You Love Your Neighbor?	Ice Breaker	14	80	No	Medium	Low	10 – 20	85
Elves, Giants and Chickens	Ice Breaker	15	250	No	Medium	Low	8 – 12	89
Evolution	Ice Breaker	16	50	No	Low	Low	10 – 20	90
Famous Pairs	Ice Breaker	16	80	Yes	Low	Low	12 – 20	91
Five Things	Ice Breaker	6	75	Yes	Low	Low	20 – 30	103
Follow the Leader	Ice Breaker	10	50	No	High	Low	10 – 18	105
Group Story	Ice Breaker	4	40	No	Low	Low	6 – 12	107
Guard the Bone	Ice Breaker	8	30	Yes	Medium	Low	6 – 15	108
Height Line	Ice Breaker	10	60	No	Low	Low	4 – 8	110
Hula Hoop Relay	Ice Breaker	9	50	Yes	Medium	Low	8 – 15	113
Hum That Tune	Ice Breaker	15	300	No	Low	Low	4 – 8	114
Human Taco (or Burger)	Ice Breaker	20	300	Yes	Low	Low	8 – 20	116
I Love You Baby, But I Just Can't Smile	Ice Breaker	10	45	No	Low	Low	6 – 12	119
I'm Thinking of Someone	Ice Breaker	10	45	No	Low	Low	10 – 20	121

Activity Name	Category	Min. # of Part.	Max # of Part.	Materials?	Activity Level	Risk Level	Minutes Required	Page
Imaginary Dough	Ice Breaker	6	50	No	Low	Low	10 – 25	122
Keep It Up	Ice Breaker	6	20	Yes	Medium	Low	6 – 15	123
Killer	Ice Breaker	16	50	No	Low	Low	10 – 20	124
Line Relay	Ice Breaker	10	60	No	High	Low	6 – 12	127
List Stories	Ice Breaker	6	36	Yes	Low	Low	10 – 20	128
Lollipop	Ice Breaker	4	30	Yes	Low	Low	15 – 40	129
M&M Game	Ice Breaker	4	30	Yes	Low	Low	15 – 40	130
M&M Swap	Ice Breaker	5	50	Yes	Medium	Low	8 – 15	131
Machine Game	Ice Breaker	10	120	No	Medium	Low	10 – 20	132
Mafia	Ice Breaker	8	25	Yes	Low	Low	20 +	133
Make a Date	Ice Breaker	8	50	Yes	Low	Low	12 – 20	136
Mirror, Mirror	Ice Breaker	8	30	Yes	Low	Low	6 – 15	139
Mrs. Mumbles	Ice Breaker	8	40	No	Low	Low	10 – 18	140
Musical Interpretation	Ice Breaker	10	200	Yes	Medium	Low	5 – 10	141
My Favorite Place	Ice Breaker	5	30	Yes	Low	Low	15 – 25	142
Number Groups	Ice Breaker	15	300	No	Low	Low	3 – 8	143
Ooo, Aaaah, Oooh!	Ice Breaker	9	32	No	Low	Low	8 – 15	144
Orchestra	Ice Breaker	10	200	No	Low	Low	6 – 10	146
Paper Bags	Ice Breaker	8	30	Yes	Low	Low	8 – 15	147
Posture Relay	Ice Breaker	8	15	Yes	Medium	Low	5 – 8	149
Puzzle Jumble	Ice Breaker	14	100	Yes	Low	Low	8 – 15	150
Raid	Ice Breaker	14	50	Yes	High	Low	10 – 20	151
Random Poetry	Ice Breaker	6	20	Yes	Low	Low	12 – 25	152
Rhythm & Motion	Ice Breaker	10	50	No	Low	Low	12 – 20	154
Rhythm Ice Breaker	Ice Breaker	10	40	Yes	Low	Low	8 – 15	155
Road Trip!	Ice Breaker	6	24	Yes	Low	Low	45-60	156
Scissors	Ice Breaker	8	28	Yes	Low	Low	8 – 15	157
Self Introduction Story Time	Ice Breaker	6	25	Yes	Low	Low	15 – 25	159
Seven-Eleven	Ice Breaker	4	60	No	Low	Low	6 – 10	162
Shoe Factory	Ice Breaker	8	40	No	Medium	Low	6 – 15	163
Shoe Sort	Ice Breaker	8	30	No	Low	Low	8 – 15	164
Sing Down	Ice Breaker	9	200	Yes	Low	Low	15 – 30	165
Slaps	Ice Breaker	8	24	No	Low	Low	6 – 12	166
Snake's Tail	Ice Breaker	12	45	No	High	Low	10 – 20	167
Snaps	Ice Breaker	10	35	No	Low	Low	12 – 20	168
Solemn and Silent	Ice Breaker	8	120	No	Low	Low	8 – 12	170
S-P-U-D	Ice Breaker	8	32	Yes	High	Low	12 – 25	173
Squeeze	Ice Breaker	12	30	Yes	Low	Low	10 – 20	174
Statues	Ice Breaker	6	60	No	Medium	Low	8 – 15	175
Stinger	Ice Breaker	15	60	No	Low	Low	10 – 20	176
Team Crossword	Ice Breaker	8	30	Yes	Low	Low	10 – 18	179
The Creature	Ice Breaker	4	40	No	Medium	Low	12 – 18	180
Think Fast	Ice Breaker	8	28	Yes	Low	Low	10 – 20	181

Activity Name	Category	Min. # of Part.	Max # of Part.	Materials?	Activity Level	Risk Level	Minutes Required	Page
Toilet Paper Game	Ice Breaker	8	30	Yes	Low	Low	12 – 25	182
T-Shirt Tales	Ice Breaker	8	35	Yes	Low	Low	10 – 25	178
Two Truths and a Lie	Ice Breaker	5	40	No	Low	Low	8 – 15	184
What I Carry	Ice Breaker	8	40	No	Low	Low	15 – 20	187
Where Were You?	Ice Breaker	6	40	No	Low	Low	15 – 25	188
Wooooooooo	Ice Breaker	10	50	Yes	Low	Low	15 - 40	189
Adjective Name Game	Name Game	8	30	No	Low	Low	8 – 20	12
Blanket Name Game	Name Game	10	30	Yes	Low	Low	6 – 15	13
Concentration	Name Game	10	30	No	Low	Low	6 – 20	15
Funny Face	Name Game	6	40	No	Low	Low	4 – 8	16
Group Juggle	Name Game	10	35	Yes	Low	Low	10 – 25	17
Here I Am	Name Game	10	25	Yes	Low	Low	5 – 10	18
Human Bingo	Name Game	10	150	Yes	Low	Low	6 – 15	19
I'm a Gigolo	Name Game	10	35	No	Low	Low	5 – 12	21
Introduction Interview	Name Game	8	30	No	Low	Low	8 – 25	22
Motion Name Game	Name Game	8	30	No	Medium	Low	6 – 30	23
My Three Objects	Name Game	4	40	Yes	Low	Low	8 – 30	24
Shabuya Roll Call	Name Game	8	24	No	Low	Low	8 – 20	25
Shoe Game	Name Game	8	40	No	Low	Low	10 – 25	26
Snort	Name Game	10	35	No	Low	Low	10 – 25	27
Whomp'Em	Name Game	10	30	Yes	Medium	Low	6 - 12	28
Build Your Own Game	Ropes	12	100	Yes	High	Low	40 – 60	33
Traffic Jam	Ropes	10	60	Yes	Low	Low	12 – 25	40
Amazing Teamcoat	Teambuilder	5	36	Yes	Low	Low	30 – 60	192
Autobiography	Teambuilder	5	30	Yes	Low	Low	15 – 40	194
Blind Golf	Teambuilder	6	50	Yes	Low	Low	10 – 20	196
Capture the Flag	Teambuilder	16	50	Yes	High	Low	30 – 75	201
Clipboards	Teambuilder	5	30	Yes	Low	Low	45 – 60	205
Debate	Teambuilder	6	16	No	Low	Low	30 – 60	206
Design Your Perfect	Teambuilder	6	40	Yes	Low	Low	30 - 45	207
Dot Brainstorming	Teambuilder	3	60	Yes	Low	Low	6 – 20	208
Each One, Teach One	Teambuilder	3	25	No	Low	Low	15 – 40	209
Egg Break	Teambuilder	9	80	Yes	Low	Low	30 – 45	210
Finger Paint Collage	Teambuilder	5	25	Yes	Low	Low	25 – 45	212
Five Things I Want to Learn	Teambuilder	15	60	Yes	Low	Low	10 – 20	213
Group Résumé	Teambuilder	4	20	Yes	Low	Low	20 – 40	215
Listening Skills Drawings	Teambuilder	6	150	Yes	Low	Low	15 – 30	220
Observation	Teambuilder	5	100	Yes	Low	Low	15 – 25	225
Peanut Butter & Jelly	Teambuilder	10	40	Yes	Low	Low	20 - 35	226
Perpetual Tag	Teambuilder	10	35	No	Low	Low	Weeks…	228
Psychiatrist	Teambuilder	10	30	No	Low	Low	30 – 60	234
Quilting	Teambuilder	10	35	Yes	Low	Low	120 +	235
Silent Cookie Baking	Teambuilder	4	12	Yes	Low	Low	40 - 60	238

Activity Name	Category	Min. # of Part.	Max # of Part.	Materials?	Activity Level	Risk Level	Minutes Required	Page
Straw Tower	Teambuilder	8	40	Yes	Low	Low	20 – 35	240
Team Acronym	Teambuilder	4	30	Yes	Low	Low	10 – 20	243
Team Jewelry	Teambuilder	6	30	Yes	Low	Low	45 – 90	244
Telephone	Teambuilder	10	30	No	Low	Low	5 – 15	245
TV Commercial	Teambuilder	5	60	No	Low	Low	20 – 40	248
Web We Weave	Teambuilder	8	35	Yes	Low	Low	15 - 30	254
Banana Relay	Ice Breaker	10	60	Yes	Medium	Medium	8 – 18	53
Barnyard Animals	Ice Breaker	15	300	No	Low	Medium	6 – 15	55
Birdie on a Perch	Ice Breaker	15	80	No	High	Medium	6 – 15	57
Bite the Bag	Ice Breaker	6	60	Yes	Medium	Medium	5 – 15	59
Blind Identify	Ice Breaker	10	30	Yes	Low	Medium	8 – 15	61
Blindfold Line-Up	Ice Breaker	7	40	Yes	Medium	Medium	5 – 10	62
Chubby Bunny	Ice Breaker	4	30	Yes	Low	Medium	6 – 15	73
Confusion Bingo	Ice Breaker	10	100	Yes	Medium	Medium	8 – 15	79
Dizzy Bat	Ice Breaker	8	60	Yes	High	Medium	6 – 15	84
Ducky Wucky	Ice Breaker	10	40	Yes	Low	Medium	8 – 15	87
Elbow Tag	Ice Breaker	14	36	No	High	Medium	12 – 20	88
Flour Game	Ice Breaker	6	24	Yes	Low	Medium	15 – 30	104
Freeze Tag	Ice Breaker	15	150	No	High	Medium	10 – 18	106
Ha!	Ice Breaker	10	30	No	Medium	Medium	8 – 12	109
Hog Call	Ice Breaker	20	200	No	Low	Medium	4 – 8	111
How You Doin'?	Ice Breaker	15	70	No	Low	Medium	8 – 12	112
Human Knot	Ice Breaker	6	40	No	High	Medium	12 – 25	115
Human Twister	Ice Breaker	6	40	Yes	Low	Medium	8 – 15	118
Ice Cubes	Ice Breaker	6	60	Yes	Medium	Medium	8 – 20	120
Lap Sit	Ice Breaker	6	300	No	Medium	Medium	6 – 10	125
Life Saver Relay	Ice Breaker	12	50	Yes	Low	Medium	5 – 10	126
Man Overboard	Ice Breaker	12	125	No	Medium	Medium	20 – 30	137
Orange Pass	Ice Breaker	7	50	Yes	Medium	Medium	6 – 12	145
People to People	Ice Breaker	12	60	No	High	Medium	10 – 20	148
Scooterball	Ice Breaker	6	18	Yes	High	Medium	8 – 15	158
Sentence Stems	Ice Breaker	4	50	Yes	Low	Medium	10 – 20	161
Sock Game	Ice Breaker	8	32	No	High	Medium	6 – 10	169
Sponge Pass	Ice Breaker	10	60	Yes	Low	Medium	10 – 20	171
Spoon Feed Me	Ice Breaker	3	13	Yes	Low	Medium	6 – 12	172
Sumo	Ice Breaker	11	30	No	High	Medium	12 – 20	177
Touchee Feelee	Ice Breaker	10	50	No	Medium	Medium	10 – 18	183
Water Balance	Ice Breaker	8	18	Yes	Medium	Medium	10 – 20	185
Waterfall Game	Ice Breaker	8	40	Yes	Low	Medium	8 – 18	186
Butt Spelling	Name Game	10	50	No	Low	Medium	8 – 15	14
All Aboard	Ropes	7	18	Yes	Medium	Medium	15 – 30	31
Blind Squares	Ropes	8	30	Yes	Medium	Medium	15 – 30	32
Log Jam	Ropes	10	26	Yes	High	Medium	20 – 30	34

Activity Name	Category	Min. # of Part.	Max # of Part.	Materials?	Activity Level	Risk Level	Minutes Required	Page
Log Roll	Ropes	10	50	No	High	Medium	5 – 10	35
Mars Probe	Ropes	5	24	Yes	Low	Medium	12 – 30	36
Affirmative Fold-Ups	Teambuilder	4	35	Yes	Low	Medium	10 – 18	191
Artist, Clay, Model	Teambuilder	6	80	No	Low	Medium	8 – 20	193
Build My House	Teambuilder	5	40	Yes	Low	Medium	20 – 30	200
Chain Back Rub	Teambuilder	4	150	No	Low	Medium	8 – 10	202
Chart a Life	Teambuilder	4	30	Yes	Low	Medium	12 – 30	203
Information Fun Sheet	Teambuilder	8	35	Yes	Low	Medium	30 - 60	217
Levitation	Teambuilder	8	100	No	Medium	Medium	8 – 20	219
Penny for Your Thoughts	Teambuilder	10	30	Yes	Low	Medium	15 – 25	227
Personal Quotation	Teambuilder	6	30	Yes	Low	Medium	8 – 20	229
Perspectives	Teambuilder	6	18	Yes	Low	Medium	30 – 60	230
Piece of the Puzzle	Teambuilder	8	40	Yes	Low	Medium	30 – 45	232
Poetry Group	Teambuilder	5	35	Yes	Low	Medium	20 – 45	233
Risky	Teambuilder	6	24	Yes	Low	Medium	20 – 40	236
Value Card Sort	Teambuilder	6	40	Yes	Low	Medium	20 – 40	249
Drip, Drip, Drop	Ice Breaker	15	40	Yes	High	High	10 – 20	86
Plane Wreck	Ropes	6	40	Yes	Medium	High	15 – 40	37
Rope Wall	Ropes	8	32	Yes	High	High	12 – 25	38
Three Person Trust Fall	Ropes	3	100	No	High	High	4 – 10	39
Trust Walk	Ropes	6	60	Yes	Medium	High	25 – 40	41
Two Person Trust Fall	Ropes	6	150	No	High	High	3 – 8	43
Willow in the Wind	Ropes	7	120	No	High	High	10 – 20	44
Fear Factor	Teambuilder	6	30	Yes	Medium	High	30 – 60	211
Flash Card Revelations	Teambuilder	12	40	Yes	Low	High	20 – 40	214
Important Item	Teambuilder	6	32	Yes	Low	High	20 – 90 +	216
Last Will & Testament	Teambuilder	8	35	Yes	Low	High	15 – 30	218
Masks I Wear	Teambuilder	7	40	Yes	Low	High	30 – 45	222
Masks Of Me	Teambuilder	6	40	Yes	Low	High	60 +	223
Self I See, Self U See	Teambuilder	6	40	Yes	Low	High	30 – 75	237
Spiritual Focus	Teambuilder	5	32	Yes	Low	High	20 – 45	239
Take a Stand	Teambuilder	8	75	Yes	Low	High	25 – 45	241
Touchstones	Teambuilder	10	60	Yes	Low	High	30 – 60	246

ACTIVITY LEVEL

Activity Name	Category	Min. # of Part.	Max # of Part.	Materials?	Activity Level	Risk Level	Minutes Required	Page
A to Z	Ice Breaker	6	200	No	Low	Low	5 – 10	46
Assassin	Ice Breaker	10	80	Yes	Low	Low	Weeks…	49
Balloon Blow Out	Ice Breaker	5	80	Yes	Low	Low	4 – 10	51
Barnyard	Ice Breaker	8	30	Yes	Low	Low	8 – 20	54
Barnyard Animals	Ice Breaker	15	300	No	Low	Medium	6 – 15	55
Basket	Ice Breaker	6	60	Yes	Low	Low	10 – 25	56
Birthday Line	Ice Breaker	12	200	No	Low	Low	1 – 5	58
Black Magic	Ice Breaker	10	40	No	Low	Low	12 – 40	60
Blind Identify	Ice Breaker	10	30	Yes	Low	Medium	8 – 15	61
Brain Benders	Ice Breaker	8	80	Yes	Low	Low	10 – 20	64
Buzz	Ice Breaker	10	40	No	Low	Low	8 – 15	66
Calls of the Night	Ice Breaker	6	24	Yes	Low	Low	12 – 20	67
Catch Me If You Can	Ice Breaker	6	200	No	Low	Low	4 – 10	68
Chalkboard Sentences	Ice Breaker	12	48	Yes	Low	Low	10 – 18	69
Charlie's Angels	Ice Breaker	12	45	No	Low	Low	15 – 25	70
Chubby Bunny	Ice Breaker	4	30	Yes	Low	Medium	6 – 15	73
Clapping Clues	Ice Breaker	6	60	No	Low	Low	10 – 20	75
Color, Car, Character	Ice Breaker	10	40	No	Low	Low	12 – 30	77
Comic Strip Chaos	Ice Breaker	20	100	Yes	Low	Low	4 – 8	78
Count Off	Ice Breaker	8	25	No	Low	Low	5 – 8	81
Dead Fish	Ice Breaker	8	50	No	Low	Low	4 – 10	82
Detective	Ice Breaker	12	50	No	Low	Low	8 – 15	83
Ducky Wucky	Ice Breaker	10	40	Yes	Low	Medium	8 – 15	87
Evolution	Ice Breaker	16	50	No	Low	Low	10 – 20	90
Famous Pairs	Ice Breaker	16	80	Yes	Low	Low	12 – 20	91
Five Things	Ice Breaker	6	75	Yes	Low	Low	20 – 30	103
Flour Game	Ice Breaker	6	24	Yes	Low	Medium	15 – 30	104
Group Story	Ice Breaker	4	40	No	Low	Low	6 – 12	107
Height Line	Ice Breaker	10	60	No	Low	Low	4 – 8	110
Hog Call	Ice Breaker	20	200	No	Low	Medium	4 – 8	111
How You Doin'?	Ice Breaker	15	70	No	Low	Medium	8 – 12	112
Hum That Tune	Ice Breaker	15	300	No	Low	Low	4 – 8	114
Human Taco (or Burger)	Ice Breaker	20	300	Yes	Low	Low	8 – 20	116
Human Twister	Ice Breaker	6	40	Yes	Low	Medium	8 – 15	118
I Love You Baby, But I Just Can't Smile	Ice Breaker	10	45	No	Low	Low	6 – 12	119
I'm Thinking of Someone	Ice Breaker	10	45	No	Low	Low	10 – 20	121
Imaginary Dough	Ice Breaker	6	50	No	Low	Low	10 – 25	122
Killer	Ice Breaker	16	50	No	Low	Low	10 – 20	124
Life Saver Relay	Ice Breaker	12	50	Yes	Low	Medium	5 – 10	126
List Stories	Ice Breaker	6	36	Yes	Low	Low	10 – 20	128
Lollipop	Ice Breaker	4	30	Yes	Low	Low	15 – 40	129
M&M Game	Ice Breaker	4	30	Yes	Low	Low	15 – 40	130

Activity Name	Category	Min. # of Part.	Max # of Part.	Materials?	Activity Level	Risk Level	Minutes Required	Page
Mafia	Ice Breaker	8	25	Yes	Low	Low	20 +	133
Make a Date	Ice Breaker	8	50	Yes	Low	Low	12 – 20	136
Mirror, Mirror	Ice Breaker	8	30	Yes	Low	Low	6 – 15	139
Mrs. Mumbles	Ice Breaker	8	40	No	Low	Low	10 – 18	140
My Favorite Place	Ice Breaker	5	30	Yes	Low	Low	15 – 25	142
Number Groups	Ice Breaker	15	300	No	Low	Low	3 – 8	143
Ooo, Aaaah, Oooh!	Ice Breaker	9	32	No	Low	Low	8 – 15	144
Orchestra	Ice Breaker	10	200	No	Low	Low	6 – 10	146
Paper Bags	Ice Breaker	8	30	Yes	Low	Low	8 – 15	147
Puzzle Jumble	Ice Breaker	14	100	Yes	Low	Low	8 – 15	150
Random Poetry	Ice Breaker	6	20	Yes	Low	Low	12 – 25	152
Rhythm & Motion	Ice Breaker	10	50	No	Low	Low	12 – 20	154
Rhythm Ice Breaker	Ice Breaker	10	40	Yes	Low	Low	8 – 15	155
Road Trip!	Ice Breaker	6	24	Yes	Low	Low	45-60	156
Scissors	Ice Breaker	8	28	Yes	Low	Low	8 – 15	157
Self Introduction Story Time	Ice Breaker	6	25	Yes	Low	Low	15 – 25	159
Sentence Stems	Ice Breaker	4	50	Yes	Low	Medium	10 – 20	161
Seven-Eleven	Ice Breaker	4	60	No	Low	Low	6 – 10	162
Shoe Sort	Ice Breaker	8	30	No	Low	Low	8 – 15	164
Sing Down	Ice Breaker	9	200	Yes	Low	Low	15 – 30	165
Slaps	Ice Breaker	8	24	No	Low	Low	6 – 12	166
Snaps	Ice Breaker	10	35	No	Low	Low	12 – 20	168
Solemn and Silent	Ice Breaker	8	120	No	Low	Low	8 – 12	170
Sponge Pass	Ice Breaker	10	60	Yes	Low	Medium	10 – 20	171
Spoon Feed Me	Ice Breaker	3	13	Yes	Low	Medium	6 – 12	172
Squeeze	Ice Breaker	12	30	Yes	Low	Low	10 – 20	174
Stinger	Ice Breaker	15	60	No	Low	Low	10 – 20	176
Team Crossword	Ice Breaker	8	30	Yes	Low	Low	10 – 18	179
Think Fast	Ice Breaker	8	28	Yes	Low	Low	10 – 20	181
Toilet Paper Game	Ice Breaker	8	30	Yes	Low	Low	12 – 25	182
T-Shirt Tales	Ice Breaker	8	35	Yes	Low	Low	10 – 25	178
Two Truths and a Lie	Ice Breaker	5	40	No	Low	Low	8 – 15	184
Waterfall Game	Ice Breaker	8	40	Yes	Low	Medium	8 – 18	186
What I Carry	Ice Breaker	8	40	No	Low	Low	15 – 20	187
Where Were You?	Ice Breaker	6	40	No	Low	Low	15 – 25	188
Woooooooooo	Ice Breaker	10	50	Yes	Low	Low	15 - 40	189
Adjective Name Game	Name Game	8	30	No	Low	Low	8 – 20	12
Blanket Name Game	Name Game	10	30	Yes	Low	Low	6 – 15	13
Butt Spelling	Name Game	10	50	No	Low	Medium	8 – 15	14
Concentration	Name Game	10	30	No	Low	Low	6 – 20	15
Funny Face	Name Game	6	40	No	Low	Low	4 – 8	16
Group Juggle	Name Game	10	35	Yes	Low	Low	10 – 25	17
Here I Am	Name Game	10	25	Yes	Low	Low	5 – 10	18

Activity Name	Category	Min. # of Part.	Max # of Part.	Materials?	Activity Level	Risk Level	Minutes Required	Page
Human Bingo	Name Game	10	150	Yes	Low	Low	6 – 15	19
I'm a Gigolo	Name Game	10	35	No	Low	Low	5 – 12	21
Introduction Interview	Name Game	8	30	No	Low	Low	8 – 25	22
My Three Objects	Name Game	4	40	Yes	Low	Low	8 – 30	24
Shabuya Roll Call	Name Game	8	24	No	Low	Low	8 – 20	25
Shoe Game	Name Game	8	40	No	Low	Low	10 – 25	26
Snort	Name Game	10	35	No	Low	Low	10 – 25	27
Mars Probe	Ropes	5	24	Yes	Low	Medium	12 – 30	36
Traffic Jam	Ropes	10	60	Yes	Low	Low	12 – 25	40
Affirmative Fold-Ups	Teambuilder	4	35	Yes	Low	Medium	10 – 18	191
Amazing Teamcoat	Teambuilder	5	36	Yes	Low	Low	30 – 60	192
Artist, Clay, Model	Teambuilder	6	80	No	Low	Medium	8 – 20	193
Autobiography	Teambuilder	5	30	Yes	Low	Low	15 – 40	194
Blind Golf	Teambuilder	6	50	Yes	Low	Low	10 – 20	196
Build My House	Teambuilder	5	40	Yes	Low	Medium	20 – 30	200
Chain Back Rub	Teambuilder	4	150	No	Low	Medium	8 – 10	202
Chart a Life	Teambuilder	4	30	Yes	Low	Medium	12 – 30	203
Clipboards	Teambuilder	5	30	Yes	Low	Low	45 – 60	205
Debate	Teambuilder	6	16	No	Low	Low	30 – 60	206
Design Your Perfect	Teambuilder	6	40	Yes	Low	Low	30 - 45	207
Dot Brainstorming	Teambuilder	3	60	Yes	Low	Low	6 – 20	208
Each One, Teach One	Teambuilder	3	25	No	Low	Low	15 – 40	209
Egg Break	Teambuilder	9	80	Yes	Low	Low	30 – 45	210
Finger Paint Collage	Teambuilder	5	25	Yes	Low	Low	25 – 45	212
Five Things I Want to Learn	Teambuilder	15	60	Yes	Low	Low	10 – 20	213
Flash Card Revelations	Teambuilder	12	40	Yes	Low	High	20 – 40	214
Group Résumé	Teambuilder	4	20	Yes	Low	Low	20 – 40	215
Important Item	Teambuilder	6	32	Yes	Low	High	20 – 90 +	216
Information Fun Sheet	Teambuilder	8	35	Yes	Low	Medium	30 - 60	217
Last Will & Testament	Teambuilder	8	35	Yes	Low	High	15 – 30	218
Listening Skills Drawings	Teambuilder	6	150	Yes	Low	Low	15 – 30	220
Masks I Wear	Teambuilder	7	40	Yes	Low	High	30 – 45	222
Masks Of Me	Teambuilder	6	40	Yes	Low	High	60 +	223
Observation	Teambuilder	5	100	Yes	Low	Low	15 – 25	225
Peanut Butter & Jelly	Teambuilder	10	40	Yes	Low	Low	20 - 35	226
Penny for Your Thoughts	Teambuilder	10	30	Yes	Low	Medium	15 – 25	227
Perpetual Tag	Teambuilder	10	35	No	Low	Low	Weeks…	228
Personal Quotation	Teambuilder	6	30	Yes	Low	Medium	8 – 20	229
Perspectives	Teambuilder	6	18	Yes	Low	Medium	30 – 60	230
Piece of the Puzzle	Teambuilder	8	40	Yes	Low	Medium	30 – 45	232
Poetry Group	Teambuilder	5	35	Yes	Low	Medium	20 – 45	233
Psychiatrist	Teambuilder	10	30	No	Low	Low	30 – 60	234
Quilting	Teambuilder	10	35	Yes	Low	Low	120 +	235

Activity Name	Category	Min. # of Part.	Max # of Part.	Materials?	Activity Level	Risk Level	Minutes Required	Page
Risky	Teambuilder	6	24	Yes	Low	Medium	20 – 40	236
Self I See, Self U See	Teambuilder	6	40	Yes	Low	High	30 – 75	237
Silent Cookie Baking	Teambuilder	4	12	Yes	Low	Low	40 - 60	238
Spiritual Focus	Teambuilder	5	32	Yes	Low	High	20 – 45	239
Straw Tower	Teambuilder	8	40	Yes	Low	Low	20 – 35	240
Take a Stand	Teambuilder	8	75	Yes	Low	High	25 – 45	241
Team Acronym	Teambuilder	4	30	Yes	Low	Low	10 – 20	243
Team Jewelry	Teambuilder	6	30	Yes	Low	Low	45 – 90	244
Telephone	Teambuilder	10	30	No	Low	Low	5 – 15	245
Touchstones	Teambuilder	10	60	Yes	Low	High	30 – 60	246
TV Commercial	Teambuilder	5	60	No	Low	Low	20 – 40	248
Value Card Sort	Teambuilder	6	40	Yes	Low	Medium	20 – 40	249
Web We Weave	Teambuilder	8	35	Yes	Low	Low	15 - 30	254
Arc Ball	Ice Breaker	14	60	Yes	Medium	Low	8 – 20	48
Balloon Tag	Ice Breaker	8	50	Yes	Medium	Low	4 – 10	52
Banana Relay	Ice Breaker	10	60	Yes	Medium	Medium	8 – 18	53
Bite the Bag	Ice Breaker	6	60	Yes	Medium	Medium	5 – 15	59
Blindfold Line-Up	Ice Breaker	7	40	Yes	Medium	Medium	5 – 10	62
Body English	Ice Breaker	6	70	No	Medium	Low	5 – 10	63
Chocalotaschnizzel	Ice Breaker	8	30	Yes	Medium	Low	12 – 20	72
Clothespin Tag	Ice Breaker	8	50	Yes	Medium	Low	5 – 12	76
Confusion Bingo	Ice Breaker	10	100	Yes	Medium	Medium	8 – 15	79
Do You Love Your Neighbor?	Ice Breaker	14	80	No	Medium	Low	10 – 20	85
Elves, Giants and Chickens	Ice Breaker	15	250	No	Medium	Low	8 – 12	89
Guard the Bone	Ice Breaker	8	30	Yes	Medium	Low	6 – 15	108
Ha!	Ice Breaker	10	30	No	Medium	Medium	8 – 12	109
Hula Hoop Relay	Ice Breaker	9	50	Yes	Medium	Low	8 – 15	113
Ice Cubes	Ice Breaker	6	60	Yes	Medium	Medium	8 – 20	120
Keep It Up	Ice Breaker	6	20	Yes	Medium	Low	6 – 15	123
Lap Sit	Ice Breaker	6	300	No	Medium	Medium	6 – 10	125
M&M Swap	Ice Breaker	5	50	Yes	Medium	Low	8 – 15	131
Machine Game	Ice Breaker	10	120	No	Medium	Low	10 – 20	132
Man Overboard	Ice Breaker	12	125	No	Medium	Medium	20 – 30	137
Musical Interpretation	Ice Breaker	10	200	Yes	Medium	Low	5 – 10	141
Orange Pass	Ice Breaker	7	50	Yes	Medium	Medium	6 – 12	145
Posture Relay	Ice Breaker	8	15	Yes	Medium	Low	5 – 8	149
Shoe Factory	Ice Breaker	8	40	No	Medium	Low	6 – 15	163
Statues	Ice Breaker	6	60	No	Medium	Low	8 – 15	175
The Creature	Ice Breaker	4	40	No	Medium	Low	12 – 18	180
Touchee Feelee	Ice Breaker	10	50	No	Medium	Medium	10 – 18	183
Water Balance	Ice Breaker	8	18	Yes	Medium	Medium	10 – 20	185
Motion Name Game	Name Game	8	30	No	Medium	Low	6 – 30	23
Whomp'Em	Name Game	10	30	Yes	Medium	Low	6 - 12	28

Activity Name	Category	Min. # of Part.	Max # of Part.	Materials?	Activity Level	Risk Level	Minutes Required	Page
All Aboard	Ropes	7	18	Yes	Medium	Medium	15 – 30	31
Blind Squares	Ropes	8	30	Yes	Medium	Medium	15 – 30	32
Plane Wreck	Ropes	6	40	Yes	Medium	High	15 – 40	37
Trust Walk	Ropes	6	60	Yes	Medium	High	25 – 40	41
Fear Factor	Teambuilder	6	30	Yes	Medium	High	30 – 60	211
Levitation	Teambuilder	8	100	No	Medium	Medium	8 – 20	219
Amoeba Tag	Ice Breaker	14	125	No	High	Low	10 – 20	47
Back to Back	Ice Breaker	8	300	No	High	Low	5 – 15	50
Birdie on a Perch	Ice Breaker	15	80	No	High	Medium	6 – 15	57
Clam Free	Ice Breaker	16	60	Yes	High	Low	12 – 20	74
Dizzy Bat	Ice Breaker	8	60	Yes	High	Medium	6 – 15	84
Drip, Drip, Drop	Ice Breaker	15	40	Yes	High	High	10 – 20	86
Elbow Tag	Ice Breaker	14	36	No	High	Medium	12 – 20	88
Follow the Leader	Ice Breaker	10	50	No	High	Low	10 – 18	105
Freeze Tag	Ice Breaker	15	150	No	High	Medium	10 – 18	106
Human Knot	Ice Breaker	6	40	No	High	Medium	12 – 25	115
Line Relay	Ice Breaker	10	60	No	High	Low	6 – 12	127
People to People	Ice Breaker	12	60	No	High	Medium	10 – 20	148
Raid	Ice Breaker	14	50	Yes	High	Low	10 – 20	151
Scooterball	Ice Breaker	6	18	Yes	High	Medium	8 – 15	158
Snake's Tail	Ice Breaker	12	45	No	High	Low	10 – 20	167
Sock Game	Ice Breaker	8	32	No	High	Medium	6 – 10	169
S-P-U-D	Ice Breaker	8	32	Yes	High	Low	12 – 25	173
Sumo	Ice Breaker	11	30	No	High	Medium	12 – 20	177
Build Your Own Game	Ropes	12	100	Yes	High	Low	40 – 60	33
Log Jam	Ropes	10	26	Yes	High	Medium	20 – 30	34
Log Roll	Ropes	10	50	No	High	Medium	5 – 10	35
Rope Wall	Ropes	8	32	Yes	High	High	12 – 25	38
Three Person Trust Fall	Ropes	3	100	No	High	High	4 – 10	39
Two Person Trust Fall	Ropes	6	150	No	High	High	3 – 8	43
Willow in the Wind	Ropes	7	120	No	High	High	10 – 20	44
Capture the Flag	Teambuilder	16	50	Yes	High	Low	30 – 75	201

About the Author

Jon Tucker currently serves as the Leadership Development Coordinator at Western Oregon University in Monmouth, Oregon. A small, public university located in Oregon's Willamette Valley, Jon finds this an optimal location to work with students on an individual basis and to make positive impacts on their lives. He is a native to Oregon and began his career at the University of Oregon before working in housing and residence life at Boise State University and Colorado State University. He lives in Oregon where he enjoys spending time with his friends and family, chasing after his three nephews, playing volleyball, tending to his house and yard and spending quality time lounging with his bulldog, Ripley.